Eu

A Creative History of the Russian Internet

Eugene Gorny

A Creative History of the Russian Internet

Studies in Internet Creativity

VDM Verlag Dr. Müller

Impressum/Imprint (nur für Deutschland/ only for Germany)
Bibliografische Information der Deutschen Nationalbibliothek: Die Deutsche Nationalbibliothek
verzeichnet diese Publikation in der Deutschen Nationalbibliografie; detaillierte bibliografische
Daten sind im Internet über http://dnb.d-nb.de abrufbar.
Alle in diesem Buch genannten Marken und Produktnamen unterliegen warenzeichen-, marken-
oder patentrechtlichem Schutz bzw. sind Warenzeichen oder eingetragene Warenzeichen der
jeweiligen Inhaber. Die Wiedergabe von Marken, Produktnamen, Gebrauchsnamen,
Handelsnamen, Warenbezeichnungen u.s.w. in diesem Werk berechtigt auch ohne besondere
Kennzeichnung nicht zu der Annahme, dass solche Namen im Sinne der Warenzeichen- und
Markenschutzgesetzgebung als frei zu betrachten wären und daher von jedermann benutzt
werden dürften.

Coverbild: www.purestockx.com

Verlag: VDM Verlag Dr. Müller Aktiengesellschaft & Co. KG
Dudweiler Landstr. 99, 66123 Saarbrücken, Deutschland
Telefon +49 681 9100-698, Telefax +49 681 9100-988, Email: info@vdm-verlag.de
Zugl.: London, London University, Diss., 2006

Herstellung in Deutschland:
Schaltungsdienst Lange o.H.G., Berlin
Books on Demand GmbH, Norderstedt
Reha GmbH, Saarbrücken
Amazon Distribution GmbH, Leipzig
ISBN: 978-3-639-14559-5

Imprint (only for USA, GB)
Bibliographic information published by the Deutsche Nationalbibliothek: The Deutsche
Nationalbibliothek lists this publication in the Deutsche Nationalbibliografie; detailed
bibliographic data are available in the Internet at http://dnb.d-nb.de.
Any brand names and product names mentioned in this book are subject to trademark, brand or
patent protection and are trademarks or registered trademarks of their respective holders. The use
of brand names, product names, common names, trade names, product descriptions etc. even
without a particular marking in this works is in no way to be construed to mean that such names
may be regarded as unrestricted in respect of trademark and brand protection legislation and
could thus be used by anyone.

Cover image: www.purestockx.com

Publisher:
VDM Verlag Dr. Müller Aktiengesellschaft & Co. KG
Dudweiler Landstr. 99, 66123 Saarbrücken, Germany
Phone +49 681 9100-698, Fax +49 681 9100-988, Email: info@vdm-publishing.com
London, London University, Diss., 2006

Printed in the U.S.A.
Printed in the U.K. by (see last page)
ISBN: 978-3-639-14559-5

Contents

A c k n o w l e d g m e n t s

I would like to thank all people whose joint efforts made the Russian Internet a rich and versatile creative environment and an exciting subject of research. I am especially grateful to those of them who showed interest in my research and found time to answer my question and to share their opinion about research issues. The list include Aleksey (Lexa) Andreev, Leonid Delitsyn, Alex Exler, Alexander Gagin, Marat Guelman, Maxim (Mr Parker) Kononenko, Artemi Lebedev, Roman Leibov, Aleksander (SAM) Malyukov, Maxim Moshkov, Anton Nosik, Dima Verner and many others without whose work and thought this project would be impossible. I am thankful to Russian Internet researchers for discussion at the seminar in Bochum and Muenster in spring 2005. To Henrike Schmidt (Lotman Institute, University of Bochum) for inspiration and editing help. To James Curran, David Morley, Sara Kember and Joanna Zelinska (Goldsmith College, University of London) for critical remarks about the early drafts and useful suggestions. To my supervisor Des Freedman for his guidance and patience. To Robert Greenall and Oliver Ready for their help with language and style and to Genia Zilberstein for proofreading. The research was supported by the Ford Foundation International Fellowship Programme and I wish to thank the members of IFP staff in both New York and Moscow. Special thanks to Andrey Tsunsky and Luba Sharij for giving me shelter in Moscow, as well as to Yuri and Anna Tsunsky for a calm and fruitful time in snow-covered Karelia. Last but not least, I am most grateful to my parents for encouragement and moral support.

List of tables

List of Figures

INTRODUCTION

1.1 Background to the research

The title of the book combines three concepts: creativity, history and the Russian Internet. These concepts define the research problem of the book, its research methods and its subject matter.

The idea of this study grew from a cognitive dissonance. At the very beginning of my career as an Internet professional more than ten years ago, my own experience, participation in collaborative projects and observation of the experiences of others drew my attention to the phenomenon of creativity on the Internet, the variety of its manifestations and its morphogenetic potential whose realization produces change on the Internet and influences society and culture at large. Over the years of working in the field, I could observe the forms of Internet creativity changing in the course of time. However, I have been unable to find a satisfactory theoretical explanation of the processes I witnessed in the available research literature. On the one hand, creativity has been conceptualized by some researchers as a fundamental source of development of the Internet as a technocultural formation (Himanen, 2001; Castells, 2001; Fischer, 2002) but these theories usually lacked solid empirical evidence. On the other hand, many particular aspects of Internet creativity have been described and discussed (see chapter 2 for detail) but they have been usually treated individually and separately from other aspects. In other words, the concept of creativity has not been applied to the Internet consistently enough to form a theoretical framework which could transcend thematic and methodological departmentalization of particular studies. This observation led to the formulation of a research question about the general characteristics of the Internet as a domain of creativity. A systematic study of theoretical and practical aspects of Internet creativity could provide an answer to that question. The goal of the book is more modest: to investigate forms and processes of Internet creativity in a specific segment of the Internet – its Russian-language part. The research findings could help to correct the generalizations of previous researchers and provide a theoretical framework for further studies of Internet creativity.

The interest in the process of change has determined the choice of historical methods as the core methodology of the research. It should be noted that the relative youth of the Internet poses serious methodological challenges for a historian. Traditional history deals normally with processes which extend to hundreds and even thousands of years; by contrast, the history of the Internet may seem too recent and brief to become a proper subject for a historical study. However, the Internet does have a history as shown by many researchers (see section 2.5 of chapter 2 for detail). The Internet is a vivid example of accelerated development: the processes of change that might take a long time in other domains occur on the Internet at a much faster pace. The Internet can thus be a subject worthy of historical study.

The choice of the Russian Internet as the subject matter of the study was primarily determined by the fact of my personal involvement in its development as a user, producer and researcher, which gave me practical experience and knowledge required for its in-depth study. A brief description of my personal background may be useful to explain my interest to the research problem and outline my standpoint. I started using the Internet in 1994 when the concept of the Russian Internet did not yet exist. In a few years, the Russian Internet as a discernable phenomenon emerged due to the joint effect of multiple factors: the development of telecommunication infrastructure in Russia which made possible access to the Internet in the country and resulted in the registration of a national top-level domain .RU; Russification of software which made possible to use the Russian script in computer communication and to produce online content in Russian language; and the activity of Russian early adopters of the Internet who developed content projects and formed a self-aware community. Working as a journalist at a Russian-language newspaper in Tallinn, Estonia, I followed the development of the Internet and reviewed its significant events. At the same time, I explored the opportunities of the Internet as a means of self-expression and creativity and communicated with Russian users in different parts of the world. In 1996, I became the editor-in-chief of Zhurnal.ru, the project which became a point of crystallization for the emerging Russian cyberculture. Two years later, I continued this work as editor of the Net Culture section in the Russian Journal. Since 2000, I have worked as an expert in cultural IT projects, electronic publishing and journalism for various organizations such as Soros Foundation, Carnegie Moscow Center, IREX, and Moscow Scientific Foundation. I also did research on Internet-related subjects. My study of the Russian Internet resulted in the edited collection *The Internet and cyberculture in Russia* (Gorny, 2000b) and *A Chronicle of the Russian Internet: 1990-1999* (Gorny, 2000c). This personal experience provided both motivation and background for the research into the history of the Russian Internet.

The study has also been stimulated by the paucity of research into the Russian Internet, especially blatant when the project just started, and a wish to introduce the Russian Internet as a subject worth of academic research into English-language scholarship. Western Internet studies until recently have almost completely ignored non-English segments of cyberspace and made their generalization on the basis of the Anglo-American Internet. This bias has been lately admitted as a problem. Thus, David Silver (2004) acknowledges "a Western, English-speaking slant" in cyberculture/Internet studies. There is a growing understanding of the need for "de-Westernizing media studies" (Curran and Park, 2000) as well as Internet studies (Gauntlett, 2000). As the editors of forthcoming anthology *Internationalizing Internet Studies* (Goggin and McLelland, 2006) point out,

> English use is now a minority in terms of overall online language use. However, communications and media scholarship, especially in the Anglophone world, has not registered the deep ramifications of this shift –

and the challenges it poses to the concepts, methods, assumptions, and frameworks used to study the Internet.

The study of the Russian Internet can contribute to a wider programme of research into non-Anglophone uses of the Internet which "might challenge certain preconceived notions about the technology and its social impacts as well as the manner in which Internet studies is taken up, valued and taught outside the circuits of understanding prevalent in Anglophone academia" (Goggin and McLelland, 2006).

1.2 Research problem and research questions

The purpose of this study is to investigate manifestations of creativity in the history of the Russian Internet. It seeks to discover the internal logic of the development of creative forms, to identify the factors that account for change and to analyse the relationship between Internet creativity and wider sociocultural contexts. To achieve these goals, the following research questions must be answered by the study:

1. Can the Internet be considered as a specific domain of creativity comparable with other domains?

2. How is Internet creativity distributed among Russian Internet users and who are the actors of creativity on the Russian Internet?

3. What is the correlation between individual and collective creativity on the Russian Internet?

4. Which historical and cultural factors have influenced creative production on the Russian Internet?

The questions are central to the structure of the book. They are addressed in chapters dealing with case studies and discussed from various perspectives throughout the text. The research problem will test previously proposed generalisations analysed in chapter 2. The constructs referred to in the research problem are high-level ones; more specific constructs are developed at the conclusions at the end of Chapter 2 and their operational definitions are developed in Chapter 3.

The research has an interpretive and a theoretical aim. The interpretive aim is to understand how Internet creativity contributes to the historical change of the Russian Internet and the way in which its forms and practices give shape to, and are themselves shaped by, core aspects of Russian culture and society. The theoretical aim is to generalize from historical instances of creative forms and practices found on the Russian Internet and to develop a theoretical framework for Internet creativity research.

The study has been informed by a commitment to empirical research, to historical research, to Internet research, to creativity research, to Russian cultural studies and to interdisciplinary studies. The methods used in the study have been integrated using the frameworks of the interpretive theory approach and grounded theory approach developed in chapter 3.

The area of the study, cultural limits and chronological limits have defined the boundaries and delimitations of the research problem by setting limits for its generalizability. These boundaries are discussed in detail in section 1.8. The data and conclusions of this research apply to the Russian Internet and they can be questioned outside these boundaries. Comparative cross-cultural research into the uses and interpretations of the Internet could help to develop broader generalizations concerning Internet creativity.

Specific research questions have been developed and answered in case studies and the emerging interpretive theories have been used to find a solution to the research problem. Essentially I argue that creativity – defined as production and communication of cultural value governed primarily by intrinsic motivation – has been a key factor in the development of the Russian Internet. Internet creativity is realized on many levels and it takes many forms; these forms are subject to constant change which is caused by a combination of internal and external factors. Like in other domains, the distribution of Internet creativity is uneven. The number of users/producers is less than the number of users/consumers; and the number of those who have introduced a significant creative contribution into the Internet is even less. There is a dialectical relationship between personal and group creativity. Various forms of creative collaboration pervade the Internet; however, in most cases there are informal leaders who inspire others by example and define the patterns of creative behaviour. The forms of Internet creativity are defined by the properties of the medium and influenced by the historical background, the contemporary sociocultural context and the cultural identity of the users. These research findings are discussed in more detail at the end of each chapter and summarized in the last chapter.

1.3 Justification for the research

The research problem is important on several theoretical and practical grounds.

At the time this project was conceptualized, there was a paucity of empirical research upon the Russian Internet. Although the situation is changing and a few research projects have recently started that study particular aspects of the Russian Internet, it is explored to a much lesser extent than other segments of the Internet. Generally, the Russian Internet remains to a great extent *terra incognita* for English-language Internet researchers. The study aims to contribute to the knowledge of Internet uses and interpretations in various cultural contexts by developing theories based on empirical and historical case studies of the Russian Internet.

No research is made in isolation from what has been done before. A short review of research into the Russian Internet is required to outline both achievements and lacunae and to justify the research problem.

Researchers pointed out that specific historic background and sociocultural context has largely influenced the development of the Russian Internet. Early studies of the Russian Internet were primarily concerned with the key role that the Internet and other information technology had played in the fall of the Soviet regime and with their potential for democratization of Russian society (Castells and Kiselyova, 1995; Castells and Kiselyova, 1998; Ellis, 1999). Researchers pointed out that the uses and interpretations of the Internet in Russia have been influenced by personal networks that have been traditionally used by Russians to circumvent limitations imposed by the authorities (Ledeneva, 1998; Rohozinski, 1999). It was also argued (Rohozinski, 2000) that the legacy of the Soviet system had continued to influence the character of the Russian Internet and expressed scepticism concerning the idea of the Russian Internet as a public sphere. Bowles (2006) who studied the development of the Russian Internet concluded that "RuNet has been, and is likely to remain, subject to conditions that are not shared by the majority of Western countries" such as traditional disrespect for copyright and a particularly centralised media structure. Developing previous research into the Russian Internet élite (Gorny, 1999c; Gorny and Sherman, 1999) she pointed out the similarity between the RuNet élite and underground intelligentsia of Soviet times, with its "ambivalent status as a social and intellectual network set apart from mainstream academic and political thought." She noted that the Russian Internet reflects characteristics of wider Russian society, such as personalism, censorship concerns and an emphasis on mutuality. Other popular research topics include the development of the communication infrastructure of the Internet in Russia (Perfiliev, 2002), issues of Internet regulation and censorship (Alexander, 2003; Trofimenko, 2004; Schmidt and Teubener, 2005b); and sociocultural implications of the Internet in Russia, particularly in the context of literary production (Now, 2000).

One of the most important centres of Russian Internet research is based in Germany. Russian net literature has been explored in the framework of a collaborative project Sphärentexte/CyberRus under the direction of Henrike Henrike Schmidt of Lotman-Institute, University of Bohum, in 2000-2003 (Schmidt, 2002a). It was followed by the Russian-Cyberspace.org project under the direction of Henrike Henrike and Kati Teubener, devoted to an 'investigation into cultural identity performances on the Russian Internet' (Schmidt, 2004; Schmidt and Teubener, 2005a, 2005c). The key themes have been the (re)construction of cultural identity on the Russian Internet; the correlation between national, international and transnational; the interplay between public and private spheres;

and the use of the Internet as a tool for political and cultural resistance. In the framework of the project, a number of research papers and articles have been published in English, German and Russian and several workshops and virtual seminars have been organized. The project resulted in the edited volume (Schmidt, Teubener and Konradova, 2006) which included versions of chapters 5 and 6 of this study. The role of the Internet in the process of cultural identification of Russians has been also studied by Robert Saunders (2004), who explored the use of the Internet in the former Soviet republics such as Kazakhstan and Latvia and concluded that "The Internet is being used by ... cyber-Russians as a tool to resurrect the universalist identity that the Soviet Union was founded on".

Academic research on the Russian Internet and cyberculture in the Russian language is relatively scant. In contrast to the situation in the West, where "[p]rofessional societies and degree-granting programs devoted to digital communication have steadily increased" (Barrett, 2001: 13), in Russia the Internet has not been considered a subject worthy of academic study until very recently. In this situation, the role of journalists from the net culture milieu, self-reflective users and semi-academic research has been key. Such publications as Zhurnal.ru, The Evening Internet, The Internet Magazine, The Internet World and Net Culture in the Russian Journal have covered and discussed a variety of issues related to Russian Internet culture. However, these writings have often suffered the usual limitations of the journalistic approach such as superficiality, partiality, overgeneralization, and hasty conclusions. Nevertheless, they are valuable sources of both information and opinions and have been used in this study among other secondary sources.

This study also relies on the author's previous research such as a collection of biographies of the "Russian Internet élite" (Gorny and Sherman, 1999), *A Chronicle of the Russian Internet: 1990-1999* (Gorny, 2000c) and an edited collection *The Internet and Cyberculture in Russia* (Gorny, 2000b). Other important sources include the online project Nethistory.ru, under direction of

Dmitri Ivanov, whose declared aim is to collect information relating to the history of the Russian Internet.

One of the recent publications on Runet history is Sergey Kuznetsov's (2004) book *Touching the Elephant*. So far, it is probably the most voluminous work on the subject. The author gathered his old articles and added extensive commentaries. He presented his work as 'a book for reading' and 'an evidence of a witness' from which the reader can know not only the official but also an unofficial history of Runet: 'who drank with whom, what drugs the founding fathers loved (or did not love)', etc. The book covers the early five or six years of Runet with occasional inclusion of later events. Although the author does not claim to be objective or even reliable, the book provides many interesting facts and anecdotal stories about the "heroic period" of the Russian Internet.

It is noteworthy that creativity has been neither a topic not a theoretical framework for the researchers. Thus, Kuznetsov (2004) lists the most frequent models that have been used to conceptualize the Russian Internet. These include: a discussion club; samizdat, archive or a library; an electronic unconscious, a place for displaced emotions and thoughts depicted by 'black mythology' of the Internet; an instrument of cooperation and collaboration; a universal mass medium; a tool of political action and provocation; a shop and auction; and, finally, a daily life utility. This study introduces a model of the Russian Internet that has not been mentioned – that of a creative environment.

Furthermore, there was a shortage of theoretical exposition upon the role of creativity in cultural production on the Internet in the English language scholarship. Although much research has been done on particular aspects of creative practices in the digital domain, there appears to have been little integration of this research, and even less evidence of attempts to link it with the broader theoretical context of creativity research. Theories of creativity and the research into Internet creativity are reviewed in chapter 2. The review concludes that there has been little interaction between the two fields: creativity researchers have not paid much attention to the Internet and Internet researchers have not used creativity theories as their theoretical framework. This project attempts to integrate these two domains of research and to develop an integral framework by combining methods of creativity research and Internet studies.

There was also a relative neglect of history as a research methodology by previous researchers. Although the historical approach has proved its usefulness and validity in both technological and cultural histories of the Internet, history is a relatively unusual methodology in the field of Internet studies which tend to underestimate the historical dimension of techno-cultural processes. However, a historical approach helps to avoid unjustified projections and overgeneralizations when certain regularities discovered at a certain place and a certain time are conceptualized as having universal significance. This study follows the principle of historicism and relies on methods of historical study outlined in section 3.4.3 in chapter 3. This allows correcting and amending of generalizations made by previous researchers as well as developing theories which account for the processes of socio-cultural change on the Internet and beyond.

The research findings will be useful for several areas of knowledge such as media studies, Internet studies, Russian studies, cultural studies, creativity research and history. They will provide a theoretical and methodological framework for further research into the history of the Internet and Internet creativity. It can also serve as a model for other researchers.

1.4 Methodology

This section provides an introductory overview of the research methodology justified and described in chapters 2 and 3.

The theoretical framework and rationale of the research is determined by a sociocultural perspective that emphases the social and cultural dimensions of the Internet as a domain of creativity. The study uses primarily qualitative research methods based substantially on the tradition of the interpretive approach which constitutes a foundation for many theories in humanities and social sciences. This approach is justified in section 3.1 of chapter 3 which discusses its general principles and its place among other approaches.

The study is at an intersection of several areas of knowledge and it combines methods from several disciplines. These include Internet studies, ethnography (including virtual ethnography as a research area within Internet studies), cultural studies, creativity research, and history. There is a hierarchy of methods accepted in the study. History is a central methodology. Other methods play a secondary role; they are used to refine research issues and generalize the findings of the main method. All research methods are integrated into a unified methodological framework by using the grounded theory approach which allows ranking of elements and procedures found in different methods in terms of research stages. The methodology is discussed in detail in section 3.5 of chapter 3.

1.5 Outline of the book

This book consists of eight chapters and a reference list.

Chapter 1 describes the background of this research, identifies the research questions, provides definitions of terms, states delimitations and key assumptions, and outlines the structure of the research.

Chapter 2 discusses the concept of creativity and reviews major concepts and theories of creativity research. Then it introduces the concept of Internet creativity and reviews relevant research literature. It identifies several research areas in the field which include histories of the Internet, actors of Internet creativity, forms of internet creativity, personal and collective creativity and the characteristics of the Internet as a creative environment. The chapter summarises and critically assesses previous research and justifies the research questions.

Chapter 3 describes the methodology used to collect data and to investigate them. It outlines general theoretical and methodological premises of the study, discusses methods by area of knowledge and provides a model of method integration in the framework of grounded approach theory.

The rest of the study is structured as a series of case studies. Each case study deals with a particular form of creativity on the Russian Internet, traces the historical dynamics of its form, relates to a certain research question stated in chapter 1 and employs a specific set of relevant methods and theories in a general conceptual and methodological framework described in chapter 3.

Chapter 4 traces the development of online media on the Russian Internet. It begins with historical background which is deemed essential for understanding functions and interpretations of the Internet and online media in Russia. Then it reviews the evolution of Russian online media focusing on the key projects that introduced significant innovations in the domain. Finally, it discusses three models of interpretation of the online media which refer to Russian historical experience and apply concepts of Samizdat, kitchen-table talks and the public sphere to the Internet.

The next two chapters deal with the 'twin pillars of cyberculture studies' (Silver, 2000) – virtual identities and virtual communities. Chapter 5 introduces virtual personae as a genre of Internet creativity and traces the historical development of the genre on the Russian Internet from Usenet to LiveJournal.

Chapter 6 focuses on the Russian community on LiveJournal. It approaches the community building as a creative act and investigates the role of innovation, emulation and imitation in this process. It also analyses and explains structural deviations of the Russian community from its English-language counterpart and discusses the correlation between national, international and transnational aspects in Russian Internet culture.

Chapter 7 provides a case study of *Jokes from Russia*, one of the oldest and the most popular web sites on the Russian Internet. It discusses the issue of "cyber-humour" and folklore in the Internet Age and focuses on the dialectics of personal and collective creativity in the project development.

Chapter 8 identifies the contribution to knowledge, summarises the research findings, compares them with generalizations found in previous research and outlines implications for further research.

16

The work ends with a list of bibliographic references.

The text has a modular structure. The continuous numeration of sections facilitates cross-references and adds a hypertext quality to the linear text.

1.6. Definition and discussion of terms

The statement of the problem and the formulation of research questions and research assumptions involve some terms which need definition and discussion. Terms which recur in these foundational statements are 'the Internet', 'Internet culture', 'creativity', 'Internet creativity', 'the Russian Internet' and 'history'. Definitions adopted by researchers are often not uniform, so key terms are defined to establish positions taken in this research.

1.6.1 The Internet

The Internet is a complex concept and its definitions depend on what aspect is emphasised. The Internet has been defined in technological, social, cultural, commercial and even mythical or metaphysical terms. The central elements of most definition are "computer technology" and "network". Some of the definitions combine several aspects. An example of such a definition is found in Wikipedia:

> The Internet, or simply the Net, is the publicly accessible worldwide system of interconnected computer networks that transmit data by packet switching using a standardized Internet Protocol (IP). It is made up of thousands of smaller commercial, academic, domestic, and government networks. It carries various information and services, such as electronic mail, online chat, and the interlinked Web pages and other documents of the World Wide Web.[1]

This research focuses on the cultural dimension of the Internet. More specifically, it approaches the Internet as a domain of creativity, that is, a specific "cultural, or symbolic, aspect of environment" (Csikszentmihalyi, 1999) in which creativity occurs.

---

[1] http://en.wikipedia.org/wiki/The_internet

17

1.6.2 Internet culture

Internet culture (synonyms: cyberculture, virtual culture, etc.) can be generally defined as the totality of cultural practices on or apropos of the Internet. It has been also approached from various perspectives (e.g. Aronowitz, 1995; Moore, 1995; Jones, 1997; Kiesler, 1997; Porter, 1997; Smith, 1999; Bell, 2000; Bell *at al.*, 2004). The key topics in Internet culture/cyberculture studies include virtuality, community and identity, as well as such derivative subjects as embodiment/disembodiment, cyborgs, cybersex, self/government and sub/countercultures that take place on the Internet.

There are two major trends in Internet culture research. Sociological theory (Sztompka, 1993) distinguishes between structure-oriented theories and action-oriented theories. The first focuses on recurring structures and an entire society or culture; the second focuses on the processes of change and individuals and groups as the agents of change. Most of Internet culture research follows the structure-oriented theories which tend to understand culture in terms of recurring patterns, established norms and typical behaviour. Introducing an innovation, shifting patterns and establishing new norms are primary subjects of action-oriented approach. Both creativity and history – the key concepts of this research into an Internet culture – involve change. This demands the use of an action-oriented approach which shifts the focus from mass adoption to individual innovation, from following the norms to establishing the norms.

From this perspective, Internet culture is a culture of users/producers rather than of users/consumers, to use the terms introduced by Castells (2001). Unlike most Internet culture researchers who have studied cultural *uses* of the technology, Castells 2001: 36) defines Internet culture in terms of cultural *production*: "Technological systems are socially produced. Social production is culturally informed. The Internet is no exception. The culture of the producers of the Internet shaped the medium." Such an approach allows introducing creativity as a key element of Internet culture. This was reflected in a working definition of cyberculture suggested elsewhere (Gorny, 2003): "Cyberculture is a creative activity in the digital media, based on the intrinsic motivation and principles of interaction and sharing." An informal definition given by Linus Torvalds (Torvalds and Diamond, 2001) suggests that cyberculture is using computers "just for fun".

Such a definition allows locating cyberculture among other typical practices/discourses found on the Internet. As it has been argued (Gorny, 2003), there are discourses of creativity, authority, business, and consumption, each representing a certain system of ideas, values, practices and motivations. The main value of cyberculture is creativity and the leading motivations are play and self-actualization. Other types of discourses are dominated by different motivations, such as power, wealth, and consumption. The Table 1 shows the correlation between these discourses.

Values / Discourse / Practice	Dominant motivation	Agents
Authority	Power, control, manipulation	Government
Business	Profit	Companies, corporations
Consumption	Entertainment (consumption of material and immaterial goods)	Consumers
Creativity	Play, self-actualization, sharing	Creators

Table 1. Locating cyberculture: values, motivations and agents.

Cyberculture, as any creative activity, involves production. The Table 2 shows its relationship to other discourses/practices by the type of motivation and productivity.

Motivations / productivity	Non-productive	Productive
Extrinsic	Authority	Business
Intrinsic	Consumption	Creativity

Table 2. Locating cyberculture: motivation and productivity.

The proposed operational definition of cyberculture is unconventional but useful in the context of discussion about Internet creativity. It should be noted that historically cyberculture has two distinct phases. Macek (2005) opposes *early cyberculture* as a past socio-cultural formation to *contemporary cyberculture* – much in the same way as I proposed elsewhere (Gorny, 2003). If early cyberculture, or Cyberculture-1, was a dualistic ideology based on the strong opposition between the online and the offline world, then its contemporary form, or Cyberculture-2, is a more holistic worldview, in which the online is inseparable from the offline and the virtual serves as an instrument of the real. However, Cyberculture 1 and 2 share a common set of values, such as creativity, freedom, sharing, and voluntary collective production, which allows us to argue that they are not two different phenomena but stages in development of the same phenomenon.

A few reservations should be made about the correlation between production and consumption, introducing innovation and following the established patterns on the Internet. First, structure and action are not absolutely opposed to each other but rather they are two interacting aspects of the Internet as a sociocultural environment. One of the strategies "attempting the synbook of 'two sociologies', the individualistic sociology of actions and the holistic sociology of structures" (Sztompka, 1993: 299) is theory of social movements. The question about if and to what extent Internet culture can be considered as a social movement is beyond the scope of this research. What is important is the idea of interconnection between structure and action, consumer uses and creative production in Internet culture. This dialectical relationship is discussed throughout the study.

Second, the opposition between producers and users is too rough to account for the whole range of dynamics of Internet culture. In many cases users are not passive recipients in the process of diffusion of innovation (Rogers, 1962) but they actively contribute to its shaping (Oudshoorn and Pinch, 2003). There are levels and degrees of innovation and creativeness among Internet producers, as well as of users' participation in and contribution to Internet culture. Fischer (2002) developed the "Consumer/Designer Spectrum" transforming the opposition to a scale: passive consumer, active consumer, end-user, user, power users, local developers, domain designer, meta-designer. This model emphasizes degrees of creativeness found in Internet culture.

1.6.3 Creativity

Most definitions of creativity found in research literature (Runco and Albert, 1990; Runco and Pritzke, 1999; Sternberg 1999) include the following structural elements: 1) *novelty* (originality, unexpectedness) of the creative work, 2) its *value* (relevance, appropriateness, significance, usefulness, effectiveness), and 3) *assessment* of something or someone as being creative by an authoritative body according to some criteria and 4) *communication* of this value to an audience. A few reservations concerning these elements should be made.

1) Originality is not a decisive feature of creative work; novelty in creativity is always based on what has been created before. Theoretically, relative and absolute, or subjective and objective novelty may be distinguished. Subjective novelty is perception of something as being new by an individual person or a group of persons; objective novelty is something that is new for all humanity in its development through ages. It is unlikely, however, that even the most knowing and knowledgeable person can be bold enough to say that he knows everything that was before and take liberty to judge things from this standpoint. Hence follows that one can never be fully confident that something is objectively new; thus, any forms of novelty are subjective or at least intersubjective, that is relative and probabilistic.

Self-aware artists, writers, scientists and other creators and innovators have always acknowledged the relativity of novelty. Newton acknowledged standing "on the shoulders of giants" in science. Goethe who was both a poet and a scientist asked the question, "What is invention, and who can say that he invented something?" and answered himself, "It is an utter foolishness to swagger about precedence. Not to admit oneself, after all, a plagiarist is just a senseless fanfaronade". Historian Thomas Carlyle maintained that "the merit of originality is not novelty; it is sincerity." Osip Mandelstam described how poetry is created saying that "scald will sing an alien song. But will pretend that it is his one." T.S. Eliot said that the difference between a good poet and a bad one is that the first steals consciously while the second steals unconsciously. And a contemporary inventor holds that the main thing that one should have to invent is a big database.

However, if even one accepts the fact of borrowing of ideas and material in creativity, one usually can distinguish – intuitively or rationally – new from old, original from banal. The reason is that the perception of novelty largely depends on the breadth of vision and the depth of historical memory. The depth of memory in covering the news on TV or newspapers rarely exceeds a few months. In that which they sell as "new", "original" and "unprecedented", a historian, philologist or psychologist can easily find recurrent patterns that were in use many ages ago. The Internet and cyberculture are not an exception. Intellectual and cultural histories of the Internet reviewed in section 2.5.2 of chapter 2 reveal numerous mythological and ideological antecedents of Internet culture. What is then the nature of perceived novelty? Arieti (1996: 4) points out, "Whereas theologians and religious people in general believe that God's creation comes *ex nihilo*, from spacial and temporal nothingness, human creativity uses what is already existing and available and changes it in unpredictable ways". These "unpredictable ways" may include creation of forms that are not in use in the creator's environment, combination of the common elements into a singular structure, deformation of the habitual form, a shift of function in which the object is used, and so forth. Thus, taxonomy of novelty turns into taxonomy of transformations.

In this study novelty is understood historically, that is in terms of contrast (with a context) and transformation (of what was borrowed). Borrowing and recurring structures are considered as the elements of novelty production. The dialectics of the old and the new in creativity accounts for both continuity and discontinuity in the historical process.

2) There is no single criterion to establish value and usefulness of a creative work. Ochse (1990: 2) points out that experimental and social criteria of usefulness are different: "'Valuable' may refer to answers that gain high marks on creativity

tests or to inventions that change the quality of human life". Researchers of creativity suggest that usefulness regarding creative products "is not meant in merely a pragmatic sense, for behavior or thought can be judged as useful on purely intellectual or aesthetic criteria" (Feist, 1999: 158). Moreover, value and usefulness depend on *Weltanschauung*, that is, the range of needs and the scope of interests of both creators and the audience. The difference between individuals and social groups with regard to needs, interests and values makes a uniform concept of usefulness problematic. The concept of usefulness results from assessment of a creative work.

3) Who does decide what is original and useful and tell creative phenomena from non-creative ones? Three typical agents of assessment and corresponding procedures may be distinguished: 1) the *creator* himself who evaluates his work by his own *internal standards*; 2) the *audience* that accepts the creative work and *popularity* (often expressed in terms of attention or in money equivalent); 3) the *experts* (gatekeepers, field) who "have the right to add memes to a domain" (Csikszentmihalyi, 1999: 324) and thus define the author's *reputation*. Historically, all three types have been used, although the predominance of a particular type varied depending on the period or social context.

Creativity research tends to focus on expert assessment. Usefulness presupposes an external evaluation, hence the social nature of creativity. This factor has been recently emphasized in the framework of the "system approach", which regards creativity as a process at the intersection of individual, social and cultural factors (Amabile, 1983; 1996; Hennessey and Amabile, 1999; Csikszentmihalyi, 1988, 1996, 1999; Woodman and Schoenfield, 1989).

The partisans of this approach tend to regard creativity as a product of social consensus, rather then a result of personal differences. As Czikszentmihalyi (1996: 29) put it,

> [W]e don't need to assume that the creative person is necessarily different
> from anyone else. In other words, a personal trait of "creativity" is not what
> determines whether a person will be creative. What counts is whether the

novelty he or she produces is accepted for inclusion in the domain. This may be result of chance, perseverance, or being at the right place at the right time. Because creativity is jointly constituted by the interaction among domain, field, and person, the trait of personal creativity may help generate the novelty that will change a domain, but it is neither a sufficient not a necessary condition for it.

However, the emphasis on the social aspect of creativity narrowly understood as the evaluation by the *field* (experts) logically leads Czikdzentmihaly to a rather absurd conclusion (*ibid.*: 30):

> According to the system model, it makes perfect sense to say that Raphael was creative in the sixteenth and in the ninetieth centuries but not in between or afterwards. Raphael is creative when the community is moved by his work, and discovers new possibilities in his paintings. But when his paintings seem mannered and routine to those who know art, Raphael can only be called a great draftsman, a subtle colorist – perhaps even a personally creative individual – but not creative with a capital C.

He maintains that "creativity can be constructed, deconstructed, and reconstructed several times over the course of history" (*ibid.*). Although this is generally true, the particular interpretation of the causes ascribing the leading role to the experts is biased. It seems a projection of the ideology of elitist managerialism and technocracy, a historically transient phenomenon characteristic for late capitalism as described by Rozsak (1969: 6-7):

> In the technocracy, nothing is any longer small or simple or ready apparent to the non-technical man. Instead, the scale and intricacy of all human activities – political, economic, cultural – transcends the competence of the amateurish citizen and inexorably demands attention of specially trained experts. <...> The technocracy is ... the regime of experts – or those who can employ the experts.

Although the experts play a significant role in the social processes of creativity, they are not the only agents of assessment. Creators and creative audiences also have their means to evaluate creativity. Their assessment can significantly diverge from that of the experts. Moreover, the field itself is not a united but highly diversified entity. The technique of "consensual assessment" of creativity (Hennessey and Amabile, 1999) relies on the independent subjective judgements of individuals familiar with the domain in which the products were made or which are recognized experts in the domain. However, this technique tends to produce uniform judgements when applied to everyday creativity or creativity in a stable field, but fails in evaluation of creative works at the "cutting edge" of any domain or in the situation of the paradigm shift when it results in a broad diversity of opinions. The arguments between schools of critics or discrepancy between popular taste and connoisseurs' judgments provide other examples of the lack of unanimity in assessing the value of a creative work.

This research combines several criteria of assessment of creative work on the Russian Internet. It considers both the audience's response to a work (popularity) and expert judgements (reputation). In the latter case, preference is normally given to the experts within the domain (Internet culture producers) than to the experts outside the domain (critics and researchers without personal involvement in and contribution to Internet culture). Self-assessment of Internet creators is also considered.

4) Communicativeness of cultural value as an essential element of creativity is emphasized by media and communications researchers (Negus and Pickering, 2004). This element is especially conspicuous in Internet creativity which involves communication in both production and distribution of creative works.

The concepts and theories of creativity are discussed in more detail in section 2.2 of chapter 2.

1.6.4 Internet creativity

Internet creativity can be defined as creativity which takes place in the Internet domain and which uses Internet technologies to produce, publish and distribute creative works.

The concept of Internet creativity has been used rarely and inconsistently. Research literature on the issue is fragmented in terms of subject-areas, underlying assumption and employed methods. Some researchers tend to equate Internet creativity with technological invention or innovation; some with techniques and skills such as HTML coding or web authoring; others with such practices as online political activism or Internet art, etc.. Some emphasize the role of individual innovators; others focus on online creative collaboration. For some reason, the concept of creativity does not enjoy popularity in Internet research. Most often studies of actual agents, forms or processes of creativity on the Internet have managed without the concept of creativity; it has been just mentioned or suggested. Although research into creative practices on the Internet reviewed in chapter 2 does not usually refer to creativity theories discussed in section 2.2 of chapter 2, taken as a whole, it covers the fundamental aspects of creativity: the creative person, the creative process, the creative product and the creative environment. However, the lack of a common conceptual framework results in incommensurability of findings and a growing compartmentalization of knowledge. The need for a broader synthesis and the development of a general theoretical framework is urgent.

In response to this challenge, this study introduces Internet creativity as one of the key concepts which constitute the foundation of its theoretical and methodological framework. Internet creativity is used as an umbrella term that covers various forms and practices of production and communication of cultural value on the Internet. To develop the concept of Internet creativity, the study applies the concepts and theories of creativity research to the Internet domain. This makes possible comparison and linking together a range of phenomena which otherwise would be perceived as separate and incomparable. On this basis, unexpected regularities can be discovered and emprirical generalizations can be made.

1.6.5 The Russian Internet

Like the Internet generally, *the Russian Internet* is understood in this study mainly in cultural terms. A working definition of the Russian Internet is as follows: it is a totality of information, communications and activities which occur on the Internet, mostly in the Russian language, no matter where resources and users are physically located, and which are somehow linked to Russian culture and Russian cultural identity. The culture-based definition adopted in this study is opposed to the geography or state-based definitions of the Russian Internet employed by some Russian official or commercial structures (Schmidt and Teubener, 2005a). The English word "Russian" corresponds to two different words in the Russian language which accounts for the divergent interpretations and which should be therefore distinguished. *Russkij* refers to ethnicity and culture, while *Rossijskij* refers to geography, citizenship and the state. Although these two concepts of Russianness often overlap, this study is generally about the *Russkij* rather than *Rossijskij* Internet.

The cultural geography of the Internet is defined mainly by linguistic factors. Presumably, the number of users using a language must reach a certain critical mass to enable the formation of a linguistically/culturally specific internet cultures. Developed 'internets' are few, similarly to grand civilizations whose number is estimated from ten to twenty. According to a recent research (GlobalReach, 2004), Internet users speaking in languages other that English make up 64.8 percent of the total Internet population. The most used non-English languages are distributed as follows: Chinese – 13.7 percent, Spanish – 9.0 percent, Japanese – 8.4 percent, German – 6.9 percent; French – 4.2 percent, Italian – 3.8 percent. Although the share of the Russian language is relatively modest – only 0.8 percent – it did not prevent the emergence of Russian Internet culture.

However, it is not only the sheer number of users but also their self-reflection which account for the development of the idea of culturally specific "internets". Schmidt and Teubnener (2005a) point out that the idea of "RuNet" (a popular abbreviation for the Russian Internet) as something which unites Russian-speaking users as "us" in implicit opposition to "them", seems to have no direct analogues in European segments of the Internet. They suggest an explanation of this fact by analysing several factors: the historical circumstances of the development of the Internet in Russia, political context and cultural situation. The opposition between "us" and "them" on the Russian Internet corresponds to the concept of Russianness popular in both Russian culture and mass consciousness. In this respect, the idea of the Russian Internet or "RuNet" is comparable with such cultural constructs as the "Russian way" or the "Russian idea" both of which suggest the uniqueness of Russia and its historical mission as well as its complex relationship to both the West and the East.

It should be accepted that the concept of the Russian Internet is fuzzy and includes marginal cases when it is unclear if something relates to the Russian Internet or not. These cases include web sites, communications or software produces by Russians in other languages as well as resources produced by foreigners in Russian. Thus, Google can hardly be considered as belonging to the Russian Internet just because its co-founder Sergei Brin is a Russian. One the other hand, works of Russian net.artists Olia Lialina and Alexei Shulgin made in English do belong to Russian Internet culture as well as to Internet culture generally, even if in different ways.

Previous researchers showed that the uses and interpretations of the Internet in Russia were rooted in historical and cultural experience of the people and argued that cultural factors are essential for understanding the Russian Internet and avoiding theoretical projections and overgeneralizations. Thus, Rohozinski (1999: 24) pointed out that

> The Russian Net's scope and character, and that of its attendant cyberspace, are strongly embedded in its specific socio-cultural context, bounded by

language and the specific needs of its users. The Russian case reminds us to be cautious in our tendency to conceptualize networks as a universal social technology, unbounded by the norms of human societies and behaviour. Perhaps we need to adopt an anthropological approach to cyberspace, which is as much defined by culture, language and circumstance as any other area of human endeavour.

The study follows this suggestion and emphasizes culture, language and history as essential factors defining the Russian Internet.

To sum up, the Russian Internet is a specific meaningful formation emerged and developing in the intersection of two areas: new information technologies, on the one hand, and Russian culture, on the other hand. The double conditionality determines the dialectics of the general and particular in the subject matter. Technologically, the Russian Internet is homogeneous with the Internet as a whole; culturally, it is a unique phenomenon. At the same time, Russian Internet culture is not the result of a mechanical combination of technological and cultural constituents but rather their synbook which results in the emerging of a new quality. It is neither identical to Western cyberculture, nor it is a mere extension of Russian culture, although it is genetically linked to both.

1.6.6 History

This study is historical *par excellence*, although is combines methods of history with other methods of humanities and social sciences. The overall methodology of the study is discussed in detail in chapter 3, including the methods of history which are discussed in section 3.4.3. This section serves as a general introduction to this discussion. It provides a definition of history and specifies the type of historical research represented by this study.

This study follows Fisher's (1971) definition of history as a reasoned argument about past events in which answers to research questions include selected facts which are arranged in the form of explanatory paradigm. The argument takes the form of a narrative in which interpretation and explanation of facts emerge from the facts themselves rather than from a certain pre-establihed theory or ideology.

History can be classified in many ways. The most common are classifications by period (chronological), by region (geographical), by nation (national), by ethnic group (ethnical) and by subject or topic (topical). All these classification principles can be used to delimit the character of this study. Chronologicaly it covers the period from the late 1980's to the present with occasional excursions into a deeper past when the historical background is discussed. It is a study in modern or recent history. Geography, nationality and ethnicity play a secondary role in the cultural definition of the Russian Internet accepted in this study. The study does not focus on a specific region because Russian Internet culture is not limited by state borders. At the early stages of the Russian Internet most of its producers and the audience were physically located outside Russia. Now most of its producers, audience and resources are concentrated in the Russian Federation and the Russian Internet is more closely associated with Russia as a country. However, members of Russian diaspora constitute a significant part of the Russian Internet population. An estimated 25 to 50 million of Russians live abroad and some of them use the Internet as a means of a "virtual reunification" (Teubener, Schmidt and Zurawski, 2005). This fact justifies the definition of the Russian Internet in terms of culture rather than geography suggested in section 1.6.5. Nationality and ethnicity are relevant to the research questions of the study to the extent to which they constitute an important aspect of self-reflection of the members of the Russian Internet. The field of this study is Russian Internet culture, and its central topic is creativity as a source of historical change.

1.7 Delineation of the research problem and key assumptions

The data and conclusions of this research apply to the Russian Internet and they can be questioned outside these boundaries. Comparative research into the uses and interpretations of the Internet in different cultural contexts could help to develop broader generalizations concerning Internet creativity.

The research problem centres upon the paucity of empirical research into the Russian Internet. It also notes the shortage of theoretical exposition upon Internet creativity and the lack of established methodology for its study. It recognizes that, while there have been *ad hoc* studies devoted to specific domains of Internet creativity, there has been little attempt at synthesizing the results and methods of this research. On the other hand, the Russian Internet remains one of the least explored segments of the Internet on both factual and conceptual levels. Although the situation has been slightly improved since the project started and a number of studies on particular topics relating to the Russian Internet have been published, they are still few and fragmented. Moreover, there has been no attempt to approach the Russian Internet from the standpoint of creativity research.

Case studies provided the basis for the development of a set of interpretive theories. They were drawn from online evidence, interviews with participants, and personal experience of the author as a participant observer. These theories have been developed through the analytical process by the researcher and linked to existing theories where appropriate.

Every researcher has some assumptions concerning the subject of study as well as a broad range of ontological and epistemological issues. These assumptions may be defined by many factors such as belonging to a particular school, culture, or époque as well as by particularities of personal experience. These assumptions influence the choice of subject of study, research questions and methodological preferences. They may provide a starting point for asking questions; however, they should not predetermine the answers. The researcher must learn to be aware of these assumptions in order to avoid bias and respect them as an epistemological basis of his work. However, it is impossible to be totally self-aware. Moreover, as Michel Polanyi (1958: 156) noted, "Any attempt to gain complete control of thought by explicit rules is self-contradictory, systematically misleading, and culturally destructive". It is impossible (and unnecessary) to describe the thought process during the research in all its details; however, it is possible to clarify its basic premises and techniques.

31

To begin with, the author's background in humanities largely influenced his interest in the 'human side' of the Internet. I received my higher education in University of Novosibirsk which had a strong tradition of linguistic, literary and historical studies and University of Tartu, the centre of Russian structuralism, semiotics and cultural anthropology. The atmosphere at these two academic centres and the living example of my professors in Tartu, Yuri Lotman and Zara Mintz, had a deep impact on the formation of my scholarly outlook. I developed a strong preference to the interpretive approach based on a scrupulous textual analysis and an awareness of historical situatedness of cultural meanings. The reverse side of this is my aversion to both the substitution of meanings by numbers found in extreme cases of quantitative approach and the substitution of empirical-based reasoning by projection of ready-made ideologies. This academic background is also partly responsible for my interests in the correlation of personal and impersonal factors in culture, historical change and creative processes.

The study proceeds from the assumption that creativity is one of the most important driving forces which account for socio-cultural transformation. In this belief I follow the great historians and sociologists of modernity such as Spengler (1928), Kroeber (1944), Toynbee (1948) and Sorokin (1957). This view is supported by the tradition of creativity research as well as recent multidisciplinary research reviewed in section 2.3 of chapter 2 which have provided valuable insights into the role of creativity in post-modern society.

The next assumption concerns the role of cultural factors (interwoven with economic, political, social and other factors) in the process of construction and interpretation of technology. Culture is understood as a system of symbols, values and patterns of behaviour shared by a community. Symbols refer to language and the totality of works created in this language as well as to semiotic artifacts based on "secondary modelling languages" (Lotman) rather than natural languages. Values inherent in a culture are indirectly connected with language but they have a non-linguistic nature. Normally, they escape discursive formulations (unlike prescribing genres such as commandments, regulations and manifestos). Values

32

can be compared to Jung's archetypes of the collective unconscious but, unlike the latter, they are conditioned by the historical experience of particular societies. They are abstract mental forms or formulas that generalize people's experience and regulate their behaviour on a deep, usually unconscious level. Their abstract formula nature makes difficult their discursive expression, because expression is always a concretization of a formula by substituting the variable with certain definite values. What is expressed is always a variant; but the invariant remains ineffable. Probably the most effective way to represent the values is with artistic or religious symbols. The emotional charge and modelling role of these 'social archetypes' reveal themselves in an especially powerful way in crisis or 'mythic' situations, i.e. in situations where reality either radically diverges from the intuitive concept about how it should be or radically coincides with it. The totality of 'social archetypes' defines the psychological profile of a nation (Kas'yanova, 2003). On the external level, it determines stable behavioural patterns, that is, a tendency to behave in a predictable way in typical situations. These stable psychological and behavioural characteristics particular to a nation in abstraction from individual differences of its members constitute the "national character" (Peabody, 1985) or, using more up-to-date terms, the "hidden rules of behaviour" (Fox, 2005) that govern cultural identity.

The next assumption concerns the relationship between culture and technology. This relationship is studied in the framework of constructivist perspectives, such as the social construction of technology (SCOT) approach (Bijker, Hughes and Pinch, 1987; Bijker, and Law, 1992; Bijker, 1995). It argues that different social groups produce different meanings of technology, which accounts for its *interpretive flexibility*. The typical way of technological development is from *interpretive flexibility* to *stabilization* of meaning and uses that lead to *closure* of technology. This implies that a technology is the most rich in meanings in its early stages. However, even a stable technology can be revitalized by a shift in interpretation and use.

Who are the agents of technological evolution (and revolution)? The SCOT approach argues that these are different social groups including both designers and users of technology who interact within the same *technological frame* (Bijker, 1995). In dynamic interaction, they "determine what technologies are, what they do, how they work, even, what it means to say that they 'work'" (Scott, 1981). If designers of a technology try "to configure (that is to define, enable, and constrain) the user" (Woolgar, 1991: 69), then users often reconfigure the 'script of technology' in unpredictable ways by 'hacking the system' and finding new uses and applications of a technology. The latter process applies to not only hackers and cyberpunk but has more universal significance. Correspondingly, the diffusion of innovation that sometimes has been portrayed as a passive adoption of what had been designed by inventors and innovators (Rogers, 1962) is rather a co-construction or co-creation of technology by both producers and users (Oudshoorn and Pinch, 2003).

Although various types of users and social groups participating in constructing technology have been studied, the role of national culture communities in the process has usually remained in a shadow. However, the triple factor of symbols, values and patterns of behaviour shared by the members of a national culture influences both practical uses and ideological construction of a technology. This position is developed and tested in this study.

1.8 Scope and delimitations of the study

The ambit of this study was potentially large, and therefore certain boundaries needed to be established in order to make it both focussed and manageable. The explicit boundaries to the research problem have been described in section 1.2, and its limitations and key assumptions have been established in section 1.7. This section summarizes both explicit and implicit boundaries of the research problem.

The first limitation concerns the literature review. Although I tried to keep an eye for ongoing research on Internet creativity and the Russian Internet during the whole period, it would be impossible to review constantly all new research without detriment to the process of writing. Therefore, the literature does not tend to be current beyond the end of 2004. Any works that appeared after that time are represented very selectively.

A similar limitation applies to data. Chapters have different time scope defined by the subject and the actual time of conducting a case study. As a rule, the higher limit is also the end of 2004 with a sporadic inclusion of later data.

Limitations of methodology are defined by the use of qualitative methods of data analysis. It would be beneficial to support the emergent interpretive theories by quantitative data but, unfortunately, it was not possible in many cases. Thus, there is no available global statistic on the patterns of friendship on LiveJournal or a solid quantitative methodology which would allows assessing the degree of users' creativity. Quantitative methods were used where it was deemed appropriate throughout the study to balance the general qualitative approach. However, more quantitative research into the subject is needed. The author hopes that the study can provide a basis for future quantitative research which would test its results and help to develop formulations that are more precise.

Case study chapters use different units of analysis: a subdomain of Internet creativity (chapter 4), a genre form (chapter 5), a virtual community (chapter 6) and a web site (chapter 7). This was made deliberately to cover various dimensions and aspects of Internet creativity. However, in-depth exploration of a few aspects of creativity on the Russian Internet may restrict the generalizability of findings. The author does hope that his project can stimulate further research in the field which would add new dimensions to the work.

1.9 Expected results

My contribution to new knowledge will be factual, methodological, and theoretical.

First, the study introduces new factual material concerning the Russian Internet which has a value of its own and which can stimulate further research.

Second, the study attempts to establish a link between multiple areas of knowledge and corresponding methodologies. Its methodological innovation is a combination of methods found in Internet studies, history and creativity theory. The attempted synthesis is a response to the challenge which the Internet provides for traditional disciplines. It contributes to ongoing debates of methodological adequacy and to the negotiation of new research strategies in Internet studies.

Third, centring the research framework on the issue creativity enables a fresh view on the Russian Internet and the Internet generally. The integral approach used in the study makes it possible to synthesize the results of case study of particular aspects and sub-domains of Internet creativity. This allows seeing a connection between phenomena which appeared unconnected as well as linking them with wider historical and cultural contexts.

Finally, the study develops a historical approach which can stimulate the introduction of history into the agenda of Internet studies by providing a model for other researchers. From the standpoint of interpretive theory, the historical approach is not only about establishing the chronology of events (this task was partially accomplished at an earlier stage; see Gorny, 2000c) but also about reconstruction of cultural meanings, concepts, models, and patterns of behaviour which provide a context for social action and account for sociocultural change.

1.10 Conclusion

This chapter laid the foundation of the research. It outlined the background to the research and introduced the research problem and research questions. Then the research was justified, definitions of key terms were presented, the methodology was briefly described and justified, the book was outlined, the limitations were given and expected results were stated. On these foundations, the book can proceed with a detailed description of the research.

Chapter 2

LITERATURE REVIEW: INTERNET CREATIVITY RESEARCH

We create values. We do this because we are alive.

Hakim Bey (1998). Information War

2.1 Introduction

This chapter builds a theoretical foundation upon which the research is based by reviewing the relevant literature to identify the research issues which are worth researching because they are controversial and have not been answered by previous researchers. The research literarure on the Russian Internet has been reviewed in section 1.3 in the previous chapter. The lack of attention to creativity on the Russian Internet was stated and the research problem was thus justified. This chapter concentrates on the area of the research problem described in section 1.2 and links the research problem with a wider body of knowledge. It reviews the concepts and theories of creativity research and background theories about the role of creativity in modern society, discusses the controversies about the Internet as a domain of creativity and then focuses on the research literature on specific aspects of Internet creativity.

2.2 Concepts and theories of creativity research

Creativity is one of the key concepts of this research. This section reviews concepts, approaches and methods of creativity research relevant to the research questions.

The research literature on creativity is enormous and highly heterogeneous. Creativity has been studied 'from so many frequently incompatible theoretical perspectives, each with its own assumptions, methodologies, biases, and even meta-theoretical views' (Brown, 1989: 3) that reviewing this field of research is not an easy task. The situation is aggravated by the lack of unified terminology and an integral view that could help to coordinate various aspects of creativity research. As Ochse (1990: 2) put it,

> 'creativity' means different things to different people – even to different psychologists. Indeed it seems that 'creativity' means different things even to the same person, and that some writers are happy to ignore the distinctions between their various conceptions of creativity – leaping blithely to conclusions about one type of creativity on the basis of facts relating to another.

Wehner, Csikszentmihalyi, and Magyari-Beck (1991) reviewed 100 doctoral dissertations on creativity from psychology, education, business, history, history of science, and other fields, such as sociology and political science and found a "parochial isolation" between various disciplines studying creativity. They discovered, for example, that business-oriented research showed preference for the term innovation and focused primarily on the organizational aspects of creativity, while psychology research used the term creativity and was concerned mostly with the level of the individual. Creativity research remains highly compartmentalized. "Creatology", a term suggested by Magyari-Beck (1990, 1999) for a cross-disciplinary study of creativity, has not been generally accepted and is rarely used.

However, significant efforts have been made to systematize existing approaches, methods, concepts and terms. There are a few annotated bibliographies on creativity (Stein, 1960; Gowan, 1961, 1965; Razik, 1965; Arasteh, 1976; Anthony, 1981; McLeish, 1992) as well as a significant number of general presentations of creativity theories (c.f. Stein and Heinze, 1960; Freeman, Butcher and Christie, 1968; Vernon 1970; Bloomberg, 1973; Busse and Mansfield, 1980; Brown, 1989; Runco and Albert, 1990; Sternberg and Lubart, 1999). Recently several compendiums meticulously discussing various concepts and approaches of creativity theory have been published (Torrance *et al.*, 1989; Runco, 1997; Sternberg, 1999; Runco and Pritzker 1999).

38

Regardless of conceptual divergences, the definitions of creativity found in modern research literature share two common elements: (1) novelty (originality, unexpectedness) and (2) value (relevance, appropriateness, significance, usefulness, effectiveness).

This type of definition can be found in the recent *Handbook of Creativity* edited by Robert J. Sternberg (1999), an authoritative collection summarising contemporary creativity research. Let us give a few examples. 'Creativity is the ability to produce work that is both novel (i.e. original, unexpected) and appropriate (i.e. useful, adaptive concerning task constraints)' (Sternberg and Lubart, 1999: 3). 'Like most definitions of creativity, ours involves novelty and value: The creative product must be new and must be given value according to some external criteria' (Gruber and Wallace, 1999: 94). 'A creative idea is one that is both original and appropriate for the situation in which it occurs' (Martindale 1999: 137). 'Creativity from the Western perspective can be defined as the ability to produce work that is novel and appropriate' (Lubart, 1999: 339). The comparison table compiled by R. E. Mayer (1999: 450) shows the unanimous use of these two elements in definitions of creativity through the whole book.

Another two elements often found in definitions of creativity are assessment and communicativeness. The discussion of the definitions of creativity and their constituting elements are presented in section 1.6.3 of chapter 1. This study adopts an integral definition of creativity proposed by Negus and Pickering (2004) who define creativity as "communication of cultural value" and analyse its relationship to such aspects of culture as convention, innovation, tradition and experience.

Creativity has been traditionally considered as consisting of four components or aspects: (1) the creative process, (2) the creative person, (3) the creative product and (4) the creative environment or situation (Arieti, 1976). These aspects are discussed below.

2.2.1 The creative process

The study of the creative process includes the following major topics: a) characteristics of the creative process, b) stages of the creative process, c) motivation, and d) forms of creative behaviour. Aspects of these topics have been discussed by major approaches to creativity.

a) The psychodynamic approach describes the creative process as a combination of two mental mechanisms, which Freud called *primary and secondary processes*; the first is archaic, illogical and is a function of the unconscious, while the second is a function of the awake mind and relies on common logic.

The psychometric approach (Guilford, 1954; Plucker and Renzulli, 1999) uses the concept of *divergent thinking* (Baer, 1993; Runco, 1991) and assesses the quality of the creative process by testing such factors as fluency (or number of generated ideas), flexibility (the variety of perspectives represented by ideas), originality (statistical infrequency of ideas) and elaboration.

Associative theory treats creative thinking as the formation of "associative elements into new combinations which either meet special requirements or are in some way useful" (Mednick, 1962). Arthur Koestler (1964) introduced the term 'bisociation' to designate "any mental occurrence simultaneously associated with two habitually incomparable contexts" which he considered the essential mechanism of the creative process.

b) The division of the creative process into stages or phases was introduced to research on scientific creativity by the physiologist Helmholtz and the mathematician Poincaré (1921). Joseph Wallas (1926) distinguished between four stages of the creative process: 1) preparation, 2) incubation, 3) illumination, and 4) verification. This division was generally accepted by the subsequent researches, sometimes with some variations of the name or number of the stages. Thus, Osborn (1953) expanded the list to seven stages: 1) orientation (pointing out the problem); 2) preparation (gathering pertinent data); 3) analysis (breaking down the relevant material); 4) ideation (piling up alternatives by way of ideas); 5) incubation ("letting up", to invite illumination); 6) synthesis: putting the pieces together; 7) evaluation: judging the resulting ideas.

c) The motivation of creators is another important aspect of creative process.

Freud (1900; 1908) explained creativity as a means of reducing the tension between fundamental biological drives and social norms and restrictions. Creativity, in this view, is a form of sublimation of socially unacceptable desires of a sexual or aggressive nature, and their replacement by symbolic forms of wish-fulfilment. In this respect, creativity performs the same function as dreams or play. Freud (1910, 1925) also tended to identify creativity with neurosis and generally considered it as a pathological phenomenon.

Other theorists, on the contrary, have described creativity as a healthy tendency to master one's own environment and to realize one's human potential. This approach can be traced back to Jean-Jacque Rousseau's view that a man is essentially good, though often corrupted by social institutions, and Nietzsche's concept of super-man. Thus, Alfred Adler and Otto Rank, both disciples of Freud, rejected Freud's suggestion that creativity resulted from the sublimation of a sexual drive, and suggested instead that it was successful expression of a positive drive to improve the self and gain mental health. Thus, Adler (1956) argued that many great creative persons developed their skills to compensate for physical or intellectual disability. He also considered fear of death as a strong motivation force for creativity since it inspires people to compensate for their feelings of impending extinction by producing something of lasting value to survive them. Rank (1968) believed that creativity is motivated by two fundamental fears – fear of death and fear of life. On this basis, he built up his typology of personal development and definitions of three kinds of persons – adaptive, neurotic, and artistic. He considered creativity as a way to a healthy personality.

This view was developed further by the Humanist school in psychology. Both Rogers (1976; 1980) and Maslow (1968; 1973; 1987) believed that creativity was motivated by the drive for self-actualization or fulfilling one's fullest potential. Maslow described creativity as the spontaneous expression of the person whose more basic needs have been satisfied. However, his definition of self-actualization as "the process of becoming everything one is able to be" (Maslow, 1968) has been later criticized as 'unrealistic and unwise' (Ochse, 1990: 20) as well as his underestimation of the factor of work and persistence in the creative process. Rogers (1976, 1980) believed that the self of the creator could be the object of creation to the same extent as more conventional creative products such as poems, paintings or technological inventions. He insisted that creativity is restricted by external evaluation and stimulated by unconditional acceptance and the possibility of free expression.

The motivation of creativity has also been understood as a search for the ideal object, 'an object that does not exist in his psychological reality' (Arieti, 1976: 30), as 'a way of repairing the self' (Storr, 1989: 143) and 'to restore a lost unity, or to find a new unity, within the inner word of the psyche, as well as producing work which has a real existence in the real world' (*ibid*: 123). Crutchfield (1962: 121) proposed the distinction between extrinsic and intrinsic motives, defining the first as such motives where 'the achievement of a creative solution is a means to an ulterior end rather than the end in itself', and the second as such motives where the person is mostly interested 'in the attaining of the creative solution itself'.

The concept of the two types of motivation has been elaborated by Amabile since the early 1980s (Amabile, 1983). Extrinsic motivation is defined as a 'motivation to engage in activity primarily in order to meet some goals external to the work itself, such as attaining an expected reward, winning a competition, or meeting some requirement; it is marked by a focus on external reward, external recognition, and external direction of one's work.' (Amabile and Collins, 1999: 299-300). Amabile identified two types of extrinsic motivators: synergistic, 'which provide information or enable the person to better complete the task and which can act in concert with the intrinsic motives' (*ibid*, 304), and nonsynergistic, which lead the person to feel controlled and are incompatible with intrinsic motives' (*ibid*).

Extrinsic motivation is opposed to intrinsic motivation, which is defined as a "motivation to engage in activity primarily for its own sake, because the individual perceives the activity as interesting, involving, satisfying, or personally challenging; it is marked by a focus on the challenge and the enjoyment of the work itself" (Amabile and Collins, 1999: 299). Intrinsic motivation is a condition of *detached devotion* (Henle, 1962), a psychological state related to creativity in which a person's intense passion, commitment, and interest in the activity are combined with a critical detachment.

Amabile proposed, in the framework of her *componential model* of creativity, the "intrinsic motivation hypothesis" which in its later form (known as "intrinsic motivation principle) states that "Intrinsic motivation is conducive to creativity; controlling extrinsic motivation is detrimental to creativity, but informational or enabling extrinsic motivation can be conducive, particularly if initial level of intrinsic motivation are high" (Amabile 1996: 119).

Csikszentmihalyi (1996: 90) also notes that typical motivation for creativity is a combination of personal interest and a sense that something is askew in the intellectual environment.

c) Policastro and Gardner (1999) distinguished between five forms of creative behaviour according to the type of goal: 1) solution of a problem (or a discovery), 2) theory building (constructing a set of concepts that account for existing data and organize them in a way that sheds light on – and points to new directions in – a given domain), 3) creating permanent works in a symbolic system (for example, works of art), 4) performance of a ritualized work (interpretation of a work such as a symphony or a ballet), and 5) high-stake performance (for example, political activism, military engagement, athletic contests, and presidential debates). They point out that 'each of these creative forms has particular strong (also not exclusive) associations with specific domains and disciplines. One expects more often to find scientists engaged in problem solving and theory building; writers, painters, composers, and inventors engaged in creating permanent works; dancers and actors involved in stylistic performances; and political leaders engaged in high-stake performances' (*ibid.*, 221). This theory relates to the research question about the Internet as a domain of creativity and its relationships with other domains as well as its subdomains.

2.2.2 The creative person

The study of the creative person includes the following major topics: a) personal traits, b) types of creative persons and c) levels or degrees of creativity.

a) Some authors argue that creativity is determined primarily not so much by characteristics of mental processes occurring in the creative act as by specific personal traits. Various lists of such traits characterizing the creative person may be found in the research literature. Thus, Davis (1999) collected over 200 adjectives and brief descriptions of creative attitudes and personality traits found in literature on creativity and sorted them into fifteen categories of positive, socially desirable traits and seven categories of negative, potentially troublesome traits. Most characteristics found in creative people may be considered as both positive and negative. However, the situation is more complicated because the creative person is characterized by mutually exclusive traits.

Csikszentmihalyi (1996: 57) maintains that the most prominent trait in creative persons is *complexity*, that is, tendencies of combining thought and action that in most people are segregated:

They contain contradictory extremes – instead of being an "individual", each of them is a "multitude". Like the color white that include all the hues of the spectrum, they tend to bring together the entire range of human possibilities within themselves.

He lists ten pairs of apparently antithetical traits that are "often both present in such creative individuals and integrated with each other in a dialectical tension" (*ibid.*: 58): 1) energy and rest: 2) smart and naïve (as in divergent thinking); 3) combination of playfulness and discipline, or responsibility and irresponsibility; 4) an alternation between imagination and fantasy at one hand, and a rooted sense of reality at the other; 5) extroversion and introversion; 6) humbleness and pride,

44

ambition and selflessness, or competition and cooperation; 7) combination of "masculine" and "feminine" traits (the tendency towards androgyny); 8) traditional and conservative, rebellious and iconoclastic views; 9) passionate and objective attitudes to their work or the ambivalence of attachment and detachment; 10) openness and sensitivity that results in suffering and pain but also a great deal of enjoyment. He conclude that, '[T]he novelty that survives to change a domain is usually the work of someone who can operate at both ends of these polarities – and that is the kind of person we call "creative"' (*ibid.*: 76)

Another often-quoted trait of creative persons is *adaptation* (Cohen and Ambrose, 1999) However, the term is used in at least three different meanings: 1) to adjust the self to fit environmental conditions through *conformity*, agreement, or *compliance*; 2) to acclimatize or apply experience to the use or selection of an environment to personal advantage; 3) to modify or transform the environment to suit the individual. The dynamic interplay between person and environment is one of the most important factors in the analysis of creativity. It is essential to understand *who* or *what* is adapting and in what sense. One the one hand, the ability to adapt to an environment is traditionally (since, perhaps, Darwin) considered as a condition of creative behaviour. On the other hand, "If the individualregards the external world merely as something to which he has to adapt, rather than as something in which his subjectivity can find fulfilment, his individuality disappears and his life becomes meaningless" (Storr, 1989: 72). Creativity necessarily includes both adaptation and its opposite: "man's adaptation to the world is the result, paradoxically, of not being perfectly adjusted to the environment, of not being in a state of psychological equilibrium" (*ibid.:* 197).

Kirton (1994) suggested that there are two poles of creative behaviour and developed a scale to measure cognitive style preferences, so called *Kirton Adaptive-Innovative Inventory*. He distinguished between innovators and adaptors. Innovators prefer looser cognitive situations that allow them to break out of the paradigm. Adaptors, on the contrary, prefer structured situations; their focus is on redefining, elaborating, modifying, and improving a paradigm. Adaptors and innovators both have distinct attributes that can be advantageous or disadvantageous, depending on the specific context.

Cohen (Cohen, 1989; Cohen and Ambrose, 1999) developed a scheme called *Continuum of adaptive creative behaviour* addressing adaptation in context as well as the creative process itself. The levels of this continuum are as follows: 1) learning something new: universal novelty; 2) making connections that are rare compared to peers; 3) developing talents; 4) developing heuristics; 5) producing information; 6) creating by extending a field; 7) creating by transforming the field.

The creative person is characterized by a high degree of *autonomy*, which is defined as a tendency to move away from or to be relatively uninfluenced by others. Autonomy is understood as a trait that "clusters around other social dispositions: introversion, internal locus of control, intrinsic motivation, self-confidence/arrogance, non-conformity/norm-doubting, desire for solitude, and asocial and antisocial leanings. These traits are social because they each concern one's consistent and unique patterns of interacting with others" (Feist 1999; cf. Cuypers, 2001). *Introversion*, which is closely tied with autonomy, is defined as a tendency to focus attention inward and to withdraw from social stimulation.

The adjacent concept of *self-management* is defined as intentional monitoring and guiding of one's own behaviour. Studies have shown the importance of self-evaluation and *metacognition* for human performance in general (Jausovec, 1994; Kitchner, 1983) and for creative thinking in particular (Runco, 1991). Self-management involves learning one's own strengths and weaknesses and finding ways to use them for creative work, awareness of what conditions and environment are more conducive for creativity and time management.

Autonomy often takes form of *solitude*. Winnicott (1969) found that "the capacity to be alone [...] becomes linked with self-discovery and self-realization; with becoming aware of ones deepest needs, feelings, and impulses". Solitude is one of the components of psychoanalytic concepts of 'ego strength' defined as capacity to maintain personal identity despite psychic pain, distress, turmoil and conflict between opposing internal forces or the demands of reality (Fried, 1980).

Anthony Storr (1989) noted that people in the late 20th century have wrongly come to view relationships as the only possible source of happiness to the neglect of one's intellectual and creative development. Moreover, creative and interpersonal skills are to some extent competing and even opposing forces. As it is, many people are often afraid of being alone and feel uncomfortable when confronted with themselves. Such is not the case with most creative people, who often have lives that not only provide much opportunity to be alone but actually require it. The high rates of norm-doubters among the highly creative suggest a willful and intentional desire to be alone and outside the influence of others (Feist, 1999). Freedom, creativity, intimacy, and spirituality are considered to often result from solitude (Long and Averill, 2003).

Curiosity and *interest* are also positive factors influencing creativity. Storr (1988: 73) notes, "Interests, as well as relationships, play an important part in defining individual identity and in giving meaning to a person's life". These are linked with *passion*, which is an important characteristic of creative people. Russian ethnographer and historian Lev Gumilev (1973/1990) introduced the term *passionarity* (from Latin *passio*, passion) to signify the ability for and urge towards changing the environment, both social and natural, or, physically speaking, towards the disturbance of inertia of the aggregative state of an environment. He defined passionarity as a psychological characteristic reproduced genetically that accounts for deviations from the normal behaviour of the species and is opposite to the instinct of self-preservation. It is always directed to changing the environment, both social and natural, and the attainment of the desired aim, which is often illusory or even destructive for the subject himself, but which seems to him more valuable than his own life. Passionarity accounts for the formation of new ethnos and various innovations in society and culture in the established ethnos. Gumilev argued, for example, that all military and political history of the developing ethnos consists of various variants of passionarity induction by which the crowds of harmonious persons are set in motion. It is also at the foundation of the anti-egoistic ethic where the collective interests, even if wrongly understood, prevail over the craving for life and concern for one's own posterity. Individuals possessing this characteristic under favourable conditions perform actions that, summing up, break the insertion of tradition and initiate change in the ethnos. Passions of various kinds such as greed, ambition, envy or love are also modes of passionarity. Czikszentmihalyi (1996: 11), although he is not using the term passionarity, describes the psychological source of creativity is a similar way:

> Each of us is born with two sets of instructions: a conservative tendency, made up of instincts for self-preservation, self-aggrandizement, and saving energy, and an expansive tendency, made up of instincts for exploring, for enjoying novelty and risk – the curiosity that leads to creativity belongs to this set.

The capacity of creative individuals to exploit their differences from the norm, converting them to their advantage, is denoted by the term *fruitful asynchrony* used by Gardner and Wolf (1988).

Among the traits that impede creativity, the most often quoted is *conformity* defined as action in accordance with customs, rules, prevailing opinions or with standards such as law, order, wishes or fashion. *Conformity* may take form of *acceptance* that involves both acting and believing in accord with social pressure or *compliance* that involves publicly acting in accord with social pressure while privately disagreeing. As it was shown by research, conformity and creativity are largely incompatible because people who tend to conform to group opinions and beliefs are usually motivated by extrinsic motives and escape taking risks connected with originality. (Crutchfield, 1962; Sternberg and Lubart, 1995; Sheldon, 1999).

Another factor negatively influencing creativity is *habit*. As William James (1908) put it:

> The force of habit, the grip of convention, hold us down on the Trivial Plane; we are unaware of our bondage because the bonds are invisible, their restraints acting below the level of awareness. They are the collective

48

standards of value, codes of behavior, matrices with built-in axioms which determine the rules of the game, and make most of us run, most of the time, in the grooves of habit – reducing us to the status of skilled automata with Behaviourism proclaims to be the only condition of man.

b) Historically, there have been many attempts to classify creative behaviour and creative persons. Rank (1932/1968) wrote about three types of persons typifying the three stages in the development of creative personality: 1) the adaptive or average man, 2) the neurotic man, and 3) the artist or man of will and deed. *Adapted man* is one who is dominated by the fear of life. Such people continually seek the security of belonging and unity with others. They tend to be dependent, and to conform. *The neurotic* is dominated by the fear of death, and continually tries to separate himself from the others, although he feels guilty for doing so, as children feel when exercising their own will against their parents. In the *artist* fears are balanced. They acquire discipline form the others while preserving their own individuality.

Taylor (1959) distinguished between five types of creativity which correspond to a certain types of creative persons: 1) *expressive creativity*, or independent expression, without reference to the quality of the product; 2) *productive creativity*, when the individual gains mastery over some section of the environment and produces an object; 3) *inventive creativity*, which requires the new use of old parts; 4) *innovative creativity*, when new ideas or principles are developed; and 5) *emergent creativity*, which requires the 'ability to absorb the experiences which are commonly provided and from this produce something quite different'.

Ochse (1990) classified various types of people and behaviours commonly described as creative into three major categories: 1) people who are designated as creative because of their lifestyle, interpersonal functioning and attitudes; 2) people who perform well on creativity tests or other given tasks that are described as creativity; 3) people who produce something of cultural value, creative geniuses.

Csikszentmihalyi (1996) similarly wrote about tree types of creative persons: 1) *brilliant*, those who express unusual thoughts, 2) *personally creative*, those who experience the world in novel and original ways, and 3) *creative unqualifiedly,* those who effect significant changes in their culture.

Policastro and Gardner (1999) proposed a typology of creators based on two factors: 1) the extent to which the creator accepts the current domain as given (as compared to challenging the delineation of domains), and 2) the extent to which the creator is concerned with a world of objects and symbols that denote objects and objects' relations (as compared with a focus on the world of persons). They distinguish between four kinds of creators: 1) *the master,* an individual who accepts the current domain as delineated and seeks to realize genres of that domain to the most superlative degree; 2) *the maker,* an individual who, whatever his or her mastery of the current domains, is driven by a compulsion to challenge current domain practices and, ultimately, to create new domains or subdomains; 3) *the introspector,* a person whose creativity is devoted to the exploration of his or her own psyche; and 4) *the influencer,* who explores the personal world, but directs his or her creative capacities towards affecting other individuals.

c) Creativity may be realized in varying degrees. There is traditionally opposition between *original genius* who introduce fundamental novelty and *talent* who merely is good at doing something. Arieti (1976) differentiated between *ordinary* and *great* creativity. The first is the function of ego of every human being, while the second is the prerogative of *genius.* These two levels of creativity are different in their functions and outcomes both on personal and societal levels: "If it is true that ordinary creativity uplifts man's morale and dispels or decreases neuroses, great creativity is responsible for humanity's great achievements and social progress" (*ibid.,* 10-11). Gardner (1993) contrasted "little C creativity" – the sort of all of us evince in our daily life – and "big C creativity" – the kind of breakthrough which occurs only very occasionally. Similarly, Boden (1991) distinguished between psychological (P) and historical (H) creativity saying that the first relates to something that is novel and original for a particular individual, and the latter to the whole of human history. Other synonyms for this opposition include mundane/mature, everyday/exceptional creativity, etc..

2.2.3 The creative product

The third aspect of creativity, the creative product may take the most various forms because creativity occurs in virtually any domain of human activity. Ariety (1976) lists the following domains of creativity: wit; poetry and aesthetic process; painting; music; religious and mystical experiences; science; philosophy (including general system theory). The difference between domains results in the problem of evaluation criterion. As Plucker and Renzulli (1999: 44) put it,

> The importance of creative product emerged in response to perceived needs for external criteria to which researchers could compare other methods of measuring creativity for the purpose of establishing validity. However, an absolute and indisputable criterion of creativity is not really available, hence the criterion problem.

The most common method for the measurement products utilizes the ratings of external judges who are experts in a given domain. *Consensual assessment technique* (CAT) is an example of this approach. This technique used for assessment of creativity and other aspects of products, relying on the independent subjective judgements of individuals familiar with the domain in which the products were made or which are recognized by the experts in the domain. This method tends to produce uniform judgements when applied to everyday creativity or creativity in a stable field. However, the use of this method at the "cutting edge" of any domain is more problematic because it often results in a broad diversity of opinions. (Hennessey and Amabile, 1999)

There have been attempts to establish attributes of form and content which distinguish great creative works from ordinary ones. Thus, Simonton (1984) used quantitative methods to explore 15,618 themes in the classical musical repertoire and found out a positive relationship between thematic fame and melodic originality. He also studied 81 plays created by five of the world's most famous dramatists (Aeschylus, Sophocles, Euripides, Aristophanes, and Shakespeare) using content analysis. He found out that great plays could not be distinguished from obscure plays on the basis of the particular themes addressed. However, they differ in the number of issues they treat but only insofar as the issues are expressed in memorable passages.

2.2.4 The creative environment

Creative environment is defined as the physical, social, and cultural environment in which creative activity occurs (Sternberg and Grigorenko, 1997; Harrington, 1999). These include *zones of concentration and absorption*, that is times and places where people can become deeply absorbed in their creative work and where they can achieve levels of concentration not available in other settings. Some researches argue that "it easier to enhance creativity by changing conditions in the environment than by trying to make people think more creatively" (Czikszentmihalyi 1996: 1).

Arieti introduced the term *creativogenic society* to describe a type of society that enhances creativity. He described nine presumably creativogenic socio-cultural factors: 1) availability of cultural (and certain physical) means (at least, for the élite of society); 2) openness to cultural stimuli (in different aspects of human life); 3) stress on becoming and not just on being; 4) free access to cultural media for all citizens, without discrimination; 5) freedom, or even the retention of moderate discrimination, after severe oppression or absolute exclusion; 6) exposure to different and even contrasting cultural stimuli; 7) tolerance for diverging views; 8) interaction of significant persons; 9) promotion of incentives and awards. He suggested that only the first factor is absolutely necessary and that 'the other eight, although important, are not such factors that a tremendous effort on the part of the creative person could not overcome or remedy their absence' (Arieti 1976: 325). He also argued that the intrapsychic elements of the creative person are more essential for creativity that any socio-cultural circumstances. Simonton (1999) who used quantitative methods found out four characteristics of supportive social environment enabling flourishing of creativity: domain activity, intellectual receptiveness, ethnic diversity, and political openness. Florida (2002) came to

52

similar conclusions in this research in his study of "creative cities", i.e. broad social, cultural and geographical milieu conducive to creativity.

2.2.5 Theoretical approaches of creativity

Sternberg and Lubart (1999) group theories and approaches to creativity into seven major approaches: mystical, pragmatic, psychodynamic, psychometric, cognitive, social-personality and a group of confluence approaches. These approaches use a wide range of methods and not all of them are relevant for this project. Thus, psychometric methods devised for the direct measurement of creative ability or its perceived correlates in individuals using paper-and-pencil tasks (Guilford, 1954; Plucker and Renzulli, 1999) are not applicable to the projects for evident reasons. The same applies to experimental approach to creativity (Runco and Sakamoto, 1999) which is similar to the psychometric approach in its methods but focuses rather on cognitive and problem-solving performance than on personality and environment.

Although a range of approaches can be applied to the Internet creativity, the most useful for this study are a) social-personality approach and b) historimetric approaches which both emphasize social and historic dimensions of creativity. They are relevant for the research questions and they correspond to the interpretive theory framework adopted in the study.

a) Social-personality approach focuses on personality variable, motivational variables, and the sociocultural environment as sources of creativity. Representatives of this approach are the componential model and the system approach.

The *componential model* (Amabile, 1983, 1996; Lubart, 1999) is an attempt to specify the set of abilities, skills, traits, dispositions, and/or processes that are involved in creative behaviour. This model suggests that creativity will be highest in that area where the three components (domain-relevant skills, creativity-related processes, and intrinsic task motivation) share their greatest overlap. In other words, people are most likely to be creative within their "creativity intersection". Identifying this intersection can be an important step towards creativity.

In a similar way, *the systems approach* regards creativity as a process at the intersection of individual, social and cultural factors (Amabile, 1983, 1996; Csikszentmihalyi, 1988, 1996, 1999; Simonton, 1988; Woodman and Schoenfield, 1989). It defines creativity as the result of "the interaction of a system composed of three elements: a culture that contains symbolic rules, a person who brings novelty into the symbolic domain, and a field of experts who recognize and validate the innovation" (Csikszentmihalyi, 1996: 6).

Domain is defined as a cultural, or symbolic, aspect of the environment (Csikszentmihalyi, 1999). Domain in an essential element for defining creativity because "creativity occurs when a person makes a change in a domain, a change that will be transmitted through time" (*ibid.*, 315). Gardner (1983) described seven domains (or, in his terminology, intelligences): linguistic, musical, logical, special, bodily kinaesthetic, interpersonal and intrapersonal; later he added to these 'naturalist's intelligence'.

Field is defined as a social aspect of creative environment. It refers to the social organization of the *domain* – "to the teachers, critics, journal editors, museum curators, agency directors, and foundation officers who decide what belongs to the domain and what does not" (Csikszentmihalyi 1999: 315). The actors of the field are called *gatekeepers*. In other systems field is often used in the meaning of *domain*.

b) The historiometric approach applies statistical methods to the study of historical data. It is defined as "scientific discipline in which nomothetic hypotheses about human behavior are tested by applying quantitative analysis data concerning historical individuals" (Simonton 1990: 3). Central topics of historiometry include the developmental psychology of exceptional creativity (life-span study of illustrious creators); the foundation of creativity (birth order, intellectual precocity, childhood trauma, family background, educational and special training, role of mentors and masters); the manifestation of creativity

54

(change of creative styles through age, differential and social psychology of phenomenal creativity); and distribution of creativity in population.

Normally historiometry concentrates on historical rather than contemporary subjects. As Simonton (1984: 17) explains, 'One rationale for this focus is that exploitation of historical populations may maximize our ability to discover any transhistorically invariant laws of creativity and leadership. Hypotheses about the nature of genius should be tested on samples with the maximum amount of cultural and historical variety, if a behavioral law holds across such diversity, then it has the highest probability of universal validity.'

However, contemporary creators can also be the subjects for historiometric study: 'historiometricians do not always study just dead people: as the hypotheses permit, the subjects can be very much alive. Creators and leaders can make history in their own lifetimes' (*ibid.*, 18). People who were honoured by inclusion in Who's Who, an encyclopedia, a historical treatise, or even a biography "can be treated like any eminent figure of the past." (*ibid.*: 18). The principle that 'eminence is the best indicator of historical genius' applies to contemporary creators as well. Other criteria are Citation Indices (in sciences, politics, arts, etc.), the size of the audience (for TV, cinema, media), sales level, the percentage of the general repertoire, etc. Two aspects of eminence should be distinguished: popularity (public opinion) and recognition (expert evaluation). The factor of continuous influence is essential to determine historical eminence.

Unlike historiometry, this study relies on qualitative rather than quantitative methods using the latter just occasionally. The significance of historiometry for this study consists in the fact that historiometry formulates "laws of creativity and leadership" that can serve as reference points for this research.

The "laws of historiometry" can be summarized as follows.

(1) Creativity can be considered as a variety of leadership. "If a leader is one whose imprint on the group exceeds that of most group members, then certainly some creators are leaders within their own cultural realms." (Simonton, 1984: 78)

The third group of the eminent are celebrities which are neither creators nor leaders and their fame is ephemeral.

(2) The potential of a creator or a leader is almost entirely established in adolescence and early adulthood, the rest of the individual's life being dedicated to actualizing this potential genius. Hence follows the importance of the study of family influences, role-models, etc.

(3) The desire to excel is a primary factor in achieved eminence, often compensating for an intellect below the highest rank. A strong need to achieve excellence was found in 90 percent of the eminent.

(4) The role of education for the development of creative potential: obtaining basic knowledge and skills is necessary; graduate education is irrelevant. The role of self-education, wide interests and a breadth of perspective is high. Versatility – the number of separate fields in which individual attains distinction – significantly correlates with achieved eminence.

(5) Certain prolific persons are responsible for a disproportionate share of the achievements in any given domain of creativity. This highly skewed distribution of creative contributions has been formulated as a social scientific law by Alfred James Lotka (1926). According to this law, the number of scientists publishing exactly n papers is roughly proportional to $1/n^2$, where the proportionality constant varies with the discipline. Lotka's law is remarkably similar to Pareto's law of income distribution, by which cumulative figures for personal earnings, as assessed in several nations over a long period of time, tend to be proportional to $1/n^{15}$. Lotka's law was refined by Price (1963). According to Price's law, half of all scientific contributions are made by the square root of the total number of scientific contributors: thus, if there are 100 scientists within a given discipline, just 10 of them will account for 50 percent of all publications. The validity of this law has been confirmed for various cultural domains and historical periods. As Simonton (1984: 81) concludes, "The inequality of productivity revealed in the highly skewed distribution of creative output is an undeniable law of historiometry."

(6) The quantity of productive output is probabilistically connected to quality of impact, or eminence. The odds of a creator's conceiving a quality product are always proportional to the quantity of products. This can be explained by Campbell's (1960) blind variation and selective-retention model of creativity which is analogous to that of biological evolution. According to Simonton (1984), the main factors of total lifetime output are the early beginning (precociousness), productivity rate and longevity.

(7) The principle of cumulative advantage or 'Matthew's effect' (Merton, 1968) is one basis for the extraordinary individual differences in eminence and influence. Matthew's effect functions to create a small group of eminent leaders: 'In leadership, as in creative endeavours, an élite few accumulate more and more influence and power, and humanity is progressively stratified into the eminent, the also-run, and the anonymous multitudes' (Simonton, 1984: 92).

(8) The productive peak in a creative career – the floriut or acme – occurs around the age of 40. As was found by Beard (1874) who studied the biographies of more than a thousand eminent persons, 70 percent of the world's best work is accomplished by persons under 45 years of age and 80 percent of it by those under 50. The absolute peak period of a career seems to fall between 30 and 45, though the half-decade from 35 to 40 is more productive than that from 40 to 45. This findings were corroborated by latter researchers (Zusne, 1976; Simonton, 1977). However, the specific location of the peak vary from one creative discipline to another (revolution is, like poetry and mathematics, a preoccupation of youth, while history and philosophy reach their creative peak at a later age).

(9) The products of genius have objective attributes that set it apart from less distinguished creations, and these beneficial attributes may in turn arise from precise biographical events or circumstances, such as life crises or age.

(10) Neither the Zeitgeist nor the genius is unimportant, though both agents must yield some explanatory ground to chance as well.

The results of empirical studies of creativity on the Russian Internet will be compared with these laws in the final part of the research.

2.3 Creativity in post-industrial society

The issues of creativity have become crucial for any society that has overcome the boundaries of the industrial system and entered into a post-industrial state of development. The main characteristics of post-industrial society, the formation of which is traced to the 1960s, are the radical intensification of scientific and technological progress, the reduction of significance of material production that is expressed in the decrease of its share in the gross national product, the development of service and information sectors, the increased role of research and innovations, and the emergence of a new social class of intellectuals, experts and technocrats (Bell, 1973).

Post-industrial society has been described as a new social formation that, as the term suggests, overcame industrial means of production as well as correlating phenomena described by Marx such as private property, market economy, and exploitation (Touraine, 1974; Masuda, 1981; Gorz, 1982; Stonier, 1983; Frankel, 1987; Rose, 1991; Hage and Powers, 1992).

As Inozemtsev (2000) notes, the objective component of post-industrial society includes the shift from material production to the tertiary sector, transition from mass production to the production of customized or unique products, and the radical change of organizational structure. The subjective component includes the increasing dependence of society on the creative potential of its members.

Creativity has become the essential factor for both the productive process and the consumption of its results because they require knowledge and developed skills to cope with new information in a creative way. What is yet more important is the essential change in motivation and character of human activity. This change in the motivational structure of activity has been generally described in terms of transition from labour to creativity. Labour, which is the main form of activity in the industrial society, is forced by the external necessity confined by the limits of satisfaction of the material needs of men. As such, it is governed by extrinsic or outward motivation and serves as a mechanism of alienation of people from the world and themselves. Creativity, on the contrary, is a form of activity in which the intrinsic or inward motivation is realized and which is stimulated not by the necessity of satisfaction of immediate physiological or social needs but rather by the need for perfection of the personality and its abilities. As such, creativity is a means of elimination of the phenomenon of alienation that pervaded industrial society. This conception can be traced back to Marcuse's works, especially his *Eros and Civilization* (Marcuse, 1955); however, in the theory of post-industrial society it has been posited as an accomplished fact rather than a project for the future. The term 'post-material' was coined by Inglehart (1977) to designate the motivation that is directed to self-realization and freedom rather than to material and social goals. He conceptualized the shift of values in post-war Western society from material to immaterial as 'the silent revolution'. The increasing domination of 'post-material' motivation in post-industrial society has had a deep impact upon the entire system of social relationships, including economic, political, and cultural relationships. The growth of 'post-material' or intrinsic motivation meant the increasing role of creativity in the formation of the new social.

Since the 1960s the theory of information society has begun to develop (Machlup, 1962, 1984; Machlup and Mansfield, 1983; Porat and Rubin, 1978; Masuda, 1981; Stonier, 1983; Katz, 1988; Sakaiya, 1991). It has been a reaction to the growing role of computers and communication technologies in the life of society. This theory maintained that information and knowledge have become governing factors determining the process of social change and that they have replaced labour in the new social order to denote which such terms as "information society", "knowledge society", "knowledgeable society", "network society" and so forth have been used. The theory of an information society is sometimes critically assessed as a part of the theory of post-industrial society that concentrates on particular aspects of the new social order such as the role of information technologies and tends to abstract from others aspects of modern society (Inozemtsev 2000). However, the concept of information society (and its analogues) remains an influential theoretical model for understanding modern society (Castells, 1996, 1997, 1998; Castells and Himanen, 2002; Webster 2002, 2003).

The theory of post-industrial society emphasizes the growing share of the tertiary sector in economics while the theory of information society focuses on the role of knowledge and information. Creativity is another factor that becames conspicuous in the new social order. Toffler (1980) distinguished between three ages or waves in human history each with a specific dominant economic resource: agricultural (land and human labour), industrial (raw materials and physical labour) and creative (knowledge and creativity). Because creativity became the driving force of economic growth which raises productivity and living standards, the concept of creative class as a leading social class has been developed. Florida (2002) described the class structure in the U.S. in 1990s as follows: Creative class (including Super-Creative Class and a broader group of creative professionals), Working Class, Service Class and Agricultural Class. According to Florida (2002: 69), the Super-Creative Core of Creative Class includes "scientists and engineers, actors, designers and architects, as well as the thought leaders of modern society: nonfiction writers, editors, cultural figures, think-tank researchers, analysts and other opinion-makers", whose economic function is "to create new ideas, new technology and/or new creative content" (*ibid.*: 8). Creative professionals include people engaged in complex problem solving that involves a great deal or independent judgement and requires high levels of education and human capital. Florida (2002) estimated that members of the creative class make up 38 percent of the nation's workforce in the U.S. He emphasized the creative ethos shared by the creative class and focused on unequal distribution of creativity between creative and uncreative areas (the concept of "creative cities") and within creative epicentres between creative and service workers.

To sum up, creativity has been established as a key feature of the modern society by theorists and researchers who approached the issue from various theoretical and methodological perspectives.

2.4 The Internet as a domain of creativity

The Internet is one of the most conspicuous symbols of the new social order discussed in the previous section and the issue of creativity applies to it in full measure. This section analyzes the relationship between the Internet and creativity and reviews the research literature relevant to the research problem.

The issue of Internet creativity is situated in a wider context of the debate on the general effects of technology. This debate has often oscillated between polar views: progressive and critical, utopian and distopian, technophilic and technophobic. On the one pole, technology has been considered as something which 'makes life better'; on the other, it has been seen it as an instrument of enslavement, alienation and dehumanization. The opposition was conceptualized in terms of enablement and determination, or liberation and domination (Hill, 1988) as effects of technology. On the one hand, technology or technique is defined as "the ensemble of practices by which one uses available resources in order to achieve certain valued ends", but on the other hand, it becomes autonomous, self-determining and it *forces* human to adapt it, turning them from subjects into objects (Ellule, 1964). Culture presumably surrenders itself to technology that turns out to be a totalitarian force (Postman, 1992).

This binary opposition has been used to initiate "discussion on the extent to which new technologies and specific hardware and software *determine* the precise nature of their human use and therefore cultural 'creativity' and the texts produced by them; as opposed to the extent to which various new technologies *enable* their users to produce distinctive new cultural forms" (Hayward, 1990: 4). However, it was argued that oppositions are a rather crude instrument of cognition and should be superseded by a subtler analysis and more complex formulations. Thus, the antithesis between determination and enablement is eroded by the fact that "the range of potential applications of advanced technologies is necessarily beyond the precise intentionality of its designers and manufacturers" (*ibid.*: 6), which makes it possible to distinguish between 'preferred' or conventional uses predetermined by the manufacturer and 'creative' or more original uses invented by the users

61

themselves. The co-construction of users and technology has become a key issue in the study of sociotechnical change (e.g. Bijker, 1995; Oudshoorn and Pinch, 2003).

The Internet, like technology generally, has been seen as 'a brave new world' in the double sense of Shakespearian optimism and Huxleyesque pessimism (Cummings et al., 2002). On the one hand, it has been seen as liberating technology enabling people to overcome limitations of social structure, cultural dissociation and human nature at large. On the other hand, some have considered it a menace to humanity, a means of surveillance, enforcement and alienation. Some opposed the internet as 'a new home of the Mind' to the old tired world (Barlow, 1996), while others argued that it is an extension of 'the world where we live in' (Robins, 1996/2000). The opposition was typical at an early stage of the Internet's diffusion (late 1980s and early 1990s). However, by the end of the 20th century when more people went online and the Internet, at least the Internet in developed countries, became 'more ubiquitous and more invisible' (Gere, 2002: 201), the intensity of the debate smoothed out and the focus of researchers' attention has shifted from "homesteading on the electronic frontier" (Rheingold, 1993) to study of "The Internet in everyday life" (Wellman and Haythornthwaite, 2002).

The metaphor of revolution applied to the new technology went out of fashion; both utopian and distopian readings of the Internet gave place to an interpretation in terms of everyday life. Thus Cummings (Cummings et al., 2002: XII) argues that, although "the internet has had a dramatic effect on discussion about free speech, business and democracy" and some of these changes are controversial, "few of us really believe that the internet is transforming society as comprehensively as it is claimed on the fringes". He is echoed by Peter Watts (Cummings et al., 2002) who ridicules the idea of cyberspace and a tendency of interpreting the Internet in the sci-fi frame of reference found in cyberculture studies (Bell and Kennedy, 2000). He argues that consumer discourse presenting individuality as a function of buying is more valid for understanding people both offline and online. He refers to empirical research that "indicates people tend to use the internet in ways that suit their already established lifestyles, rather than adapting themselves to the medium" (Cummings et al., 2002: XV) and maintains that "in a world where more and more the discourse of the individual consumer shapes how the people know themselves, that understanding will more likely than not underlie how they engage with and understand the technology, when they seek and create content and when they communicate with each other" (*ibid.*, 17). However debatable this generalization may be, it exemplifies the dominant current trend to consider the Internet in terms of an extension of real life.

It would be an overstatement to say that Internet creativity has totally escaped the attention of researchers. However, it has mostly been touched upon indirectly in relation with other issues. The convergence of technology, science and culture as well as its impact on society is a topic of ongoing debates reflected in such concepts as technoscience (Aronowitz, 1995; Ihde and Selinger, 2003), technoculture (Robins and Webster, 1999), cyberculture (Dery, 1996: Bell *et al.*, 2004) and "information arts" (Wilson, 2002). The analysis of structural properties and aesthetics of new media (Manovich, 2001) provides an insight into how the new media are used to produce and distribute content and how the new forms and procedures become a model for the conceptualisation of other cultural domains. Although Manovich does not focus his attention specifically on the Internet, his observations apply to the Internet as a part of the new media. There has been research on artistic practices on the Internet under an umbrella-term of Internet art (Green, 2004). The use of the Internet for promoting technological and social change has been discussed in contexts of hacking (Levy, 1984/2001; Vaidhyanathan, 2004) and cyberactivitsm (Meikle, 2002; Jordan and Taylor, 2004). However, these and other creative uses of the Internet have been usually discussed separately and the general concept of Internet creativity has not been developed.

Thus, Castell's (1996; 1997; 1998) powerful and influential theory of network society managed without the concept of creativity. Pekka Himanen (2001), Castells's younger collegue, compensated for this omission. His work titled *Hacker Ethic and the Spirits of the Information Age* presents itself as a modern version of

Max Weber's *The Protestant Ethic and the Spirit of Capitalism* (1904-1905/1992). Himanen argues that creativity, not work is the ethos of the Information age. Seven fundamental values of the Protestant ethics described by Weber are money, work, optimality, flexibility, stability, determinacy, and result accountability. To these the author opposes symmetrically seven values of the hacker ethic (the concept first introduced by Levy [1984/2001]): *passion*, that is, the intrinsic interest that brings energy and joy to activity; *freedom* in lifestyle and in the rhythm of creative work; *work ethic*, which melds passion with freedom, *money ethic*, which does not regard money as value in itself but uses it to motivate activity with the goals of social worth and openness; *nethic* or the attitude towards networks which is defined by the values of activity and *caring* which means concern for others as an end in itself and, finally, *creativity*, that is, 'the imaginative use of one's own abilities, the surprising continuous surpassing of oneself, and the giving the world of a genuinely valuable new contribution' (Himanen, 2001: 141).

Himanen's conceptualization of the hacker ethic introduces creativity as one of the central elements of the Age of Information which makes it stand out from other theoretical approaches to the Internet which normally have ignored the concept of creativity. In his epilogue to Himanen's work Castells acknowledged, "In my own analysis, as well as the contribution of other scholars, this essential dimension of Informationalism has been touched upon but not really studied" (*ibid.*: 178). In his update to his own theory, Castells (*ibid.*: 177-178) introduces cultural creativity as an essential element of network society:

Informationalism was partly invented and decisively shaped by a new culture that was essential in the development of computer networking, in the distribution of processing capacity, and in the augmentation of innovation potential by cooperation and sharing. The theoretical understanding of this culture and of its role as the source of innovation and creativity in Informationalism is the cornerstone in our understanding of the genesis of the network society.

Himanen's idea of the hacker ethic and Castells's extension of his theory of network society can help in formulating research questions and provide a theoretical framework for the study of Internet creativity. However, both should be approached *cum grano salis* as they tend to universalize their findings and, in particular, underestimate the role of cultural differences. An interpretive approach outlined in section 3.2 of chapter 3 grounded in factual evidence and using predominantly inductive methods to generate concepts and theories can help to assess the validity and reliability of these theories. Before proceeding to this task the research literature on the dimensions and aspects of Internet creativity should be discussed.

2.5 Histories of the Internet

2.5.1 Internet as a collective creation

The Internet emerged as the result of collaborative creative efforts of many individuals and organizations. In 1957, the US formed the Advanced Research Projects Agency in response to the launch of Sputnik, the first artificial earth satellite, by the USSR. In 1969 the Advanced Research Projects Agency Network (ARPANET) was established under the sponsorship of the United States Department of Defence (DoD). Its aim was to develop a computerized distributed system of information transmission which would be able to withstand the destruction of nodes in wartime. In 1983, the TCP/IP networking protocol was implemented which provided interconnectivity between different computer networks and thus laid the foundation for the Internet as we know it today. In 1986, the National Science Foundation (NSF) began construction of a university network backbone (NSFNet). Apart from the military, the Internet became available in academic and research and institutions. In 1991, Tim Berners-Lee advanced the idea of the World Wide Web based on HyperText Markup Language (HTML). However, WWW became publicly accessible only in 1993, when Mosaic, the first web browser was released. This led to an explosion of the Internet (at 341,634 percent annual growth rate of service traffic). By 1996 the word 'Internet' became common public currency, but it was associated mostly with the World Wide Web. However, the Internet embraces many other services such as e-mail, Usenet newsgroups, file sharing, Instant Messenging, IRC, MUDs, webcasts and weblogs.

A timetable of Internet-related events shows how dynamically the Internet has been developing. The fist e-mail program to send messages across a distributed network was invented by Ray Tomlinson in 1971 (the following year, he introduced the '@' sign, meaning 'at' in an email address). USENET, a system of news groups, was established in 1979. The same year the first MUD (Multi-User Domain, or Dimension or Dungeon), a role-playing game where participants construct and interact in virtual text-based worlds, was established at University of Essex. In 1983, FidoNet, a system of off-line exchange of electronic messages, was developed by Tom Jennings. The same year, the name server was developed at University of Wisconsin, no longer requiting users to know the exact path to other systems. Domain Name System (DNS) was introduced the following year. In 1985, the first registered domain appeared (it was symbolics.com). The same year, the WELL (Whole Earth 'Lectronic Link') started; this electronic bulletin-board system (BBS) was latter used as an exemplary model of virtual community by Rheingold (1993). In 1988, Internet Relay Chat (IRC) was developed by Jarkko Oikarinen. In 1990, ARPANET ceased to exist. The same year, the first American commercial provider of Internet dial-up access appeared (world.std.com). The same year Mitch Kapor established the Electronic Frontier Foundation (EFF) to defend the rights of the 'netizen'. In 1991, Gopher, a system with some hypertext features was released at University of Minnesota. In 1992, the Internet Society (ISOC) was chartered. The same year, Veronica, a gopherspace search tool, was released by the University of Nevada. Also, the term 'surfing the Internet' was coined by Jean Armour Polly. In 1993, InterNIC was created by NSF to provide domain registration and other services. In 1995, Real Audio, an audio streaming technology, was introduced. First search engines (AltaVista) and catalogues (Yahoo) appeared. Netscape and some other Net related companies went public and the Internet boom began, which crashed in 2000. However, by that time the

Internet had become almost ubiquitous in developed countries producing a profound impact on work, leisure, knowledge and worldviews.

If the technological structure of the Internet has been developed by specialists in computer and information science, the development of Internet content and social applications has involved direct user participation and it is a striking example of "how users matter" (Oudshoorn and Pinch, 2003). The Internet is probably the most participatory medium which allows users to create content and to contribute to the development of the medium itself. 'Interactive creativity' (Berners-Lee, 1997) and 'the hi-tech gift economy' (Barbrook, 1998) have been essential features of the Internet since its very beginning.

According to a recent Pew Internet Report (Lenhart, Fallows and Horrigan 2004), 44% of Internet users in U.S. have created online content through building or posting to Web sites, creating blogs, and sharing files. Kevin Kelly (2002) points out that in just six years after the Netscape web browser 'launched the web in the mind of the public', 'we have collectively created more than 3 billion public web pages. We've established twenty million web sites. Each year we send about 3.5 trillion email messages'. (Add to this more than 1 terabyte per day generated by Usenet.) This incredible growth, he argues, 'is less a creation dictated by economics than it is a miracle and a gift'. He estimates that about seventy percent of web pages have been created by enthusiasts and non-commercial organizations and he predicts that 'as the Internet continues to expand in volume and diversity without interruption, only a relatively small percent of its total mass will be money-making. The rest will be created and maintained out of passion, enthusiasm, a sense of civic obligation, or simply on the faith that it may later provide some economic use.'

According to Tim Berners-Lee's vision (1997), the Web

> had to be not only easy to 'browse', but also easy to express oneself. In a world of people and information, the people and information should be in some kind of equilibrium. Anything in the Web can be quickly learned by a person and any knowledge you see as being missing from the Web can be

quickly added. The Web should be a medium for the communication between people: communication through shared knowledge.

From the very beginning, the tools allowing users to create and share content have been central to the Internet development. Thus Netscape Navigator, one of the first WWW browsers, included an HTML editor in its software package suggesting, in full accordance with Berners-Lee's vision that users would not only browse the Web but also create and publish their own content. It cannot be said that this vision was realized in its fullest in the development of the Internet. There are several reasons for this. First, because 'a large number of new media are designed from the perspective of seeing and treating humans primarily as consumers' (Fischer, 2002). Second, because a large number of users are hardly interested in anything beyond consumption and passive entertainment. However, the Internet provides numerous opportunities for various types of creativity for those who want to create. In order to delineate its potential for creativity, histories of the Internet have to be discussed in more detail.

2.5.2 Technological histories

There has been much research on the history of the Internet as a technological innovation (Abbate, 1999; Moschovitis, 1999; Wolinsky, 1999; Gromov, 2002; Loughran, 2003; Sherman, 2003). Different authors chose different points of reference for their chronologies. Thus, Moschovitis's chronology of telecommunications (1999) begins in 1843 with Charles Babbage's calculating machine and moves through the 19th century with entries on Morse and the telegraph, Bell and the telephone, and the innovation of Herman Hollerith and his electric tabulating system. Entries trace the early 20th century through the invention of the electronic binary computer (1939) to Arpanet (1969). He pays most attention to the period from 1970 and brings his story to 1998 when America Online bought Netscape. The chapter on future trends covers topics such as the Microsoft trial, advertising on the Internet, and Internet2. Abbate (1999) concentrates on a more modest time span – from the early networking breakthroughs formulated in Cold War think tanks and realized in the Defense Department's creation of the ARPANET to the emergence of the Internet and its initial growth. The numerous Internet timelines which can be found online belong to the same category. There are also a few country-specific Internet histories covering such countries as Australia (Clarke 2001, 2004), UK (Kirstein, s.a.), Finland (Karttaavi, 2004) and Russia (Gorny, 2000c).

Many authors writing about the Internet put it into a context of the history of technology and/or find its analogues in the histories of ideas. Internet has been often compared with earlier communication technologies such as telegraph and telephone (Winston, 1998; Bray, 2002) and interesting parallels have been found: the overestimation of the beneficial effects of a new technology on society in the early phase of its development; a common vector of gradual adoption of technology by different categories of users (scientists to the military to entrepreneurs to the general public); the progressive simplification of the interface and a corresponding transition from 'expert use' to 'dummy's use'; non-intended uses of a technology (for example, for practical jokes or flirt) and emerging on the basis of technological cultures. Misa (2004) begins his history of the Internet from the Renaissance. Briggs and Burke (2002) go even further into the depths of time and begin their account from the invention of printing. The Internet is thus situated within a long history of means of communication and it turns out to be rather a consistent stage in media evolution than a revolutionary break with the preceding tradition.

2.5.3 Intellectual and cultural histories

Another line of research consists in revealing the hidden ideological structure of the Internet and comparing its elements with other historical configurations of ideas. This approach regards the Internet in the framework of the history of ideas or intellectual history. Early works on cyberculture (Benedikt, 1991/2000; Escobar 1994/2000) emphasized metaphysical, mythical, mystical and magical roots of cyberculture. Mark Dery (1996) documented numerous instances of what Erik

Davis (1998) called TechGnosis, i.e. a combination of archaic worldviews with the new information technology. Margaret Wertheim (1999) in her study of the concepts of space from Dante to Internet showed that the ideology of cyberculture is closer to the medieval view, with its definition of the world as spiritual space, than to the modern physics' emphasis on the physical or abstract nature of space. The dualism between the material and the immaterial evoking Gnostic teachings and the idea of cyberspace as a shared soul space where people regain freedom from the dead weight of their bodies and where Mind reigns over matter (e.g. Barlow, 1996) stimulated spiritual aspirations but, as Wertheim concludes, it resulted in the ultimate failure of cyberspace to satisfy spiritual needs.

The mythological approach to the Internet is represented also by Mark Stefik (Stefik and Serf, 1997) who applies Jungian psychoanalysis to the study of the Internet and reveals metaphors and myths underlying its interpretation. He finds four persistent metaphors – digital library, electronic mail, electronic marketplace and digital world. He analyses archetypes related to four corresponding myths (since metaphor is nothing else than a condensed myth): the keeper of knowledge (the digital library), the communicator (electronic mail), the trader (electronic marketplace), and the adventurer (digital world). The Internet is thus seen as a realm of projection of the collective unconscious. Other authors take a different approach to Internet metaphors. Thus, Roman Leibov (1997) analyses the metaphor of movement and place used to describe the Internet in Russian language, while Annette Markham (2003) considers descriptions of the Internet as way of being, place and tool.

An edited volume *Prefiguring cyberculture: An intellectual history* (Tofts, Jonson and Cavallaro, 2002) seeks "to find ancestors, explore family connections and claim relations" of cyberculture recovering its antecedents in the history of ideas, pointing out that "technology alone is not sufficient to understand the evolution of cyberculture". The range of found analogies is impressive. Eric Davis demonstrates 'a profound if often unconscious Cartesianism' underlying cyberculture with its division between body and mind. Catherine Waldby explores

70

how technoscience since the 17th century eroded the limits between the natural and artificial (one of the central themes of cyberculture), using Mary Shelley's Frankenstein as a case study. Elizabeth Wilson discusses the presumptions of Alan Turing's concept of 'electronic brain' from which his famous test emerged and the correlation of intellectual and emotional in his theorizing about computers. Evelyn Fox Keller discusses Wiener's cybernetics that applied 'the principles of Life to work in the world of non-living'. Samuel J. Umland and Karl Wessel analyse the relationship between mind and complexity in the Philip K. Dick essay "Man, Android and Machine". Zoe Sofolius comments on Haraway's (1985/1991) Manifesto celebrating the figure of cyborg as an emerging form of experience and subjectivity traversing the opposition between male and female, natural and technological. Donald F. Theall traces the idea of cyberculture back to James Joyce's 'chaosmology', Teihard de Chardin's concept of 'noosphere' and Marshall McLuhan's ideas of the externalization of the senses and the global village and also mentions Borges' ironic image of 'The Total Library'. According to the author, the common element of these concepts as well as the idea the Internet is a merging of reality and dream.

Finding literary precedents of cyberculture is another preoccupation of the contributors to the volume. Thus, Bruce Mazlik reviews Samuel Butler's novels Erewhon (1872) and The Way Of All Flesh (1903) and discusses their central theme of "continuity among man, animals and machines and the inextricable links between these categories within cyberculture" (Mazlik, 2002: 238). McQire John Potts' (2002: 240) article directs attention to Marinetti's Futurist Manifesto and traces "utopian impulse as it ran through the futurists in the early 20th century and follows this impulse through to its current manifestation in the zone known as cyberculture". Margaret Wertheim (2002) describes the evolution of cyberculture in terms of transition from More's to Bacon's utopia. Russell Blackford (2002) analyses *Profiles of the Future* and other works by Arthur Clarke in the light of cyberculture. Richard Slaughter (2002: 264) "contextualizes cyberculture in a wider stream of human response to transformed future". This includes works of

71

science fiction writers such as John Brunner, William Gibson and Neal Stephenson; film such as Blade Runner, Terminator and The Matrix; non-fictional writings of H.G. Wells, Lewis Mumford, Herbert Marcuse and Theodor Roszak; and the institutional research of future-oriented NGOs such as World Future Society and The World Futures Federation. The main attention is paid, however, to critical analysis of Alvin Toffler's Future Shock (1970). He is criticised for his "habit of privileging aspects of the outer empirical world (facts, trends, change processes) and overlooking the inner interpretive ones (worldviews, paradigms, social interests)" (Slaughter, 2002: 270). The author concludes that "what Toffler, and indeed many futurists, overlooked is that *the future domain is primarily a symbolic one*" (*ibid.*, italic in the original) and suggests as an alternative to a technocratic approach to the future exemplified by Toffler the work of transpersonal synthesist Ken Wilber. It seems inappropriate to discuss in detail every article in this collection. However, what has been already said is enough to argue that the variety of ideological motifs and analogies the book reveals can be reduced to a few lines: the split between body and mind; confluence of natural and artificial, human and mechanical; the extension of senses and intellect through technology; religious and social utopianism; and, finally, the decisive role of dreams, fears and hopes in prediction of the future, retrospection of the past and interpretation of the present.

There are many other examples of the intellectual history approach to the Internet. Thus, Manovich (1999) argues that computer culture evolved from avant-garde practices developed by Russian constructivists and by Bauhaus artists in Germany in the 1920s whose artistic principles have been transformed into the conventions of modern human-computer interface and software. He also points out that the production and distribution of information on the Internet is typologically closer to the eighteenth century literary salons and similar small intellectual communities than to those of the Industrial Age. Gere (2002) suggests that digital culture was formed by heterogeneous social and cultural forces and inherited many ideas from the past. Among ideological components of digital culture he lists "techno-scientific discourses about information and systems, avant-garde art practice, counter-cultural utopianism, critical theory and philosophy and subcultural formations such as Punk" (*ibid.*: 14). In conclusion, he emphasizes the importance to acknowledge these elements in order "to be able to resist and question the relations of power and force" (*ibid.*: 201) embodied in current digital technology which becomes more and more ubiquitous and, therefore, invisible. Moreover, as he points out, some elements concealed in digital culture may provide models for such questioning.

Having considered the histories of the Internet let us now to proceed to the agents of Internet creativity.

2.6 Actors of Internet creativity

2.6.1 Typologies

Paraphrasing the title of Simonton's (1994) book the question can be put as follows: "Who makes the Internet history and why?" Following the system approach to creativity discussed in section 2.2.5, the agents of Internet creativity can be defined as users who introduce valuable innovation into the Internet as a technocultural domain. Late Castells (2001) differentiates between two types of Internet users: producers/users and consumers/users. He defines producers/users as 'those whose practice of the Internet feeds directly back into the technological system' and consumers/users as 'those recipients of applications and systems that do not interact directly with the development of the Internet, although their uses certainly have an aggregate effect on the evolution of the system' (Castells 2001: 36). He lists the four major actors of Internet culture who contribute to the Internet developments:

(1) Techno-élites, members of academia and research institutions who have developed the technical infrastructure and protocols of the Internet. Their supreme value is technological discovery; they form communities coordinated by authoritative figures; and they follow 'the basic rule of scholarly research under which all findings must be open' (Castells, 2001: 40).

73

(2) *The New Hacker's Dictionary* (1996:231) defines hackers as "expert programmers and network wizards", technological innovators who develop hardware and software. They share a set of values known as the Hacker Ethic (Levi 1984; Himanen, 2001) and are driven by an "inner joy of creation" (Castells, 2001: 47). Unlike techno-élites, 'they do not depend on the institutions for their intellectual existence, but they depend on their self-defined community, built around computer networks' (Castells, 2001: 47);

(3) Virtual communitarians, the 'users who brought into the Net their social innovations with the help of limited technical knowledge' (Castells, 2001: 52) by creating online communities (Rheingold, 1993/2000) around common interests.

(4) Internet entrepreneurs, the "heroes of the Net-economy", a 'composite of persons and organizations, made up of inventors, technologists and venture capitalists' (Castells, 2001: 58).

It follows from this categorization that a creative contribution to the development of the Internet domain occurs on several levels: scientific, technological, social, cultural, organizational, entrepreneurial, etc.; that Internet creativity is distributed across sub-domains of the Internet and that it takes various forms. It can also be manifested in varying degrees and the value of creative contribution may differ. The latter fact was conceptualized, for example, in Fischer's (2002) "Consumer/Designer Spectrum" mentioned in section 1.6 of chapter 1.

Castell's typology can serve as a working hypothesis for the research question about the agents of Internet creativity on the Russian Internet. It will be tested in case studies chapters. The next two sections discuss the relevant research literature and justify the research question about the correlation between individual and collective forms of Internet creativity.

2.6.2 Internet heroes

As has been shown above, the degree of user contribution to the Internet domain may vary significantly. Creativity on the Internet, as in any other cultural domain, is distributed unequally. Those whose creative contribution is recognized by the majority of users obtain the status of eminent creators, leaders and cultural heroes. The study of such persons' lives and creative achievements constitutes a specific line of Internet creativity research.

The biographical approach focuses not so much on the history of ideas as on the personal creativity of individuals who have expressed, promoted and realized these ideas. An extensive body of literature is devoted to those who made a conspicuous contribution to the Internet's development on various levels from technological invention to cultural interpretation. Internet pioneers, experts, wizards, heroes, digerati, Internet élite, Internet visionaries, Internet geniuses and other terms have been used to designate the significance and eminence of these personalities.

The term 'Internet élite' (very popular for some time on Runet) was used as early as in 1997 in an Advanced Technology Staffing report that investigated the IT work market (Brief, 1997). It surveyed 1,700 independent information technology consultants and hiring managers to gain insight into the new emerging workforce of 'free agent' professionals and analysed corresponding technology trends and demographics of independent IT consultants. It concluded that the post-industrial market, influenced by the explosion in electronic commerce and the growing global network infrastructure, 'was attracting the best and brightest technology specialists in the market, including many of the most highly skilled Internet and Intranet professionals'. These professionals were referred to as the Internet élite.

This term was also used by Laura French (2001) who related stories of Internet pioneers and innovators such as Andrew Grove, Lawrence Ellison, Ann Winblad, Esther Dyson, Steve Jobs, William H. Gates, Steve Case, Jeffrey P. Bezos, Jerry Yang, and Linus Torvalds. Similarly, Harry Henderson (2002) 'offers students insight into the lives and personalities of important figures who share a common vocation, cause or calling' in developing computers, the Internet and World Wide Web, navigating tools and electronic commerce with an emphasis on developers and entrepreneurs in the field. Many titles speak for themselves: *Steve Jobs: computer genius of Apple* (Brackett, 2003); *Jeff Bezos: business genius of Amazon.com* (Garty, 2003); *Bill Gates: software genius of Microsoft* (Peters, 2003a); *Esther Dyson: internet visionary.* (Morales, 2003b); *Larry Ellison: database genius of Oracle* (Peters, 2003b); *Steve Case: Internet genius of America Online* (Peters, 2003c). Leslie Hiraoka (2004) shows "how technical advances, financial engineering, and entrepreneurial genius are building the information highway" by analysing case studies relating to technical and financial areas of the Internet revolution. It is not always that Internet genius was measured by financial success; ideological influence also matters. Biographies of Linus Torvalds (Brashares, 2001; Torvalds and Diamond, 2001) and Richard Stallman (Williams, 2002) can serve here as examples.

The term *digerati* has seems to have slightly more intellectual connotations that cyber élite. As Wikipedia[2] explains,

> The digerati are the élite of the computer industry and online communities. Like "glitterati", the word is a portmanteau, derived in this case from "digital" and "literati." Famous computer scientists, tech magazine writers and well-known bloggers are included among the digerati.

It lists the following meanings of *digerati*: opinion leaders who, through their writings, promoted a vision of digital technology and the Internet as a transformational element in society; people regarded as celebrities within the Silicon Valley computer subculture, particularly during the dot-com boom years; anyone regarded as influential within the digital technology community. ('They are not on the frontier, they *are* the frontier', as the famous saying goes.)

In two books with *digerati* in the title, the term is used as a synonym to *cyber élite* in one case (Brockman, 1996) and *high-tech heroes* in the second (Langdon and Manners, 2001). One more synonym is *protagonists of the digital revolution* (Sottocorona and Romagnolo, 2003). It seems noteworthy that *digerati* are often

---

[2] http://en.wikipedia.org/wiki/Digerati

classified by the roles they play in the communication revolution. Thus, Brockman's (1996) list includes forty figures, each with a nickname signifying their archetypal function (cf. Stefik and Serf, 1997): for example, The Coyote (John Perry Barlow); The Scout (Stewart Brand); The Pattern-Recognizer (Esther Dyson); The Software Developer (Bill Gates); The Scribe (John Markoff); The Radical (Bob Stein) and The Skeptic (Cliff Stoll).

A special case of Internet geniuses are hackers. Hackers are considered to be one of the major driving forces behind the development of the Internet as both technology and culture.

The term "hacker" is ambiguous: it can relate both to 'heroes of the computer revolution' (Levi, 1984/2001) and to the 'extraordinary underworld' (Mungo and Clough, 1992) of 'outlaws on computer frontier' (Hafner and Markoff, 1991), 'masters of deception' (Slatalla and Quittner, 1995) and 'digital delinquents' (Thorn, 1996). It can be used to describe Hacker Ethic that embodies the Spirit of the Information Age (Himanen, 2001) as well as 'crime in the digital sublime' (Taylor, 1999).

There are numerous biographies of hackers and stories about their (un)famous deeds. The figure of Kevin Mitnick, most wanted computer outlaw, martyr of American justice and a model for many hackers, stands out in this context. His story was told many times from different perspectives (Hafner and Markoff, 1991; Shimomura and Markoff, 1996; Littman, 1996). Having served his term, Mitnick (2002, 2005) himself wrote books explaining the 'art of deception' and the 'art of intrusion', this time from the standpoint of a security consultant.

Hackers have often been considered as an embodiment of technological and Internet creativity. Thus, McKenzie Wark's (2004) *Hacker Manifesto* applies Marx's ideas to the age of digitization and intellectual property and defines hackers as a class of information producers who are exploited by the 'the vectorialist class' of owners/expropriators of information. Hackers are explicitly equated to creators in any domain (Wark, 2004: 004):

77

Hackers create the possibility of new things entering the world. Not always great things, or even good things, but new things. In art, in science, in philosophy and culture, in any production of knowledge where data can be gathered, where information can be extracted from it, and where in that information new possibilities for the world produced, there are hackers hacking the new out of the old.

Wards' understanding of hackers is reminiscent of Florida's (2002: XXVII) concept of creative class: 'If you are scientist or engineer, an architect or designer, a writer, artist or musician, or if you use your creativity as a key factor in your work in business, education, health care, law or some other profession, you are a member.'

Internet heroes and visionaries, digerati and hackers are obviously direct heirs of the concept of genius which held its position in European culture through Renaissance and Romanticism until our days, even if some researchers considered it 'an impediment to scientific research of creativity' (Sternberg and Lubart, 1999: 5). The concept of genius is closely connected with the idea of *alienation*, which suggests that "*the self is divided from the self* and that *the self is divided from the world*" (Currie, 1974: 9), and a possibility to overcome it in a creative act by the power of an exceptional personality possessing some extraordinary qualities. The work of a genius brings liberation to other people and this is the reason why creative geniuses become leaders and heroes. However, Internet creativity is not only about individual endeavour. It involves cooperation and collaboration which is the subject of the next section.

2.6.3 Collective creativity

One difficulty in evaluating Internet creativity is determined by the fact that it is often not individual but collective. The dialectical opposition between these two types of creativity is a subject of ongoing theoretical debates in both Internet studies and other social disciplines. The concept of collective creativity is often considered controversial. One the one hand, the Internet, as Hine (2000: 147) put it, is 'a text that is both read and written by its users'. On the other hand, the Western ideology of creativity (Lubart, 1999) has been traditionally associated with the concepts of individual personality and emphasized the role of solitary genius in the creative process. Non-individual, anonymous or group creativity have usually remained at the periphery of critical interest, and different evaluation criteria have been applied to such works. As Negus and Pickering (2004: 142) note, speaking about the situation in the arts, 'Eventually, the products of individual artistic creation in economically privileged countries are displayed in art galleries, while the artworks of so-called primitive or underdeveloped societies largely relegated to museums of ethnography or anthropology.' The different attitude towards these two kinds of art is caused by the fact that one is individual and the other is collective. The same principle applies to Internet creativity. A great deal of Internet creativity is collaborative in nature, which results in considering it as a fact of virtual ethnography (Hine, 2000) rather as a genuine creative work.

Group creativity has attracted the attention of researchers relatively recently, and although there is a growing body of research into the role of creative collaboration in music (Gillis, 1966), theatre (Sawyer, 2003), film industry (Travis, 2002), psychotherapy (Lewin, 1997), group communication (Frey, 2002), in the process of innovation (Paulus and Nijstad, 2003) as well as general discussion on creative collaboration (Schrage, 1995; Bennis and Biederman, 1997; Hargrove, 1998; John-Steiner, 2000); Gundry and LaMantia, 2001; Honig and Rostain, 2003), group forms of creation are still often considered as inferior to individual creativity.

However, many successful projects on the Internet from open source software to the popular web sites are products of collaborative creative efforts. The Internet blurs the borderline between users and producers. As Laslo Fekete (2001) pointed out that 'cyberspace requires the virtual presence of users, who are at the same time its creators'. He emphasizes the role of creative contribution of users on the Internet, contasting cyberspace economy to traditional capitalist economy:

Cyberspace could never have come into being or survived until now if it had separated entrepreneur from consumer or server from served (servant?), as does the reigning economic paradigm. The Internet is not pay-per-view TV, nor is the virtual community a pay-per-use society. Cyberspace, after all, is the place where symbolic goods, knowledge, and culture are manufactured, exchanged, and defined. It is a manifestation of the production and exchange of special goods to which earthly economics, based on the law of scarcity, does not apply, since the more freely we can access it, the faster it grows and the greater the profit it generates for all.

Although the role of collective forms of creativity on the Internet is indubitable, usually creative projects online have been inspired, initiated or guided by the charismatic individuals who have won laurels as outstanding creators or leaders. The dialectictical tension between the individual and the collective is one of the key topics in the discussion of Internet creativity and it will be addressed throughout the current project. The rest of this chapter reviews the research literature about typical forms of creativity on the Internet.

2.7 Forms of Internet creativity

2.7.1 Hypertext and hypermedia

When Michael Heim (1987) was writting his *Electric Language*, the word processor was a novelty, and like any technological innovation, it inspired dreams about radical changes of the human condition. Heim developed a philosophy of word processing with references to Plato, Aristotle, Heraclitus, Heidegger and other high minds of the past. His main idea was that word processors could amplify and augment thought:

> The encoding of letters in the ASCII (American Standard Code for Information Interchange) computer code not only permitted the transmission of natural-language at electronic speed; encoding natural language on

computers makes possible a new approach to language as directly manipulable in new ways (Heim, 1987: 82).

Although Heim acknowledged the negative effects of word processing raging from degeneration in handwriting skills to a decrease in the authoritativeness of the printed word, his overall conclusion was optimistic: electric language would reduce the need for time-consuming manual work demanded by writing, editing and publishing which would help develop a creative habit of the mind thus increasing human intellectual and creative potential.

The same vein of thought was characteristic of early conceptualizations of hypertext. The history of hypertext usually counts off from Vannevar Bush's (1945) article "As We May Think" in which he described a mechanical device called a Memex used for automation of library references of various kinds which would also follow references from any given page to the specific page referenced thus facilitating human cognition. Although the project was never realized, Bush's ideas inspired other inventors. In the early 1960s, Douglas Engelbart of the Stanford Research Institute began working on the On-Line System (NLS), the world's first implementation of what was to be called hypertext. The aim of the entire project, the Augmentation Research Centre (ARC), was to provide means of 'asynchronous collaboration among teams distributed geographically'. Engelbart's work directly influenced the research at Xerox's PARC, which in turn was the inspiration for Apple Computers. Influenced by both Vannevar Bush and Douglas Engelbart, Ted Nelson coined the word "hypertext" in 1965. Soon the first working hypertext systems appeared such as Apple's HyperCard or Nelson's Project Xanadu but they were overshadowed by the success of Tim Berners-Lee's World Wide Web introduced in 1993 which has become the de facto standard hypertext and hypermedia technology.

Bukatman (1995) defined hypertext as follows:

"Hypertext" designates texts that utilize non-linear (or multi-linear) structures through their composition and display on computer terminals. On screen, the text is separated from its physical existence on a hard disk, and becomes a malleable, "virtual" text. A unit of text might be "linked," through a click of the mouse or touch of a key, to another unit or text: a glossary or annotation, or another work by that author, or from that period, or one influenced by the first. Further, these additional texts, or units, can incorporate illustration, video, sound, as well as music or movie samples.

Even before the advent of WWW, Woodhead (1991: 71) referred to hypertext as 'a new information paradigm' which is 'needed to manage the growth of information in general.' Hypertext, he believed, provided an additional dimension of perception and conceptualization for the knowledge-worker as well as new 'means of distributing the finished products.' He considered hypertext and hypermedia as having 'the potential to become the dominant software paradigm of the 1990's' (*ibid.*: 93). According to Landow (Landow, 1997; Delany and Landow, 1991), hypertext leads to reconfiguring the text, the author, the narrative and literary education. Hypertext and hypermedia (Berk and Devlin, 1991; Lennon, 1997) has been conceptualized not only in the framework of writing and reading (Bolter, 1991) but also as sociomedia (Barrett, 1992) a powerful tool for the social construction of knowledge.

Having reviewed the history and theory of hypertext, Muller-Prove (2002) concluded that

> The designers of early hypertext and graphical user interface systems shared a common objective: the development of a personal dynamic medium for creative thought. Not very much is left from this original vision. Retrospect reveals promising insights that might help to reconcile the desktop environment with the Web in order to design a consistent and powerful way to interact with the computer.

Hypertext and hypermedia technologies have served as a basis for new artistic genres such as net literature and cyber literature which use the opportunities provided by hypertext and multimedia technologies for artistic purposes. However, these are only a small (and primarily text-based) fraction of what has become known as Internet art.

2.7.2 Internet art

Digital and communication technologies have transformed established artistic practices (Manovich, 2001) and led to the emergence of new forms of art. Although digital media has embraced most of the old media such as painting, print, radio, television, theatre and cinema and has become a meta-medium with an opportunity of easy transcoding between particular media, there is a class of artistic phenomena which relates to the Internet in a more direct way since they explore and use its properties to produce aesthetic effects. The interrelation of the Internet and the arts has been topic for a host of authors since the early years of the online world (Jacobson, 1992; Lanham, 1993; Kelly, 1996; Scholder and Crandall, 2001).

There are three fundamental aspects of the relationship between art and the Internet. Firstly, the Internet is used as a medium for presentation and distribution of any digitalized artworks regardless of their original domain of creativity such as literature, music or visual arts.

Secondly, there is Internet art, that is, art which uses the specific properties of Internet technologies and communication space of the Internet for aesthetic ends. There are many kinds, forms, and functions of Internet art. Green (2004: 8) lists six major art forms related to the Internet: web sites, software, broadcast, photography, animation, radio and email. Wikipedia[3] gives a rather different list: Internet-based or networked installations, online video, audio or radio works, networked performances and installations or performances offline as well as spam art, click environments and code poetry. Shulgin (1998) proposed a detailed typology of Internet art consisting of nine categories. Because his text was written in Russian and is not therefore accessible for the English-language audience, I shall review it in more detail. Shulgin's typology is a generalization derived from his own experience as a net artist as well as from his reflection on other's net artists' work.

---

[3] http://en.wikipedia.org/wiki/Internet_art

It takes into account both the material and the functions of Internet art and refers to both Western and Russian Internet art works. It includes the following categories:

1) storytelling (Lialina's non-linear hypertext love story *My Boyfriend Came Back From the War* is an example);

2) travelogue ('a favorite genre of people better known as curators');

3) interactive projects using HTML forms and CGI scripts (examples includes Jane Prophet's *TechnoSphere* and Roman Leibov's and Dmitry Manin's *The Garden of Divergent Hokkus*);

4) approaching the Net as an aesthetic object (representation of 'visual aspects of hypertext, modem connection, browser and animated GIF'; examples include works of jodi.org, Michael Samyn' *Zuper* and *Form Art* of Shulgin himself);

5) subversion ('the Net as an instrument of attack against the high and mighty – authorities and transnational companies'; examples include Rachel Baker's *Tesco Sansbury Clubcard* which merges the identities of the two UK trading networks; Unknown's *Heath Bunting: Wired or Tired?* – a fake article ascribed to the net artist; and Vuk Cosic's *Documenta: done* – the stealing of the web site of a prestigious exhibition of contemporary art by an Eastern European hacker);

5a) creation of faked identities ('an artist behind someone else's mask to realize his or her secret desires or just for fun'; Katya Detkina is an example);

6) software art, including download art (examples are SERO's *Dump Your Trash* recycling web pages and turning them into 'hard' forms and I/O/D's *Web Stalker*, a non-functional browser showing the hypertext structure of a web page);

7) communication projects erasing the line between creation and communication (the 7-11 mailing list is an example);

8) finally, self-promotion ('one can be a well-known net artist without producing any works because working on a project often takes time which can be used for being in a right place at a right time'; Geert Lovink is an example).

It seems noteworthy that the list includes 'creation of faked identities', which is not normally considered as a form of Internet art. This can be explained by the fact that Shulgin refers to artistic practices on the Russian Internet where this particular form was well developed (see chapter 5).

However, no classification can embrace all possible uses of the Internet for artistic purposes. Probably, any form, element or feature of Internet technology, presentation and communication can become material for art. This is because what makes art is not material but function. Art emerges when the pragmatic function is substituted (or at least supplemented) by the aesthetic function.

Thirdly, there is a kind of Internet art in which the primary subject of reflection and representation is the Internet itself. This can be called Internet meta-art. To use a literary analogy, one can say that "art on the Internet" is prose, "the use of the Internet to create art" is poetry and "Internet art about the Internet" is poetry about poetry. Many artists have produced works that can be considered Internet meta-art. However, historically, this third kind of Internet art is associated with a small group of artists who chose the term net.art (with a dot) to designate their activity. It was formed around a mailing list called nettime in 1994 and included such artists as Vuk Ćosić, Jodi.org, Alexei Shulgin, Olia Lialina, and Heath Bunting. The group was active for only about five years but it has had a deep influence on Internet and media art.

Two recent books provide insights into the realm on Internet art. Julian Stallabrass (2003) concentrates on the confrontation between the art world and dematerialized online art. He analyses how online art has responded to consumerist ideology and suggests that it may have radical implications for such concepts as art's authorship and ownership and contribute to reconsideration of the nature of art itself.

In a similar vein, Rachel Greene (2004) considers diverse forms of Internet art such as email art, websites, artist-designed software as well as projects that blur the boundaries between art and design, product development, political activism and communication. She discusses the tools, skills and equipment used to create Internet artworks as well as the wider cultural context. She also traces the evolution of Internet art over time and provides a timeline and glossary as guides to the key works. She shows how artists have employed online technologies to enhance the sphere of artistic expression and used new art forms to explore important social, political, and ethical issues. Greene (2004: 8) points out that Internet art is difficult to define because of 'its relative youth; its dematerialized and ephemeral nature; its global reach'. She discusses art-historical context for Internet art (*ibid.*: 2004: 19-29) and notes that the latter is a rather 'marginal and oppositional form, often uniting parody, functionality and activism under a single umbrella' (*ibid.*: 11-12). However, the motivation for Internet art is the same as for more traditional forms of art (*ibid.*): 'Though their tools and venues differ, internet art is underwritten by the motivations that have propelled nearly all artistic practices: ideology; technology, desire; the urge to experiment, communicate, critique or destroy; the elaboration of ideas and emotions; and memorializing observation and experience.'

A slightly different perspective can be found in Stephen Wilson's (2002) *Information Arts* that focuses on the convergence of arts, science and technology. The book provides a review of contemporary efforts of artists to integrate scientific research into their work and to use new technology for both artistic and research purposes. He examines research that crosses the intellectual terrains of biology, physics, cognitive science, astronomy, engineering, medicine, architecture, as well as social and information science. Wilson argues that technology and science are themselves a kind of poetry, especially in our time of blurring the boundaries and proposes an integrated view of these domains of creativity that have been opposed as bearing two different languages and worldviews (Snow, 1959). To support his argument, he lists cultural forces that made this re-examination critical: the influence of technological and scientific innovations on ordinary life; their changing effect of basic ideas such as time, space and identity; the impact of critical and cultural studies, which deny the borders between low and high cultures and between separate cultural domains providing a larger psycho-political-economical-cultural framework, and the increasing level of artistic activity using computers and the Internet.

Discussing the research function of artistic works, Wilson distinguishes between several approaches: exploration of new possibilities; exploration of the cultural implications of a line of research; the use of the new unique capabilities to explore themes not directly related to the research; and, finally, incidental use of technology. He defines technology as any creation system beyond the basic apparatus of the body. He notes that technological art is a movable phenomenon and its interpretation is changeable over time. "The artistic gesture to move into an area of emerging technology that is radical in one era can end up being unnoteworthy a few years later" (Wilson 2002: 9) If at an early stage 'it is a challenge to work with a medium before anyone defines it as a medium' (*ibid*.: 10) then later, when it becomes a common activity, it does not have the same meaning anymore. Artistic experimentation with a new technology is quickly (commercially) assimilated as it enters mainstream culture. Wilson poses an interesting question: does mainstream assimilation destroy the validity of the work of art? Is it possible to speak about technology-driven art in terms of a *masterpiece*? Or do we need to reconsider our concept of masterpiece as something *timeless* and to accept the shorter life expectancy of these new forms of art?

In the chapter on art and telecommunications Wilson describes the following domains of creativity: telephone, radio and net-radio; teleconferencing, videoconferencing, satellites, the internet, telepresence; and various forms of web art. He concludes the chapter (*ibid*.: 600) by noting that 'artists have been among the leaders in exploring the technological and cultural possibilities of the Web. They have also been among those most willing to question the euphoria.'

Wilson's massive volume (more than 900 pages!) contains descriptions and commentaries of the work of more than 200 artists, organised loosely by research discipline. This compendium of innovative techno-artistic practices is undoubtedly useful. The author demonstrates that creative use of technology is an important way of asking essential questions about man and the world, a means of adaptation and humanization of technology and a source of its further development. The weaknesses of the book, which result from its merits, are its mostly descriptive character; limited temporal scope (1995-2002); and focusing on the fringes of techno-culture. Artists become the few 'chosen ones' who dare to ask questions, create values, play with technology and define its future uses for others. The issues of other agents of technological-based creativity remain beyond the book's scope. However, creativity cannot be reduced to art. Internet activism is another important form of Internet creativity.

2.7.3 Internet activism

Internet activism is the use of Internet technology for bringing social, cultural or political change. It is used by various agents – from hackers, culture jammers and corporate saboteurs to established political parties and online charity groups. Internet activism has become a popular topic in recent years (Denning, 2000; Meikle, 2002; Jordan, 2002; McCaughey and Ayers, 2003; Atton, 2004; Gan, Gomez and Johannen, 2004: Jordan and Taylor, 2004). What is important in the context of the current project is that Internet activism can be considered a form of Internet creativity. This complies with the definition of creativity given in section 1.6.3 and developed in section 2.2 and the working definition of Internet creativity given in section 1.6.4.

Internet activism presupposes ideological struggle or, at least, an ideological tension between different worldviews. To locate Internet activism Graham Meikle distinguishes between two ideological models of the Internet which he calls Version 1.0 and Version 2.0. He summarizes their differences as follows (Meikle, 2002: 12-13):

> Version 1.0 offers change; Version 2.0 offers more of the same. Version 1.0 demands openness, possibility, debate; Version 2.0 offers one-way information flows and a single option presented as 'choice'. Version 1.0 would try to bring the new space of virtually possibility into the world as we know it; Version 2.0 would take the world as we know it – politics-as-usual, the media-as-before, ever more shopping – and impose it upon cyberspace. Version 1.0 would open things up. Version 2.0 would nail them down.

He notes that the opposition between Version 1.0 and Version 2.0 is not absolute; there are many examples of their mixture and interplay. Thus, the Hunger Site is a non-profit web site which encourages users to help fight hunger in poor countries by clicking on banners and viewings ads. In exchange for this, the site's sponsors pay for a donation of a serving of wheat, rice or maize. The goals of Version 1.0 are reached through the means of Version 2.0. On the other hand, Amazon.com, a commercial enterprise of the Version 2.0 type, realizes the idea of *open publishing* characteristic of Version 1.0, enabling anyone to supply the content in the form of reviews.

The strategies used by Internet activism include networking, publicising, educating, organizing and mobilizing. Activism as it is practiced in *new* media often uses *old* means. Meikle (2000: 25) lists examples of this backing into the future:

> The whole repertoire of tactics developed through the twentieth century, from Suffragettes to Civil Rights, from Greenpeace to ACT UP, from Gandhi to Greenham Common, have found their digital analogies, as social activism moves into cyberspace. Letter-writing, phone and fax trees, petitions. Newsletters, newspapers, samizdat publishing, pirate radio, guerrilla TV. Ribbon and badges, posters, stickers, graffiti. Demonstrations, boycotts, sit-ins, strikes, blockades. Sabotage, monkeywrenching, outing. Even online benefit gigs and virtual hunger strikes.

He also points out that 'so far, there's little evidence of entirely new tactics developed specifically to exploit the unique properties of the Net' (*ibid.*, 24). In his analysis he refers to Brian Eno's idea of "unfinished" media. He point out that, 'if the 'interactive' is about consuming media in (more or less) novel ways, the 'unfinished' is about people *making* new media themselves' (*ibid.*, 32). The opposition between *consumption* and *making* gives grounds to consider Internet activism as a form of creative activity whose aims may vary from political to artistic.

2.8 Conclusion

This chapter identified and reviewed theoretical dimensions of the literature, justified the research problem and discovered research questions worth researching in later chapters. The key role of creativity in modern society was demonstrated; the problem of Internet creativity was outlined; types of Internet histories were discussed; dimensions, actors and forms of Internet creativity were presented. Although research into creative practices on the Internet does not usually refer to creativity theories, taken as a whole, it covers the fundamental aspects of creativity described in section 2.2: creative persons, processes, works and environment. The conclusion is that research into creativity on the Internet is fragmented and that there is a need for an integral approach to Internet creativity. The next chapter builds up a theoretical and methodological framework for such an approach.

Chapter 3

METHODOLOGY

3.1 Introduction

As follows from the previous chapter, the developing body of literature on aspects of Internet creativity, while informing the fundamentals of this study, does not address in any cohesive sense the key issue of Internet creativity as a multifaceted but discernable phenomenon. This chapter explores methodological options available to address the research problem and research questions outlined in chapter 1, and reviews appropriate methods from several areas of knowledge. It proceeds to justify the use of the interpretive approach and grounded theory approach to integrate these methods by ordering elements and procedures of research methods in terms of research stages. An introduction to the methodology was provided in section 1.4 of chapter 1; this chapter aims to build on that introduction and to provide assurance that appropriate procedures were followed.

Any research topic presents a number of methodological and theoretical options. The development of research design and the choice of methodology are defined by research questions and by the capacity of selected methods to deal with them in an optimal manner.

The study has been implemented at the intersection of several fields of knowledge: Internet studies, Russian studies, history, cultural anthropology, ethnography, and creativity theory. Its multidimensional character reflects the complexity of the design of the study which (1) develops a historical approach to (2) creative processes (3) on the Russian segment of (4) the Internet and puts it (5) in a broader cultural context. Every field of knowledge and each particular research question requires using a specific set of methods. This creates a danger of methodological eclectics and provides a methodological challenge for the researcher. The response to this challenge was a development of an integral methodological framework. Multiple research methods have been integrated into a common research framework by using the methodologies of the interpretive theory approach and the grounded theory approach.

In his decision, the author has been influenced by the integral theory approach that proposes "to draw together an already existing number of separate paradigms into an interrelated network of approaches that are mutually enriching" (Wilber, 2003: 17). The transdisciplinarity of this study is also consistent with the current trends in Internet research (Hunsinger, 2005).

A range of approaches could be used to address the issues raised by the study, depending upon the actual research question being answered. As each chapter focuses on a specific aspect or dimension of Internet creativity and addresses a specific research question, different sets of methods and relevant theories were chosen to approach particular cases.

At the same time, the study seeks to avoid methodological eclectics and fragmentation of knowledge by uniting the research process's methods and its findings into a coherent whole. To achieve this aim, it follows research procedures outlined in the grounded theory approach as a methodological framework into which particular methods can be integrated.

The overall methodology is qualitative. However, quantitative methods have been used in some chapters to verify, specify or support the results obtained by qualitative methods. The choice of qualitative methodology and grounded theory for the study demands some reservations which are made further in this chapter.

3.2 Theoretical framework

A "theory" is generally defined as a set of concepts and generalizations presented in the form of a logically self-consistent model or framework used to understand a certain class of natural or social phenomena. Theories can be categorized in a number of ways. Some theories proceed from general ideas and come to a conclusion by logical reasoning (deductive theories). Others proceed from observable facts and result in a hypothesis or generalizations which can be further verified or rejected by the means of new observations (inductive theories). Most theories combine inductive and deductive procedures. An example of the latter is Grounded Theory developed by Glaser and Strauss (1967) and often used as a methodology for social science. It combines deduction and induction in abductive reasoning (a category borrowed from the works of Charles S. Peirce). The three basic elements of Grounded Theory, according to Strauss (Legewie/Schervier-Legewie, 2004) are (1) *theoretical sensitive coding*, that is, generating theoretical strong concepts from the data to explain the phenomenon researched; (2) *theoretical sampling*, that is, deciding whom to interview or what to observe next according to the state of theory generation (which implies starting data analysis with the first interview, and writing down memos and hypotheses early); and (3) *comparison* between phenomena and contexts in order to make the theory strong. These are thought of as three distinctive stages of research which can be reiterated until new data does not change the emerging theory anymore.

Another classification divides theories into explanatory and interpretive theories (Jorgensen, 1989). Explanatory theories are composed of logically interrelated law-like propositions and provide causal explanations. (Wallace, 1971). Explanatory theorizing, especially in the form of hypothesis testing, involves a "logic of verification" (Kaplan, 1964). This logic operates by (1) defining a problem for study in the form of a hypothesis or hypotheses derived from or otherwise related to an abstract body of theoretical knowledge (from examples, from philosophical assumptions), (2) defining the concepts contained in these hypotheses by procedures for measuring them (called "operations"), and (3) providing precise measurements of the concepts, preferably *quantitative* (by degrees or amounts). The verification of an explanatory theory is based on experiments as well as on testing the logical coherence of concepts. Explanatory theories are aimed at explanation, prediction, and control of natural or human phenomena. By contrast, interpretive theories (1) emerge as means to understand observable facts; (2) they may proceed from a general idea but without specific hypotheses; (3) they are aimed at interpretation rather than explanation and control;

(4) they use primarily *qualitative* methods; and, finally, (5) they do not generate universal, law-like propositions but rather provide generalizations applicable to a limited range of phenomena.

In a rather different way, Read (2004) outlines a three-fold typology of epistemological approaches found in contemporary theoretical and philosophical discourse. These are realist, normative and interpretive approaches.

A realist approach sees social phenomena as not fundamentally different from the natural ones: both exist outside of their linguistic representations; both can be studied by the means of controlled experiments; both are governed by laws that can be discovered and generalized. According to this view, theory performs a double function: first, it provides a foundation for experiments; second, it serves to cleanse the mind of the researcher from distortions of ideology, prejudices and common sense opinions. A realist approach is engaged in *explanatory critique*, which aims (1) to explain observed social actions and patterns of social action as well as (2) to point out others' false explanations for these observed actions and structures. Often, the realist approach provides a political agenda for social action because it knows what is really true and how things must be done. As Read (2004) concludes, 'Realism fails to recognize the particularity and meaning-constructed nature of social life, and furthermore fails to adequately account for the standpoint of the social scientific investigator from which explanations are made.'

The normative approach considers theory as a creative and politically oriented enterprise, a 'reflective, self-consistent, and self-interrogating meditation on the meaning of various moral and ethical visions.' It presents itself as an alternative to scientism found in the realist approach by emphasizing the need to engage "ideology" from the inside, and shifts interest from the search for "objective truth" to the issues of interpretation, contestation, resistance, human consciousness and agency. As Reed (2004) argues, serving as a means of cultural critique and self-reflection through interpretation of social reality in terms of a normative axiology, the normative approach fails to distinguish itself from literature and criticism.

94

The interpretive approach 'entails a radical ontological and epistemological break from realist and normative perspectives on the social, the sources of sociological knowledge, and the nature of sociological explanation' (*ibid.*). It seeks to explain social reality by reconstructing the meaningful contexts of social actions and historical events. The interpretive approach, unlike the realist approach, does not equate the social with the natural. It argues that social reality is inseparable from human conceptions of it and it is deeply imbedded in discourse practices. Therefore, a researcher must not oppose himself to cognitive and moral structures found in a social reality or disclose them as manifestations of "false consciousness" but rather to reconstruct their meaning for subjects of study. On the other hand, his own "background assumptions" are seen not as a hindrance to be "cleansed" but rather as a starting point for understanding and explanation of other social actions and structures. Unlike the normative approach, these assumptions, however, are not imposed on the others' reality but are subject to reflexive understanding and change in the course of research. A dialogue on equal terms, rather than a critique of "false consciousness" or projection of one's moral values, is the method of the interpretive approach. The interpretive approach follows the hermeneutic tradition which constitutes a philosophical and methodological foundation for various trends in humanities and social studies. The interpretive theory focuses upon meaning which is understood as a constitutive feature of social relations to provide an explanation of 'actually existing events and patterns of action in terms of actually existing structures' (*ibid.*). The process of developing concepts in the interpretive theorising is not purely inductive, nor deductive; rather it is defined as 'reflexive systematization of experience for the purpose of comparing meaning and comprehending difference' (*ibid.*). These concepts are both specific (in their origin and development) and general (as they apply to understanding social reality in other spaces and times).

3.3 Methodological framework

Method is defined as 'a systematic procedure, technique, or mode of inquiry employed by or proper to a particular discipline or art' (Merriam-Webster Dictionary), as 'a codified series of steps taken to complete a certain task or to reach a certain objective' (Wikipedia). Basically, methods used in social sciences are divided into two categories: quantitative methods and qualitative methods. Quantitative methods deal with measurable quantities and operate with numbers. The result of the research is a series of numbers which are often presented in tables, graphs or other forms of statistics. Qualitative methods deal with the aspects of phenomena that cannot be counted but can be understood. They deal with meaning and construction of meaning; they are narrative-oriented; and they use classifications and interpretations rather than statistics to present research results.

There has been an ongoing debate about the adequacy of quantitative or qualitative methods in the social sciences and humanities. Adherents of quantitative methods claim that only by using these methods scientific truth can be discovered. Adherents of qualitative methods accuse them of simplification and reductionism and argue that non-measurable factors are the most important in understanding social and cultural phenomena. Epistemologically, quantitative methods correlate with the realist approach to knowledge, while qualitative methods correlate with the interpretive approach (see section 3.3). However, from the integral point of view, there is no inherent antagonism between the two methodologies. They focus on different aspects of reality and may supplement each other rather than be considered as mutually exclusive. On the one hand, quantitative methods require some qualitative frame of reference, and the numbers they produce should be interpreted by qualitative methods. On the other hand, using quantitative methods should allow testing of qualitative ideas and giving them precise expression.

The choice of research methodology is defined by a number of factors which include research questions, the purpose of the research, and the character of the object of study. Marshall and Rossman (1989: 46) point out that the use of

96

qualitative methods is most appropriate for research that is "exploratory or descriptive and that stresses the importance of context, settings and subjects' frame of reference". The characteristics of objects of study best fitted for qualitative research include complexities and processes, unknown societies, innovative systems, informal and unstructured linkages and processes as well as phenomena to which experimental techniques are not applicable for practical or ethical reasons (*ibid.* 45-46). The proposed study displays each of these characteristics in varying degrees. The research questions concerning creativity on the Russian Internet are complex. Experimental methods are not applicable to the historical evidence which constitutes the factual basis of the research. Internet creativity is a multidimensional process and involves innovation rather that following established patterns. There is little research about the Russian Internet and it is to a large extent unknown. Many of the linkages between the subjects and processes in Internet creativity are likely to be informal and unstructured. The totality of these factors accounts for the choice of a qualitative methodology for the study.

The use of qualitative methods allows us to develop concepts and generalizations formulated as interpretive theories, as discussed in section 1.5. Interpretive theories not only have a value of their own but they also may be used to critically examine existing hypotheses and theories and to provide directions for making practical decisions (Chenitz and Swanson, 1986).

Qualitative methods are used in fields relevant for the project: history, anthropology/ethnography, sociology, and cultural studies. Each of these fields employs a specific set of methods. However, they have common elements and follow the same succession of procedures, which provides the basis for their integration into a unified methodological framework. The following sections provide a twofold categorization of the methods used in the study. Firstly, methods are grouped by disciplines; secondly, they are described in a cross-disciplinary manner, in terms of research stages and procedures as they are represented in the grounded theory approach.

3.4 Research methods

3.4.1 Internet studies

Internet studies (known also as cyberculture studies or Internet research) evolved as a distinct discipline in the latter half of 1990s when the Internet became widely accessible to the public in many parts of the world. It can be considered as a subfield within media studies, as it deals with the new medium of computer-mediated communication (CMC). Internet research has two different meanings. First, it is the practice of using the Internet for conducting research in any area. Second, it is research having the Internet as its subject. The second meaning defining Internet study as a discipline includes the first one but it is not reducible to it. Internet studies deal with a variety of phenomena found on the Internet and consider technological, sociological, psychological and cultural aspects of Internet communications.

Internet studies have no single methodology but rather use traditional methods found in a variety of disciplines from communication theory to sociology, anthropology and cultural studies (e.g. Herman and Swiss, 2000). Rice (2005) reviewed academic publications in Internet studies and summarized interests and concepts used in sessions, papers and abstracts of the 2003 and 2004 Association of Internet Researchers conferences. He found out that most frequent words appearing in the paper abstracts included Internet, online, community, social, technology, and research. The 2003 papers emphasized topics such as the social analysis/research of online/Internet communication, community and information, with particular coverage of access, individuals, groups, digital media, culture; role and process in e-organizations; and world development. The 2004 papers emphasized topics such as access; news and social issues; the role of individuals in communities; user-based studies; usage data; and blogs, women and search policy, among others. It seems noteworthy that creativity is not among the interests of Internet researchers.

Internet studies use both quantitative and qualitative methods such as surveys, content analysis, conversation analysis, cluster analysis and network analysis. However, the properties of the new media, such as intertextuality, nonlinearity, textual ephemerality and the use of multimedia (Manovich, 2001), to list just a few, make it difficult to apply traditional methods to the electronic environment. The new media environment provides a serious methodological challenge to researchers. Steve Jones (1999: 11), the editor of the *Doing Internet Research* collection discussing critical and methodological issues of Internet studies, stresses the need for academic reflexivity in the field and wonders if 'the Internet can restore a bit of lustre to the faded glory that came with being a PhD'. However, as Hunsinger (2005) points out, Internet studies still suffer from the lack of methodological clarity, fragmentation of understanding, the disunity of research, and the resulting inadequate public reception. He argues that there is an urgent need for the development of a transdisciplinary approach in Internet studies. This project makes a step towards that end by providing a methodological synthesis which combines methods from a few disciplines described below.

3.4.2 Ethnography

Ethnography (from the Greek *ethnos*, "nation" and *graphein*, "writing") is a branch of anthropology that studies contemporary cultural and ethnic groups. Similar to history, ethnography relies on qualitative description, but unlike history, which deals primarily with written evidence, ethnography is based on fieldwork, interviews and participant observation.

Participant observation is defined as a 'research strategy which aims to gain a close and intimate familiarity with a given group of individuals … and their practices through an intensive involvement with people in their natural environment' (Wikipedia). The usefulness of participant observation for humanitarian research is hard to overestimate. As Jorgenson (1989: 9) points out, 'Direct involvement in the here and now of people's daily lives provides both a point of reference for the logic and process of participant observational inquiry and a strategy for gaining access to phenomena that commonly are obscured from the standpoint of a nonparticipant.' He argues (*ibid.*, 13) that participant observation is especially appropriate for scholarly problems when 1) little is known about the phenomenon; 2) there are important differences between the views of insiders as opposed to outsiders; 3) the phenomenon is somehow obscured from the view of outsiders (private, intimate interaction and groups); 4) the phenomenon is hidden from the public view. All of these points apply to the study of the Russian Internet in a similar manner as the use of qualitative methods at large (cf. 2.2).

Participant observation focuses on the meanings shared by the group in whose activities the researcher participates. These meanings constitute reality for the group members, in the sense that they define their interpretation of reality and influence their behaviour (Berger and Luckmann, 1966). The insiders' concept of reality is not directly accessible to aliens, outsiders, or nonmembers, all of whom necessarily experience it initially as a stranger.

Participant observation involves the following procedures: gaining entrée to a setting; participating in the daily life of a community; adapting a social role or a set of roles; gathering data by observation, interviewing and personal experience; taking notes, records and files; analysing and theorising (Jorgensen, 1989).

Ethnographic methods have largely been used in Internet studies where they were adapted to the specificity of electronic interactive environments. The term "netnography" was coined (Kozinets, 1998) to denote the use of ethnographic methods on the Internet; however, it is associated mostly with applied research in marketing and advertising. The terms "Internet ethnography", "virtual ethnography" and the like are more common in Internet research. The use of ethnographic methods was discussed in detail by Hine (2000). She argued that cyberspace should be understood as "both cultural construct and cultural artifact" (Hine, 2000: 64) and that the ethnography of mediated interaction should be described as "mobile than multi-sited" and "based on connection and difference" rather that in terms of a stable "field".

There is a growing body of literature on Internet ethnography studying the mutual influence of technology and culture in various contexts. The ethnographic approach to the Internet challenges and revises universalizing assumptions of the early literature on cyberspace. First, it avoids using metaphors of revolution, utopia or Eden; instead, it focuses on the everyday practices of Internet uses by common people. Second, it goes beyond the discourse of globalization and homogenization of culture and assumes mutual influences of cultures and technology. It insists that the uses and interpretations of a technology vary culture to culture and that they depend on sociocultural context, cultural patterns and contingencies of history. The main method of ethnography, virtual or not, is participant observation, and the main genre is a case study. A brief review of virtual ethnography research follows below.

Miller and Slater (2000) conducted an ethnographic study of the Internet in Trinidad. They found out that, contrary to early cyberculture theorization based on the opposition between on-line and off-line words and depicting cyberspace as a transcendence of national and cultural differences, Trinidadians approached the new media 'in ways that connected to core dimensions, and contradictions, of their history and society.' They described the processes of "alignments" or "elective affinities" between Internet use and the Trinidadian daily life on different levels such as relationships (including the system of kinship), national identity, political economy, business, and religion. They concluded that 'the Internet as a meaningful phenomenon only exists in particular places' and argued that empirical ethnographic studies of Internet use in particular cultures are the only firm foundation for solid generalizations and abstractions.

An edited volume *Culture, Technology, Communication: Towards an Intercultural Global Village* (Ess and Sudweeks, 2001) assembled twelve papers from a 1998 conference which include a few case studies of Internet use in culturally and linguistically specific contexts. The list of countries included Germany, France, Switzerland, Kuwait, Japan, Korea, Singapore and Thailand. The collection tried to avoid technocentric bias and to bring culture as an important component of Internet studies. It also showed an advantage of native scholars for providing an adequate perspective on culturally specific segments of the Internet.

Nakamura (2002) developed earlier research into racial issues of cyberspace (Kolko, Nakamura and Rodman, 1999). She emphasized the importance of national and race identity for Internet users which contradicts the early views on the Internet that race, gender and age are unimportant in cyberspace, and which accounts for the popularity of such "raced" enterprises as AsianAvenue.com and Blackplanet.com.

Kalathil and Boas (2003) analysed the Impact of the Internet on authoritarian rule in Vietnam, Cuba, Burma, Egypt, China, Saudi Arabia, Singapore, and the United Arab Emirates using four major categories: civil society, politics and the state, the economy, and the international sphere.

Asia.com: Asia Encounters the Internet, edited by Ho, Kluver and Yang (2003) represented a diverse range of disciplinary backgrounds such as mass communication, information technology, and social science (including political science, business management, and law). The papers provided case studies of various aspects of Internet usage in Asia including Indonesia, Malaysia, India and Singapore with an emphasis on the economic, legal, and political aspects. The authors pointed out the contrasts in reception and appropriation of Internet technology between Asia and the West and analysed the sources of these contrasts such as institutional infrastructures, government policies, economic structures and socio-cultural values.

Ignacio (2005) studied Filipino diasporic community formation on the Internet using an online newsgroup, soc.culture.filipino, as a case study.

A collection of papers on Japanese Cybercultures (Gottlieb and McLelland, 2003) focuses on three aspects of the daily use of the Internet in Japan – popular culture; gender and sexuality; and politics and religion – and shows how the Internet technology afforded new opportunities for individual expression within Japanese society through interpersonal communications and issue-oriented group networking.

According to Hine (2000), an ethnographic approach to the Internet has two distinct aspects: a study of Internet use which focuses on the off-line context and a study of the emerging Internet culture which takes place on-line. In his review of her work, Zuravski (2001) points out that this dichotomy can be overcome by approaching the Internet in terms of social practice (which includes narratives about its uses and perception). The present study follows this third way: it focuses on the processes in Russian Internet culture and links them to wider social, political and cultural contexts.

The main disadvantage of Internet ethnography (and well as of traditional ethnography) from the standpoint of the study of creativity, is that it is focused on recurring patterns of everyday behaviour rather that on production of change and generating innovation. The ethnographic approach is generally "structure-oriented" rather than "action-oriented" (Sztompka, 1993). Moreover, participant observation and the case study approach are of limited use if the aim is to understand a complex system and to trace its change over an extended period of time. Therefore, while the current project uses some elements of ethnographic approach to the Internet, it supplements it with the historical approach based on a textual analysis of recorded evidence – even in those cases where the author was personally involved in the process as a participant observer.

3.4.3 History

Internet studies generally lack historical consciousness. The Internet technology has been often treated as either completely new and, therefore, not rooted in history, or as something just present here and now. In both cases, the Internet appears as something timeless, as something that has no roots in the past or internal dynamics of its own. As the current project considers the dynamics of creativity on the Russian Internet over a period of time, the introduction of an historical dimension was deemed necessary.

History is generally defined as the study of past events and culture based on recorded evidence. Historical narrative deals with real rather than imaginary people and events and this intended authenticity distinguishes history from fiction. At the same time, history shares with fiction some important features: 'The historian, like the literary critic and art historian, is a guardian of our cultural heritage, and familiarity with that heritage offers insight into the human condition – a means to heightened self-awareness and empathy with others' (Tosh, 1984: 23).

Fisher (1971: XV) defined history as a 'process of adductive reasoning' in which adductive answers are given to specific questions about past events. Questions and answers are 'fitted to each other by a complex process of mutual adjustment'. The answers include selected facts which are arranged in the form of explanatory paradigm. The resulting paradigm, Fisher points out, may take many different forms such as a statistical generalization, a narrative, a causal model, a motivational model, a collected group-composition model, or an analogy. Most paradigms, however, consist of a combination of these components. In any case, history is presented in the form of a reasoned argument. This research is guided by this understanding of history.

Since history is not only a record of events but also a reconstruction of their meaning, the form of a reasoned argument – a historical narrative – inevitably includes two discursive elements or modi: a description of facts and events, and a meta-description (their explanation). The balance between these two modi has been historically realized in different ways, which define various sub-genres of historical writing. The dominance of description approximates history to fiction; the dominance of meta-description – to philosophy. Herodotus' *Histories* can serve as an example of the former, Hegel's *Lectures on philosophy of history* as an example of the latter. Historical explanation can also employ quantitative and qualitative methods found in various disciplines, and can concern itself with social, economic, political, psychological and other issues. As a rule, contemporary historical study is generally characterized by a greater degree of theorization than earlier histories.

Generally, the study of history is based on textual knowledge of a great number of sources and it demands taking into account numerous factors contributing to historical change. Historical study deals with unique events which defy formalization. It is the reason why the historical method generally has been defined as "systematic common sense" (Tosh, 1984). It is also the reason why historical intuition and empathy – the basic methods of classical historicism – still retain their significance. Intuition provides a holistic vision and it is indispensable in situations when the quantity and variety of information exceeds the possibilities of rational ordering. Empathy provides understanding of events and persons by means of reconstruction of the subjective situation of meaning production. According to Dilthey (1976), *Einfühlung* ("empathy", "intuition") is a fundamental method of human science which, unlike exact science, deals with human experience and meanings. These methods, elaborated in the framework of hermeneutics and phenomenology, have been widely used in social science and humanities under the names of sympathetic introspection (Cooley, 1930/1969), *Verständnis* (Weber, 1949), a humanistic coefficient (Znaniecki, 1935), sympathetic reconstitution (MacIver, 1942), etc.

The work of a historian or a social scientist has been understood as revealing the meaning of particular historical or cultural formations. Given that both the historian and the object of study are historically situated, no statements of ultimate truths or universal laws are possible. Instead, the work of the researcher is thought of as an ongoing dialogue with the past. History differs from exact science and it relates to humanities because it is not value-free, and involves interpretation and personal involvement of the historian. As Dray (1964: 25) put it, 'How can the historian write about *anything*, unless he is able to recognize its nature; and how can he grasp such objects of study as these without placing a value upon them?'

Historical study is subject to specialization of place (regions), time (periods) and theme (topics). The latter specialization accounts for the division of historical study into several different branches such as political, intellectual, economic and social history. A branch of history may be defined by subject matter (diplomacy, war, technology, art, etc.), type of sources (oral history) or approach (thus, cultural history studies cultural interpretations of virtually any phenomena in a particular culture over an extended period of time). The position of this study with regard to these dimensions was outlined in section 1.6.6 in chapter 1. History seems to have no restriction in regard to its subject matter and it has a broad valence which allows it to marry with other knowledge areas. As Lord Acton pointed out, "History is not only a particular branch of knowledge, but a particular mode and method of knowledge in other branches". This fact is reflected in the concept of historicism.

The term "historicism" refers to a 'critical movement insisting on the prime importance of historical context to the interpretation of texts of all kinds' (Hamilton 1996: 2). Historicism is defined by two ideas: one is that succession of historical events is not accidental but has a logic which can be revealed and explained; the second is that this logic is not the same in all times and places but depends on local conditions and peculiarities of a culture.

Classical historicism believed that historical explanation could naturally emerge from the historical evidence when it is studied with enough diligence. The idea was probably most clearly expressed by Leopold von Ranke who argued that the aim of history was "to show how things actually were (*wie es eigentlich gewesen*)". Later generations of historians might criticize this programme as naïve, but the tendency to avoid 'external' interpretive codes to "decipher" the meaning of historical events, and the wish to deduce their meaning and logic from the historical facts themselves, have persisted in contemporary history. This approach has been re-established by New Historicism.

New Historicism is defined as a 'critically self-aware form of historiography which took on board a sense of history as narrative, anecdote, power or discourse' (Colebrook, 1997: VI). New Historicism is an umbrella term covering a wide range of approaches represented by such names as Michel Foucault, Clifford Geertz, Pierre Bourdieu, Michel de Certeau, Raymond Williams, Lois Althusser and others. The progenitor of New Historicism is a narrower sense is Stephen Greenblatt.

An important trait of New Historicism (which brings it closer to cultural anthropology and ethnography) is an attempt to understand cultures on their own terms rather than according to some predetermined set of values, such as Christian predestination, Hegel's reason or Marx's theory of class struggle. The abstention from any universal models of culture is based on the idea that there are many cultures which differ in their characteristics and operations. Moreover, cultures describe themselves by using different "languages of description". These representations of a culture are not disregarded as illusion or deceit, propaganda or ideology; they are rather seen as symbolic and effective practices that contribute to the production of the culture they describe. Hence, the attention to cultural (self-) representations which are neither exposed not interpreted in the traditional sense of the word. Instead of revealing what texts *mean*, New Historicism shows what they *do*. Thus, for example, speaking of the Elizabethan grand narrative of the "great chain of being", Greenblatt (1988: 2) noted that 'visions of hidden unity seemed like anxious rhetorical attempts to conceal cracks, conflict and disarray'. This erodes the opposition between the text and the context: the text is not only an expression of a culture but also a way of cultural production. This approach is adopted by the proposed project.

Other methodological principles of New Historicism found in Greenblatt's works which are deemed to be relevant for this study are as follows: the avoidance of any general or trans-historical theories of culture; attention to anecdotes and human stories which are considered as "disturbances" in the surface of things providing insights into a culture; interest "in books and people" rather than in "texts and cultural constructs", as in postmodern theory; and the understanding of creative works as cultural formations shaped by "the circulation of social energy".

One limitation of New Historicism is that it has primarily studied the Western capitalist society (more specifically, Renaissance as the beginning of Western capitalism). Following its own logic, the findings of this research cannot be directly applied to not quite capitalist and not quite Western societies such as Russia, and to such a specific cultural milieu as the Internet. Therefore, the study combines some techniques of New Historicism with the general principles of the study of history such as source knowledge and adductive reasoning. It takes a broad temporal perspective, employs critical analysis of heterogeneous sources and considers texts and the context as interrelated phenomena.

Other fields of knowledge relevant for this study include creativity research and the study of Russian culture and history. Major concepts and theories of creativity research have been discussed in section 2.2 of chapter 2. There is no general review of Russian studies; however, references to particular findings in the field can be found in case studies chapters.

3.5 Research stages

However different are methods used by particular disciplines, they have common elements and succession of procedures that can be described in terms of research stages. This is facilitated by the fact that the project is intrinsically related to the frame of reference of the interpretive theory approach presented in section 3.2 which is empirically grounded, based on qualitative methods and relies on induction as its primary method of building theories. All these factors contributed to the choice of grounded theory as a methodological foundation of the study. Creswell (1998) lists five qualitative research traditions which include biography, phenomenology, grounded theory, ethnography and case study. Although there are many intersections between them, one advantage of grounded theory is its neutrality in regard to particular fields of knowledge or disciplines. This allows ordering methods in terms of research stages rather than disciplines. A review of grounded theory principles is deemed useful before we proceed to the description of research stages and corresponding methods.

3.5.1 Grounded theory framework

Grounded theory is not a system of ideas but rather a set of methodological principles devised specifically for qualitative research. Strauss (1987: 5) notes that 'it is not a specific method or technique' but rather 'a style of doing qualitative analysis that includes a number of distinct features.' One of the advantages of grounded theory is that it provides methods of developing theories 'without any particular commitment to specific kinds of data, lines of research, or theoretical interests.' The process of discovery in grounded theory is primarily inductive and this fact differentiates it from that of the logico-deductive approach, 'since the theory has been derived from data, not deduced from logical assumptions' (Glaser and Strauss, 1967: 30).

According to grounded theory, the research cycle includes several discernable stages. It begins from an initial interest in the subject and formulation of questions. Then follows the stage of collection of data. The amassed material often leads to redefining the focus of the study and a more precise formulation of its issues and problems. It is followed by the analytical stage at which generalizations and theories are produced from data.

The project had several interrelated phases which are described below.

3.5.2 Literature review

The main goals of this stage were as follows: formulation of the problem area and research questions, refining the theoretical background, linking ideas from different subject areas and preliminary selection of relevant research methods.

The interdisciplinary character of the study required conducting a literature review in two separate subject areas: Internet creativity research and the study of the Russian Internet. These were presented in chapter 2 and section 1.3 of chapter 1 correspondingly.

The review of existing literature helped to refine research questions, gaining awareness of multiple approaches and arranging materials explored at a later stage. Although a literature review, from the grounded theory standpoint, is not necessary demanded at the outset of research but can be made in the process of analysis of data, it was useful in many ways.

3.5.3 Data collection

Different disciplines use different sets of methods for data collection. A historian relies mostly upon recorded evidence; the primary method of an ethnographer is participant observation; a sociologist uses such methods as surveys, interviews, focus groups, etc. As the Internet tends to blur the borderline between fieldwork and desktop-based work, an Internet researcher finds himself in an intermediate position which allows him to combine these methods – which was the case in this study.

3.5.4 Data selection

Any research is inescapably selective in both data and the presentation of the results. Albert Cook in his research on methods of writing history from Herodotus to the present pointed out that 'a historical work is and must be synecdochic for having chosen and connecting its details from a number of others that have been omitted' (Cook, 1988: 11). He argued also that 'synecdoche applies as a technique not just to some historians but inescapably to all' (*ibid.*, 200). Michel de Certeau (1975/1988: 5) pointed out that historiography is based on a 'selection between what can be understood and what must be forgotten in order to obtain the representation of a present intelligibility'.

The same principle applies to ethnography. Clifford and Marcus (1986) showed that ethnographic writing is necessarily selective and represents a textual construction of reality rather than the "truth" of existing "real" culture. In the realm of "virtual ethnography", Hine (2000: 82) also admits that data are "necessarily partial". However, it does not necessary lead to interpretive relativism or "deconstruction" but it rather means that many interpretations of the same ethnographic phenomenon are possible. The best interpretation would be one that explains in a coherent manner the most part of the data.

The problem of selection concerns not only the gathering of data but also the presentation of the results. Intelligibility is closely connected with style, and the style is the result of selection and omission. The chapters of this study have been revised and rewritten many times (some have as much as eight different versions). Much written material, analytical as well as factual, has been sacrificed in the process of editing for the purpose of clarity of the argument and consistency of the structure.

3.5.5 Types of data

The basis of any historical study is work with documentary evidence or sources. Traditionally, historical sources have been divided into two groups: primary and secondary sources. Primary sources provide evidence of facts, events and opinions 'contemporary to the event of thought to which it refers' (Tosh, 1996: 29). Secondary sources are commentaries and interpretations of past events made at a later time. The delimitation of source is not always clear-cut: evidence 'can be primary in one context and secondary in another' (*ibid.*, 30). For example, a commentary on an event on the Russian Internet made the next day after the event took place in an online column can be considered either as secondary source if we oppose it as an interpretation to the actual event or as a primary source if we treat this interpretation itself as a significant event causally linked to the original event. The fact that Internet history is quite recent and the temporal distance between sources is less than normally required by traditional history problematises the division of sources even further. However, this division can be made relatively easily if we consider the function and actual use of a source in the context of research.

Sources used in the study can be divided into three categories according to their form of publication: online, printed and oral evidence. Online sources include a variety of genres: personal, corporate and public websites, online media, creative literature and criticism, art projects, forums, memoirs, diaries and blogs, e-mails, transcripts of interactive communications (such as IRC or ICQ), official records and statistics. When sources have been absent from their original location, I relied on archives in which copies of the documents can be found (if the concepts of original and copy are applicable to electronic documents). This includes the Internet Archive (archive.org), collections of documents at websites, and my personal archives. Printed sources include books, journals and magazines. These are mostly secondary sources providing research and criticism. Oral sources include formal and informal interviews with informants. The selection of sources of the study has been defined by their relevancy to the purpose of the study. Every attempt has been made to explore the full extent of the sources. However, it is impossible to embrace everything: the end of 2004 was set up as the upper chronological limit of the study; although some sources may belong to later time, no claims of being exhaustive are made. Other limitations of this study were discussed in section 1.8 of chapter 1.

3.5.6 Data management

Huberman and Miles (1994: 428) defined "data management" as 'the operation needed for a systematic, coherent process of data collection, storage and retrieval'. This section details those operations.

Data collection and recording were conducted in accordance with the guidelines suggested by the proponents of grounded theory technique (Glaser and Strauss, 1967; Strauss, 1987; Marshall and Rossman, 1989; Strauss and Corbin, 1990).

The computer-aided storage and retrieval system facilitated the retention of the material and its successful manifestations, as recommended by Huberman and Miles (1994: 451). They suggested 11 items which should be retained for several years after the project to assist in establishing replicability. They included the raw material, partially processed data, coded data, the coding scheme or thesaurus, memos and other analysis; search and retrieval records, data displays, analysis episodes, report text, general chronological log or documentation and the index of the above material. The above categories were used as a guideline in research process.

The process of data storage and retrieval was as follows. The primary data for the study were collected by reviewing Internet sources and saving relevant documents or quotations to a database on a laptop computer. The documents were analysed for their relevance to particular research questions and selection made on this basis. The material was classified, sorted and distributed to folders according to the subject matter and relevance to research questions. In those cases when only a part of the documents was relevant, quotations were extracted and a bibliographic description attached. The original files were kept for later reference.

Many types of software were used for acquiring, processing, storing and retrieving the data. The most important computer technologies and programmes were as follows. Search engines such as Google, Yandex and Rambler were used for searching relevant documents on the Internet. The two latter search engines have an advantage in comparison with Google as they take into account the morphological structure of the Russian language. However, unlike Google, they are limited in their scope and restrict themselves to the Russian Internet, whatever it may mean. Google desktop search technology was used to search and retrieve documents from the database. TreePad software was used to manage concepts, ideas and quotations by organizing them into treelike hierarchies and establishing hypertext links between the items. A reference database was compiled which included both online and print publication. EndNote was used to manage bibliographical references. Drafts and different versions of the chapters were stored separately, which enabled version comparison and monitoring of research progress.

3.5.7 Critique of the sources

The work of a historian is often compared with that of a detective or a judge in court: a detective looks for evidence, a judge evaluates evidence, and a historian does both. It is argued that no source can be taken at its face value; they should all be treated with suspicion and disbelief. There is definitely a grain of truth in this statement, even if the researcher follows an "understanding" rather than a "revealing" approach.

There are two major aspects in critical evaluation of sources: external criticism which aims to establish the authenticity of documents and internal criticism which deals with the interpretation of a document's content.

External criticism seems less important for Internet studies than for the study of more distant époques. It is unlikely that any palaeographic methods are applicable to web pages or e-mails. However, forgery and mystification are not uncommon on the Internet; therefore, establishing the original author as well as the date and place of a document's creation may sometimes be required. The most common method here is comparison of sources: examining the document for consistency with facts known from other documents. In the case of establishing authorship, stylistic analysis may be used.

Internal criticism examines the reliability of documents and reveals intentions and biases of their authors. It uses a wide range of textual analysis methods and interpretation techniques (see below for details). Personal experience obtained by participant observation – a key source of information in ethnographic studies – is also subject to criticism and constant re-evaluation. The subjective position of this researcher has been shifted several times during the research process, as well as his interpretive strategy. The general vector of these changes was from explanative theories to emergent theories and from the standpoint of involved participant to that of detached observer who has access to insider information and understanding of the principles of reality construction shared by members of the studied group.

3.5.8 Data analysis

Jorgensen (1989: 110) defines analysis as 'breaking up, separating, or dissembling of research materials into pieces, parts, elements, or units.' When material is broken down into manageable pieces, 'the researcher sorts and sifts them, searching for types, classes, sequences, processes, patterns, or wholes.' The result of this process is a theory, that is, 'an arrangement of facts in the form of an explanation or interpretation.' Theorising usually involves categories, terms and concepts not found in the factual evidence. These are opposed to facts, as meta-description is to description.

According to Jorgensen, the analytic process involves a number of strategies. One analytic strategy is to identify and label a phenomenon in terms of its *basic components* and examining phenomena for its *essential features*. Another analytic strategy involves looking for *patterns and relationships* among facts. A third strategy is *comparing and contrasting* facts or identifying *similarities and*

114

differences among phenomena, which enables the researcher to arrange them into *classes, types, or sets*. The relationships between the classes are also analysed and an *emergent typology* is built on this basis which can be applied to other related phenomena.

Turner (1981: 231) developed a nine-point listing of the stages which accommodated the strategies and procedures described above in the framework of grounded theory study. Turner's stages were:

1) Develop categories (by labelling data);

2) Saturate categories (by providing examples);

3) Develop abstract definitions (by stating criteria for putting together instances into a category);

4) Use the definitions (as a guide to emergent features in the material and as a stimulus for theoretical reflection);

5) Exploit categories fully (by being aware of additional categories suggested by those that have been produced; their inverse, their opposite, more specific and more general categories);

6) Note, develop, and follow links between categories (establishing relationships between categories);

7) Consider the conditions under which the link holds;

8) Make connections, where relevant, to existing theories (build bridges to existing work at this stage, rather than at the outset of the research);

9) Use extreme comparisons to the maximum to test emergent relationships (identify the key variables and dimensions and see whether the relationship holds at the extreme of these variables).

These stages were used as a guideline for this research.

However, data analysis in not always a linear process. As the stages and procedures are recurrent, the process can be best described as an *analytical cycle* (Jorgensen, 110-111).

While individual chapters differed in research questions, the basic units of analysis, types of sources and methods, they shared the stages and procedures described above.

3.6 Conclusion

This chapter gave a detailed description of the theoretical framework and the methodology. Although the interdisciplinary approach adopted in the study provides more perspective on the phenomenon being studied, it also provides a methodological challenge because methods used in particular disciplines may seem incompatible. The chapter first justified the methods in terms of research questions and literature review and then united them in terms of research stages using the grounded theory approach as a methodological framework.

Chapter 4

RUSSIAN ONLINE MEDIA

4.1 Introduction

This chapter introduces a series of case studies covering dimensions of Internet creativity in the history of the Russian Internet. It is concerned with the development of online media on the Russian Internet. The online media are defined as Internet publications updated on a regular basis which are not mere channels of distribution of the content of "traditional media" but which produce original content. They can have or not have a counterpart in traditional media such as print publication, radio or TV programmes. The production of new content is what distinguishes online media as they are understood here from "online versions" of traditional media. The focus of this chapter is on the processes of creativity and innovation that account for the development and evolution of online media.

Structurally, the chapter consists of three parts. The first part describes a historical background. It reviews information policy in the Soviet Union and its fundamental change with the collapse of the Soviet regime. Further, it traces the evolution of the mass media system in the New Russia. Without this, it would hardly be possible to understand the role of online media in Russia, to explain the trajectory of their development and the peculiarities of their uses. The second part analyses the evolution of Russian online media focusing on the key projects that introduced significant innovations in the domain. The third part discusses the functions of online media in Russia in a wider sociocultural context. It analyses three widespread models of interpretation, which use the concepts of Samizdat, kitchen-table talks and the public sphere.

4.2 Historical background

4.2.1 Information policy in the Soviet Union

The October revolution of 1917 was not only the appropriation of power, but also appropriation of meaning (Bonnell, 1997). The Bolsheviks since the very beginning used propaganda for mass mobilization (Kenez, 1985) and controlled the flow of information (Remington, 1988). In the Soviet time, Russia seemed for foreigners an information vacuum. Newspapers and radio teemed with stories of 'unprecedented growth and all-round development' of the Soviet Society, but down-to-earth information was rationed and restricted, especially when it concerned anything that had gone wrong or had gotten out of hand (Smith, 1990). Soviet authorities were obsessed by secrecy – in the same way as their czarist predecessors. 'In Russia secrecy presides over everything; secrecy – administrative, political, social,' the Marquis de Custine wrote in 1839, and in the Soviet Russia this attitude persisted.

One could find no reports about domestic catastrophes, accidents, air or train crashes, or crime in the Soviet press. It was only in the West that such things could happen. The audience was treated like a child that should be protected from any negative information and should be fed with moralizing and inspiring stories. Or, in another interpretation, it was treated as slaves that should not think because thinking could prevent them from effective work, disturb their mind and provoke them to disobedience. Often, however, there were no visible reasons for the informational deprivation except the 'sheer bloody-mindedness or an ingrained, habitual, arrogant Soviet disdain for "the little man" ' (Smith, 1990: 428). Street maps and telephone books were unavailable for ordinary people since they were considered "military secrets." There was no basic consumer information or advertisements so people had to rely on inside tips from well-placed friends or else do without. As Smith (*ibid.*, 433) notes, 'Like the rest of Soviet life, information is not a matter of money, but connections. The better his connections, the better

118

informed a Soviet can be because information, like consumer goods, is rationed out according to rank.'

Theoretically, in Soviet society, all people were equal, but in fact, like in Orwell's Animal Farm, some were more equal than others. Although the traditional class structure of society had been obliterated by the 1917 Revolution, Soviet society in many respects was a caste system. Not money, but rank within the hierarchy, was the decisive factor in distribution of both consumer goods and information. The system of carefully parcelled privileges for different groups of society, rooted in the hungry years of war communism and reinforced by Stalin, permeated the entire social life. As party bosses and *nomenklatura* obtained caviar and sausages through the system of "closed distribution centres" (*zakrytye raspredéliteli*) so they received access to the information unavailable to "normal people".

Thus, TASS (the Telegraph Agency of the Soviet Union) delivered its daily news reports in three different versions for different categories of people. Apart from regular reports, there were also so called "white" and "red" TASS. The first circulated to government ministries, Party headquarters, and key newspaper offices and contained far richer and more detailed selection of foreign news and comments that ordinary TASS reports, including 'accurate and revealing information on Soviet domestic affairs, such as reports on air and train accidents, statistics on crime, word of health epidemics, serious production deficiencies, crop reports and similar material that the regime would find embarrassing to print openly' (Smith 1976: 433). Red TASS was an even more rarefied edition of TASS distributed only to chief editors, the highest government officials and Communist Party bigshots. It is noteworthy that both "secret" versions did not contain any information that would be classified in the West; most of the materials would be ordinary news to a Western newspaper.

To prevent ordinary citizens from accessing books that were considered potentially harmful for their mind, they were published in limited "special editions" and were available only "for administrative use" (*dlya sluzhebnogo*

119

pol'zovaniya). All copies were numbered individually to facilitate tracing their use and could be obtained in the library only by the holders of special permits. Examples of such books included Bertrand Russell's *History of Western Philosophy*, Hitler's *Mein Kampf*, Solzhenitsyn's *The Gulag Archipelago* and George Orwell's *1984* published in Russian translation "only for service libraries" exactly in 1984. (The control over distribution of these "classified" publications was far from being perfect and they could be obtained by connections either in the original form or in photocopies).

Large libraries normally had two different catalogues, one of which was open to the general readers and another was "closed", that is, accessible only for security-cleared staff. The general alphabetic catalogue including all library holdings was a secret. The unauthorized materials were kept in a special room with restricted access called *spetskhran* which literally means the special holding, or more accurately, the secret stack. They included books, periodicals, maps and other materials. It should be noted, however, that in spite of these limitations people still had access to a great variety of information and culture.

Press, books, theatre performances, films, concerts – everything was censored. Censorship was multilayered and included military censors, literary censors, and most important, political censors. The lists of taboo names and topics were sent to every place that dealt with information – from daily newspapers to discos. This was supplemented by eavesdropping on telephone calls, perusal of private mail and the widespread system of KGB informers. Nobody could ever be sure that one was not watched or listened to by Big Brother. The consequences of inappropriate behaviour could be very serious – from "heart-to-heart conversation" at the First Department (a KGB office at an industrial enterprise, educational institution or military unit) to arrest or exile.

Propaganda and indoctrination started in kindergartens and continued through the adult life in a variety of forms. Marxism-Leninism, political economy of socialism and the history of the Communist party were compulsory subjects in colleges and universities. The main learning methods were abstracting texts and learning quotations by heart. Independent interpretation was not encouraged; at examinations, it was normally required to reproduce the lecture's explanations verbatim. At the same time, an interest in philosophy and religion and the reading of corresponding literature was enough excuse to put a person into a mental hospital. Soviet psychiatry used such diagnoses as "continuous sluggish schizophrenia" and "syndrome of metaphysical philosophical intoxication". The latter was defined as 'monotonously abstract intellectual activity directed to finding an independent solution by means of pondering upon and resolving the eternal problems about the meaning of life, the destiny of humankind, the ending of war, as well as the search of philosophical and world outlook systems. It may include the ideas of invention, self-perfection, as well as intellectual and aesthetic passion of various kinds' (Baranov and Nosachev, 1995: 94). Not only political dissidents, or literary people, or the "alien-minded" (*inakomyslyashschie*) would be forcedly put into a madhouse with such diagnoses, but any person who showed interest in philosophy, literature or art.

The ability for independent thinking had always been taken with suspicion by the Soviet authorities who considered it a threat to the pursuit of communism. It was Lenin who said that the intelligentsia is not a brain of the nation but its shit, *govno* (in a letter to Maxim Gorky on 15 September 1919). In the Soviet Union, all domains of intellectual life had been kept under the strict control of the Party. The ideologization and politicization of culture began in 1920s. In the 1930s and 1940s, a significant part of the intelligentsia was persecuted and exterminated in the Stalinist labour camps. In the latter years the situation had softened but the dominating role of the censor, the authoritarian atmosphere and the lack of intellectual freedom had still impeded the development of the Soviet society.

In science, some theories became official dogma and any deviation was considered heresy. Thus, The New Theory of Language developed by academician Nikolai Marr in 1920s had reigned in Soviet linguistics for about thirty years. Marr applied to language the doctrine of historical materialism. He considered language as a superstructure over economic relations in society and a weapon of class

121

struggle. He also rejected language families, linguistic borrowing, denied comparative and historical linguistics as a bourgeois pseudo-science and argued that all languages evolved from four primary roots - *al, ber, yon*, and *rosh*. His "Japhetic Theory" of language was for a long time an indisputable dogma and its opponents were treated as political enemies and sometimes physically repressed. It was only after the publication of Stalin's article *Marxism and the issues of linguistics* in 1950 smashing Marr's theory that it was finally abandoned (Neroznak, 2001).

Whole scientific disciplines were censored and their development was blocked. Thus, genetics was suppressed in the times of Stalin and Khrushchev while Lysenko's theory reigned in biology, maintaining that characteristics of environment could be transmitted in the evolutionary process (Medvedev, 1969; Soyfer, Gruliow and Gruliow, 1994; Roll-Hansen, 2004). Similarly, cybernetics was labelled in the 1950s a reactionary pseudoscience and a weapon of imperialist ideology. Its recognition coincided with Khrushchev's "thaw" when it was perceived as a tool of radical reform of the Stalinist system of science (Gerovitch, 2002). Another example is the development of Russian semiotics, which had to use a deliberately obscure terminology (such as a "secondary modelling system" for language) to escape Party's critique. It also disguised itself in order to be able to explore interesting topics under the cover of official science. Thus, problems of stylistics were discussed using the material of Lenin's writings and the issues of semiotics of behaviour and cultural anthropology were elaborated within the framework of military space research whose aim was to teach Moon research vehicles (*Lunokhody*) to communicate with each other (Gorny and Pil'schikov, 2000). Restrictions on the flow of information and the Party's control over channels of scientific contact with the West resulted, among other things, in the technological inferiority of the Soviet Union to the West.

4.2.2 The époque of Glasnost

Glasnost', proclaimed by Gorbachev in 1987, was initially thought of as an instrument of the fight with conservative forces in the party and aimed at the consolidation of the socialist system in USSR. Gorbachev understood that economic and political reforms would be impossible without getting rid of the Party's stifling dogma and giving voice to the people. Pluralism, freedom of expression and encouraging creativity in social life were conceived as important factors for reforms (McNair, 1991; Gibbs, 1999). Therefore, Glasnost (openness, freedom of speech, speaking out, from the Russian *golos* or *glas*, 'voice') should become a basis and indispensable component of *perestroika* (reconstruction or reformation, from the Russian *stroit'*, 'to build', 'to construct').

Gorbachev's experiment consisted in liberating mass media and culture in the hope that it could change life for the better. This liberation was limited; information in mass media were still being sifted through the filter of party's censors. Thus, information about the accident at the Chernobyl nuclear power plant on April 25-26 1986, where the power of the nuclear explosion exceeded Hiroshima's by 600 times, was kept secret or distorted until 1989 (Melihova and Abalkina, 2003). The long concealment of the information about the scale and consequences of the Chernobyl accident, which caused direct or indirect damage to more than 9 million people, reflected the viciousness of the Soviet system with its deep-rooted disdain of the people, ubiquitous negligence, disregard of industrial safety and, last but not least, the hypocritical nature of the Soviet mass media.

But, to use Gorbachev's expression, 'the process had started'. Soon it became clear that it would be practically impossible to reverse it. Media was changing. Gradually, it became a political power that led to the crash of the Union in 1991, when the media ceased to be Soviet. Researchers pointed out that the fundamental contradiction between the Soviet system based on the control of information and the processes of innovation and diffusion of information technology was one the major factors contributing to the collapse of the Soviet Union (Castells and Kiselyova, 1995). Democratization of the Russian media in the latter half of the

1980s played the central role in this process. Freedom of press meant the fall of communism (Shane, 1995).

Western countries that for many years had led "information warfare" against the Soviet Union contributed to this process (Hixson, 1997). Popular programmes in Russian language broadcast from abroad included Voice of America, Radio Liberty, BBC and Deutsche Welle. They attracted a significant audience. Leonid Makhlis (2006) who worked for Radio Liberty since 1971 points out that in the mid-1980s about 11 million Soviet citizens listened to Radio Liberty at least once a week. He refers to Time newspaper data that USSR spent more money to jam Western radio stations in five years that the English government spent for one year broadcasting in the Russian language. Thus, only in 1980 USSR spent 93 million roubles on jamming. Although they were systematically jammed by the state, Western radio stations were listened to by many people – not only by dissident intelligentsia but also by ordinary people. However, the major factor was that people on all social levels were sick of the blatant hypocrisy of Soviet propaganda, which nobody believed anymore, including the propagandists themselves. The gap between the official version of reality and the reality itself had become so enormous that a slight push would suffice to disturb the fragile balance of the Soviet system.

The liberalisation of information started by Gorbachev provoked a chain reaction that resulted in a social explosion and led to the crash of the entire system. The media inspired the population in Russia and other Soviet republics to elect democratic reformers on republic, regional and city levels. The reformers, in turn, pressed Gorbachev and the Party to give more freedom to the media. The decisive factor in this process was the emergence of public opinion, which on the one hand was created by the independent media, and on the other, found its voice through the media.

Since 1987, the media came to the forefront of political opposition to the Communist party hierarchy. Because of the lack of civil society institutions in the country, their functions were largely appropriated by the media. As Smith (1990: 149-150) explains,

> No organized political force had yet emerged to galvanize mass support. And so muckrakers in the media, especially those on television who had a mass following, were leading the challenge against the Party Apparat. They were exposing official corruption, the privileges of the élite, and the inept mismanagement of the economy, as well as giving vent to public grievance.

The leading role belonged to television as the most mass of all mass media. Television greatly contributed to the "dethronement of the political power" by revealing its mechanisms which had been kept secret for so long. (Paasilinna, 1995; Mickiewicz, 1997).

In the late 1980s, there appeared a number of television programmes which had a tremendous popularity and influence on the audience of about 100 million. The Moscow *Vzglyad* (*Glance*) and Leningrad *Shestsot sekund* (*600 Seconds*), both launched in 1987, were probably the most popular ones. They broke the taboos of Soviet television one after another and showed materials unthinkable on television before.

600 Seconds with presenter Aleksander Nevzorov featured crime chronicles. In sharp contrast with the Brezhnev era when information about crime in Russia was secret and television drew a rosy picture of the happy prosperity of Socialist society, these programmes confronted the audience with horrors and terrors of "real life" in an aggressive and impressive manner. Nevzorov's topics ranged 'from how rotten meat is ground into sausages at a Leningrad factory, to how radioactivity emanates from old Soviet helicopters in a children's park, to a trip to the morgue to report on the tragic suicide leap of a woman and her two small children' (Smith, 1990: 154). However, it was not only criminal chronicles but also a smashing critique of the rotten regime. Soviet politics and politicians were depicted in terms of criminal chronicles. Nevzorov's programme, shocking and innovative for Soviet television, was extremely popular. For four years, *600*

Seconds held the highest rating. In summer 1990, it reached more than 90 percent. Many disliked Nevzorov's inclination to "dark topics" as well as his "state patriotism" and called him a "necrophile" and "information killer". On the other hand, the programme was praised and supported by many public figures, including Yeltsin himself (Krotov, 1993).

Vzglyad (translated as "Glance" or "View") appeared on television on 2 October 1987 and became a national hit. Its popularity exceeded all other programmes by six or seven times. Millions of people watched it every Friday throughout the country. *Vzglyad* shocked, informed and entertained the audience, shattering old myths and stereotypes. It received fifteen thousands letters a month. Similarly to *600 Seconds*, '*Vzglyad* used hard-hitting reporting on problems that Soviet propaganda used to relegate to the capitalist West – prostitution, police corruption, and drug addiction' (Smith, 1990: 168). Like *600 Seconds*, it went beyond criminal chronicles and featured "crimes of the regime". Thus, it showed how Soviet army and security forces killed nineteen people while suppressing a peaceful demonstration in Tbilisi, Georgia, on April 9, 1989, and presented evidence of the slaughter of thousands of Polish army officers at Katyn, in Byelorussia, in 1940 by Stalin's NKVD. In one of the issues, *Vzglyad* broadcast a discussion that suggested removing the Lenin mausoleum from Red Square and burying him in the regular way at a cemetery – which in a still communist country sounded blasphemous and provoked an ardent discussion. It showed revealing footage of Russian troops in Afghanistan; parodied *Vremya* (*Time*), the official news program; showed impersonations of political leaders and performed an allegory about the possible end of the perestroika. Some of the segments and, occasionally, entire programmes were banned, but what remained was enough to bother the authorities and to win audiences. One of the innovations of *Vzglyad* was the introduction of rock music to the mass audience. They showed Western bands from Pink Floyd to Bon Jovi as well as Soviet rock groups largely belonging to underground culture such as Akvarium and DDT with their obscure or sarcastic lyrics. Note that rock music was perceived differently in the Soviet Union than in

126

the West – it had no commercial connotations and its liberating influence on the youth's minds was significant (Ryback, 1990). Writers, artists, and philosophers were given voice as well. It was a breach of the information blockade in which the population had lived for so long.

The freedom of information launched by Gorbachev finally turned against him. Reforms he had started led to food shortages, crippling strikes, a deteriorating economy, ethnic unrest, ethnic warfare and movements toward sovereignty or independence in the republics. People were fed up with his demagogy, inconsistency and his Southern-Russian accent. And they rebelled. Given a choice, they rejected the candidates of communism and chose as their president Boris Yeltsin and his program of decentralization, democracy, and economic reform. On 12 June 1991, Yeltsin became the first democratically elected Russian President. Soon, party conservators struck back.

On 19 August 1991, Yanayev, Pugo, Yazov and some others announced a coup and established the National Committee on the State of Emergency (GKChP). They shut down major newspapers and seized the television centre. The state channel showed concerts of classical music and Swan Lake ballet instead of information programmes. But the media did not support them. At a press conference organized by GKChP and first shown in live broadcast, a journalist from the Independent Newspaper shouted at gloomy and nervous Yanaev, "Do you understand yourself that you made a coup d'état?" The operator showed a close-up of Yanaev's trembling hands to the entire country. Many people listened to Radio Liberty, which reported the news from Moscow non-stop (the more fortunate also watched live reports on CNN). Gorbachev was kept under home arrest at his state dacha in Phoros on the Black Sea; Yeltsin spoke to the crowd from atop a tank and then barricaded himself in the Parliament building. Many people came out to the streets of Moscow in a massive protest that helped bring down the junta. Everything was over in three days. On return to Moscow on 21 August, Gorbachev resigned from his position as the General Secretary of CPSU. In six months, on 25 December 1991, he announced his resignation and the USSR ceased to exist.

4.2.3 Media-political capitalism

Paradoxically enough, the victory of democracy led to the end of the époque of Glastnost. In a few years, the Russian mediascape changed dramatically. For a few years, the media in Russia remained an independent social institution, a "fourth estate" (in Russian, *chetvertaya vlast'*, i.e. "fourth power"), in some respects more powerful than political power. However, very soon the privatization of the media began – first, in the form of state subsidizing and economical support of the media (1990-1992), then in the form of commercialization and concentration of the media, "control of the media by capital" (1993-1995), which led to the next stage – the formation of the media-political system when the mass media became the main medium of political communication as well as an instrument of competitive struggle (Zasurski, 2001).

One of the most conspicuous traits of the Yeltsin period was the convergence of power, business and organized crime. In a situation of chaos, the lack of adequate laws and weakness of government, violence and coercion was widely used and played a crucial role in creating the institutions of a new market economy (Handelman, 1995; Volkov, 2002). Already in late 1980, it became clear that the market economy emerging in Russia was based on a simple principle: commercial success depends on political influence. In 1991, a small group of Russians emerged from the collapse of the Soviet Union and enjoyed one of the greatest transfers of wealth ever seen, claiming ownership of some of the most valuable petroleum, natural gas and metal deposits in the world. They were called oligarchs. Their list included Alexander Smolensky, Yuri Luzhkov, Anatoly Chubais, Mikhail Khodorkovsky, Roman Abramovich, Boris Berezovsky, Vladimir Gusinsky and others. Before perestroika, they lived the lives of Soviet citizens, stuck in a dead-end system, cramped apartments, and long bread lines. But as Communism loosened, they found gaps in the economy and reaped their first fortunes by getting their hands on fast money. As the government weakened and their businesses flourished, they grew greedier. The state auctioned off its assets, and they grabbed the biggest oil companies, mines, and factories. They went on wild borrowing sprees, taking billions of dollars from gullible western lenders. When the rouble collapsed in August 1998, the tycoons saved themselves by hiding their assets and running for cover (Freeland, 2000; Hoffman, 2001; Goldman, 2003). "The looting of Russia" (Klebnikov, 2000) took place on a great scale. As a result, instead of a great new democracy, the ugly reality of Russian life became the rise of the oligarchs and organized crime, the bitter, bloody wars along ethnic lines, the assassination of democratic leaders by gangsters protecting their turf, abetted by the government, the growing poverty of the populace, corruption and injustice (Meier, 2003).

Under conditions of economical crisis and almost complete suspension of the state's funding of the press, there was a dramatic drop in the circulation of newspapers and magazines. The total circulation shrunk from 37,949,556 copies in 1990 to 7,507,715 in 1998. (Zasursky, 2001) The role of television, already high, grew even more. However, mass media, including the state radio and television, which had obtained freedom from the Party, gradually became dependent upon the oligarchs' capital (Androunas, 1993).

The tendency towards business control of Russian mass media strengthened after the presidential election in 1996. Due to the negative media coverage of the Chechen war as well as scandals concerning the President's drinking habits and the state of his health, Yeltsin's popularity dropped dramatically. In early 1996, his rating was only 6 to 10 percent. There was a real threat that communists would win the elections. In this situation, major financial groups pooled their resources to give Yeltsin both financial and media support. "Political technologies" emerged as the art of manipulation of public opinion by media images and myths. A massive propaganda campaign resulted in Yeltsin's re-election. In gratitude for this support, Yeltsin gave the oligarchs privileged access to media which had been controlled by the state. It led to the formation in 1997-1998 of oligarchic media empires, meaning that powerful financial groups obtained control over key national media.

The most powerful of the media oligarchs were Vladimir Gusinsky and Boris Berezovsky. Gusinsky's Media-Most company owned NTV, a private national television channel which was created in 1993 and obtained a license for all-Russia broadcasting in 1996, the radio station Ekho Moskvy as well as a number of publishing houses, magazines and newspapers. It developed commercial satellite channels, created the regional television network TNT, controlled the lion's share of Russian cinemas and launched a number of ambitious Internet media projects. Berezovsky's Logovaz News Corporation controlled the state television channel ORT and a number of influential newspapers. Other financial groups that owned important Russian media included Potanin's Oneksimbank, Mikhail Lesin's private advertisement agency Video International, Gazprom-Media and others (Zasursky, 2002).

It should be noted, however, that the oligarchs' control over the media was functionally different from that of the Communist Party in the Soviet period. There was not a unified course and a single ideology; the interests of particular groups diverged resulting in a pluralism of outlooks. Moreover, they tended to control only information concerning their specific business and political interests, providing freedom to journalists in other areas. In this period, the advertising market developed, substituting the ideology of consumerism for the ideology of communism, to fill the disillusionment of people in a country where 'the death of an ideology has displaced millions' (Meier, 2003). At the same time, the professional level of journalism was high, the diversity of information was tremendous and the pluralism of opinions flourished.

The gradual transformation of the media into an area of a "political spectacle" (Zasursky, 2001) serving the interests of a few powerful political and business groups resulted in the crash of the myth about the media as the "fourth estate". As the result, many people, including journalists, abandoned the idea of changing society and gave themselves to their private pursuits and hobbies. The programmes popular during the Perestroika were closed; their creators were either killed or lost their interest in politics and changed their occupation.

The case of Nevzorov can be used to illustrate this shift from politics back to private life. In this time of transition between two epochs, speaking truth and being creative acquired the significance of a political act. Journalism and politics were inseparable for Nevzorov. It was a dangerous combination. On 12 December 1990, in a city vacant lot, Nevzorov, late at night, had an appointment with an unknown person who promised to provide him with compromising materials on a state leader. But instead of information, Nevzorov got a bullet in his chest. Some newspapers suggested that it was a self-inflicted wound, which Nevzorov made to enhance his prestige, but he denied this.

600 Seconds was suspended for short periods several times, and it was finally closed in March 1993 by Bella Kurkova, the new director of the Leningrad television centre, when Nevzorov was accused of 'appealing for violent change of the social order' and in 'the alteration of psycho-emotional state of the audience towards aggravation of negative tendencies such as anxiety, depression and aggression'.

During the 1991 presidential election, Nevzorov supported candidates Vladimir Zhirinovsky and Albert Makashov, both known for their nationalist bias, on his programme. Two years later, he went into national politics himself and became a deputy of State Duma (Russian parliament). Since 1993, he has been a member of parliament (re-elected in 1995, 2000 and 2003). In 1997, he became the Saint-Petersburg mayor's advisor on cinema, television and radio. In late 1994, he supported the beginning of the military operation in Chechnya, and in January 1995, he shot the documentary 'The Northern Front' and in 1997, the controversial feature film 'Purgatory' about the first Chechen war. The genre of the latter was defined by critics as 'hard horror'. It justified the activity of Russian troops and included many naturalistic scenes. The film was shown for the first time in March 1998 on the state TV channel ORT and won one of the highest ratings: in Moscow, it was watched by 34 percent of the audience (Petrova, 1998).

But then, all of a sudden, Nevzorov lost interest in both journalism and politics and turned his talent to his long-standing love – horses. In 2004, twelve series of his *Horse encyclopaedia* was shown on the First Channel. Asked by a journalist

(Romanova, 2004) how the *Horse encyclopaedia* corresponded with *600 seconds* from which his television career begun, Nevzorov answered,

> Do you know Evgeni Schwartz's play *Shadow*? So consider *600 seconds* and politics as my shadow. It was my shadow that was a public figure. It was my shadow that participated in coups, rebellions, GKChP. It was my shadow that acted, not me. Now you cannot make me come back into this mud called politics. I had many opportunities to become certain that this activity is senseless. People themselves have channelled their way through the roughness, the putrefaction of life. I bow low to today's state that it doesn't obstruct me, for example, from doing my work.

In his other interview (Kozhemyakin, 2003), he confessed that he felt ashamed for *600 Seconds*, even if it was "a devilishly talented programme" and suggested that the time of "information killers" is over because the audience has acquired immunity to media manipulation.

The career of the members of *Vzglyad* team followed a similar trajectory. In 1991, *Vzglyad* disintegrated into a number of different projects but none of them ever reached the popularity of the original programme. *Vzglyad*'s presenters – Listiev, Lyubimov, Politkovskij, Zaharov, Mukusev – were people's favourites. But the team's unity did not last long; soon their paths parted. During the putsch in October 1993, Lyubimov and Politkovsky advised the audience to go to bed. This political indifference of showmen and successful capitalists was symbolic. Alexander Lyubimov became one of the richest television journalists in the country and made a breath-taking administrative career. Vlad Listiev, the most loved hero of people's television, became general director of ORT (Public Russian Television). He was killed on 1 March 1995 after making an attempt to reorganize the advertising market. Boris Berezovsky, who was by that time the *de facto* owner of ORT, was often named among possible instigators – for example by Paul Klebnikov (2000) who was in his turn killed in Moscow on 9 June 2004 – but in spite of long police investigation, Listiev's killers were never found.

The evolution of the Russian post-Soviet media-system (Zasursky, 2001) in 1985-1999 can be summarized as follows. During the years of Perestroika, the institution of independent media emerged which, in the context of weakness of political power and economical chaos, was often considered as the "fourth estate". In a few years, the situation changed. Privatization and commercialization of the media, investments of politicized capital and the growing role of television in the life of the population led, on the one hand, to the diversification of the media, and on the other hand, to the emergence of a "public scene" as a substitute for the "public sphere", in a landscape of underdeveloped civil society institutions. The media became an arena of "political spectacle", the main instrument for manipulation of public opinion and a weapon in the fight between various financial groups that were building their media-political empires.

4.2.4 Back to centralization and state control

In his television address to the sitizens of Russia a few minutes before the coming of the year 2000, Yeltsin confessed his errors and sins and declared his resignation from the position of the President of Russia. He also announced the name of his successor. It was Vladimir Putin, a KGB officer from St Petersburg appointed as the Prime Minister a few months ago. A new era had started.

When Putin came to power in 1999, a return to state regulation of the media began. It was evidenced by the "war against the oligarchs", as well as by the steady movement towards centralization of the media-political system. The époque of oligarch television had ended. Media magnates Gusinsky and Berezovsky were deprived of their media empires and were forced into exile. Khodorkovsky, who attempted to support the opposition, was prosecuted and put into prison. The "dictatorship of the law" and the "vertical of power" imposed by Putin who was called a "German man in Kremlin" were accompanied by tightening control over information. However, the restoration of control to the same degree that it used to be in the Soviet times has become impossible, as the number of communication channels has increased dramatically. And, apart from traditional media, a new medium has emerged and developed in Russia, with its unlimited channels beyond government control, which provided a space for free speech and apparently unrestrained creativity – the Internet.

4.3 The development of Russian online media

4.3.1 Early uses of the Internet as media

The advent of the Internet in Russia coincided with the collapse of the Soviet Union. This coincidence is significant: the Soviet system was based on almost total control of information, at least in theory, while the Internet provided unprecedented freedom of information outside of state control. One of the first uses of the Internet to circumvent state censorship occurred as early as in 1991. When newspapers and television were closed or severely censored during the 1991 coup aimed at the restoration of the communist system, the Internet was used to disseminate information about the events (Belsie, 1991; Hogan and Hogan, 1991; Press, 1991; Rohozinski, 1999). However, at the time the Internet was used as a channel of communication between a few users (and the West), rather than a public medium. To become a mass medium, the diffusion of the Internet needed to reach a certain critical point. Internet first had to become a mass phenomenon.

In Russian, the mass media are called SMI (*Sredstva massovoj informatsii*, Means of Mass Information). The acronym is a legacy of the Soviet information system; it suggests that information is provided by a central authority and distributed to the masses who act as passive recipients. The SMI served not so much as a source of information and opinion but rather as a "collective propagandist, collective agitator and collective organizer" (Lenin). In the years of Perestroika, the centralized system of the Soviet SMI collapsed. One of the catchwords of the époque became *pluralism*, a variety of opinions and interpretations. The process of media liberation was apparent in the press, radio and television. At the same time, the Internet in its early stage was not considered a real medium; rather, it was describes in terms of a toy, play and self-expression.

134

First online periodicals on the Russian Internet were developed by early adopters, or users/producers in Castells's (2001) terms. They expressed their interests and values and formed the emerging Russian Internet culture. These early online media normally took the forms of e-zines or columns posted to the web with certain regularity, and they can be considered as distant predecessors of blogs. Their primary subject was the Internet itself treated from both a purely technical and a more human point of view.

The first Russian e-zine was launched in November 1993 on the server of the communication company Mark-ITT based in Izhevsk. Its editorial board consisted from one person – the company's director for technology Alexander Ermolaev. The e-zine's title – *Tyatya, tyatya, nashi seti...*[4] – referred to Pushkin's poem *Drowned* (1825) whose first stanza (translated by Genia Gurarie) goes as follows:

Children run into their izba,

Hail their father, drip with sweat:

"Daddy, Daddy! Come - there is a

Deadman caught inside our net."

The e-zine covered only a few subjects, all of them concerned with technical issues: "a description of services available via e-mail", "the family of TCP/IP protocols", and "a brief description of the Hypertext Markup Language (HTML)". Although it included contributions from different authors, it was not actually a zine because it did not come out in issues. It was something between a personal home page (Babayev, 1999) and early web-based zines such as Crazyweb[5] which had issues, a multiple authorship and even an English-language version. *Tyatya, tyatya, nashi seti...* was soon discontinued and it is remembered mostly because it was the first. However, its title was echoed in another project – Anton Nosik's column *Nashi seti* ('Our nets')[6] – which had far greater consequences for the development of online media in Russia.

---

[4] http://www.mark-itt.ru/FWO/
[5] http://www.crazyweb.ru; available via Archive.org
[6] http://sharat.co.il/vesti/zametki.html

4.3.2 The Evening Internet: Creating the audience

Nashi seti was an online version of the column which Nosik wrote for the Israeli Russian-language newspaper *Vesti*. The young popular journalist renowned for his economic commentaries took the role of an Internet guru. He taught free classes on how to use computers and wrote stories on a variety of Internet-related subjects. On the server Sharat.co.il, launched by Nosik, he published 66 issues of his column.

In December 1996, Nosik started a new, this time purely online project, which reinforced his fame as an Internet commentator. His new column *Vecherny Internet* (The Evening Internet)[7] appeared on Christmas Eve and would come out daily without breaks for a year and a half. It was hosted on the server of Cityline, a new Moscow ISP company founded by Nosik's friends, and it was a part of its marketing strategy. Cityline needed promotion and it put its bets on providing content on its web site to win attention of prospective customers of its telecommunication services. Nosik acted as a content provider. He posted the first issues of the column from Israel but in the early 1997 he returned to Moscow. His efficiency is legendary. His topics ranged from reviews of new software to commentaries on actual events on the Russian Net and included many references (and hyperlinks) to political, economic and cultural issues. Each issue consisted of hypertext, stuffed with links, 12-20,000 characters in total (2-2,500 words). He used to sit up in front of his computer 17 hours a day. Of course, this was an extreme experiment for both Cityline and Nosik himself. And it turned out to be a success. In a short time, *The Evening Internet* won an audience of about 2000 users daily – a considerable number for those years. It created an audience accustomed to daily reading of an online publication. It also gave voice to this audience: hundreds of readers discussed the issues Nosik wrote about, or started new topics in *The Evening Internet*'s guest book which became a kind of collective medium.

---

[7] http://www.cityline.ru/vi/

136

The Evening Internet was essentially a phenomenon of early cyberculture. It focused on computer and Internet technologies rather than on the "news of the world" and was addressed to the audience of early Internet adopters. It expressed values typical for the users/producers of the Russian net community representing a "self-reflection of the Internet". Like other early content projects on the Russian Internet, it created not only content but the audience as well. However, the the audience was changing, not only quantitatively but also qualitatively. Cyberculture ideology and the form of one-person media became too narrow to satisfy the growing need for relevant and diverse information. Soon Nosik's experience as online content producer was sought for the creation of ambitious projects that transformed the Russian Internet into a real mass medium. But before proceeding to the post-cyberculture stage of online media let us consider a project in which Russian cyberculture reached its highest peak.

4.3.3 Zhurnal.ru: The rise of the Russian net community

In summer 1996, an idea 'to make a journal about the Internet' occurred to the Moscow publisher Dmitri Itzkovich and his partner Mikhail Yakubov. They asked Eugene Gorny, who was known as one of the few journalists writing about the Internet at the time, to head the project. Gorny accepted the offer and entered into a correspondence with active Russian Internet content producers. The Russian Internet was in its infancy; there were just a handful of Russian content projects. All of the creators were well known in the community – the number of users/producers did not exceed a few dozen. Therefore, it was not difficult to identify and contact virtually all of them. Gorny (1996a) described the programme of the project and invited them to contribute their ideas or to join the editorial staff[8]. The programme stated that the journal should be in Russian, for the Russian audience (independently of citizenship and the physical location); should focus on the issues of the "Russian Internet" and provide a "Russian view" of the Internet

---

[8] A few messages of summer 1996 about the journal project are kept in Moshkov Library. See: http://lib.ru/WEBMASTER/gorny.txt.

generally; should be published both in print and online; and should promote the Internet as a space for cultural creativity. The goals of the journal were defined as follows:

> Narratives about trends of development, and discussion of the successes and problems of the Russian web, could perform, in our view, not only an informational function but also, in a sense, an educational (*kulturtregerskuyu*) function. It is crucial, we believe, to present the Internet not only as a source of information and a means of entertainment but also as a domain of lively creativity. If the first generally suggests a consumerist attitude to the Net, then the second can inspire people to their own creative endeavours. Only then the Russian web (*pautina*) will develop.

The programme also suggested that the journal would consolidate users/producers of the Russian Internet ("the people who do real work on the web"), serve as a place where they could share experience and ideas and also give them a chance to reach a wider audience. It promoted the idea of a "virtual association of the creators (*deyateli*) of the Russian web" which would form around the journal[9].

As the result, an editorial staff was formed in which just two or three people worked in Moscow, including Gorny who had moved from Tallinn. Most contributing members were physically based abroad. Thus, Anton Nosik (Israel) established a mailing list, Leonid Delitsyn (US) drafted an online prototype of the journal, Artemy Lebedev (Moscow) designed the web site, Roman Leibov (Estonia) and Vadim Maslov (US) contributed articles, Shohdi Naguib (Egypt) translated a text from English... In was one of the first vivid examples of creative collaboration in Russian-language cyberspace.

The journal was christened Zhurnal.ru (abbreviated as ZR). Zhurnal in Russian means 'journal', and '.ru' is an Internet acronym for Russia. The name resulted

---

[9] The idea was realized a year latter by the establishment of the International Internet Association EZHE, a non-official trade union for Russian Internet professionals.

from an insight. For a long time the journal had remained nameless and was referred to in the correspondence as simply a 'journal' or 'our journal'. When the time came to register a domain, Itzovich and Gorny complained to Eugene Peskin who worked at that time at Russia-on-Line that they could not think of a good name. He exclaimed, 'But you've got a great name already!' This was probably the first use of combination of a generic term and a first-level domain name as the name of a server on the Russian Internet. Later online media such as Gazeta.ru ("gazeta" in Russian means 'newspaper') followed this model.

A subtitle that appeared in the second issue defined ZR as "The Herald of Net Culture" (*Vestnik setevoj kul'tury*) and introduced the concept of net culture. The concept was not a passive adoption of the English term but rather a homemade invention. It is noteworthy that Zhurnal.ru was genetically linked to the Tartu semiotic school, the centre of Russian structuralism, semiotics and cultural anthropology headed by Professor Yuri Lotman. Three key figures in ZR – Itzkovich, Leibov and Gorny – were Lotman's disciples and graduates of the Department of Russian literature at University of Tartu. Mikhail Yakubov who contributed to the emerging ideology of ZR was linked with Tartu by family rather than academic ties (he met his wife there). However, it was he who first introduced Leibov and Gorny to the Internet in 1994 when, upon his return from the U.S., he found out that the Computer Centre provided free access to the Internet to the students and staff of Tartu University. The founders of ZR had a solid background in humanities and theories of culture which defined their interest in the Internet as a techno-cultural phenomenon and an environment for creativity and experiments. In this framework the idea of net culture was developed. It was influenced by the ideas of early cyberculture which opposed the values of online and offline worlds. The first issue of ZR featured a Russian translation of John Perry Barlow's *Declaration of the independence of cyberspace* as well as a collection of sarcastic quotes about censorship (a few obscene words used in the text created some problems with distribution of the issue). The new culture emerging on the Internet rejected the principles of violence, lies, established status and hierarchies of "official culture" and proposed itself as a space of unrestricted self-expression, freedom and creativity. Net culture was therefore a form of cultural resistance. However, the emphasis was on production and communication of new values rather than the negation of what seemed obsolete. As Itzkovich put it in an interview, 'from "abort", "retry", "ignore" Zhurnal.ru chooses "ignore" '(Ovchinnikov and Ivanov, 1997). The connection of ZR ideology to that of counter-culture movements was evident. It is not surprising that one of the epithets applied to ZR members by outsider critics was "net hippies".

The active phase of ZR lasted about two years. Seven issues of the journal were published (of which five came out in print). Every issue featured both original and translated articles and had a central topic such as e-business, net sex, music, extremism or science and education in the age of the Internet. The last issue summarized the development of Runet over the preceding two years under the half-ironic motto "1000 years of The Russian Internet" and featured interviews with prominent Runet figures and stories about the most successful Russian web sites.

Most people who participated in ZR did it on a voluntary basis. Only a few of the core staff working full-time received a salary, albeit relatively small. The driving force that determined the flourishing of early Russian net culture was not commercial interest but the creative drive of the participants. Partly this was the result of an editorial strategy based on the idea of focusing the dispersed creative energy in one point to increase its effect and reach new syntheses. ZR FAQ, published on November 18, 1996 (Gorny, 1996b) emphasized user participatory creativity:

> Zhurnal.Ru (further ZR) is a journal for Internet users published in Russian in print and online. Moreover, ZR is a site on the World Wide Web (WWW) which includes, apart from the journal, many interesting things, and where a permanent creative process takes place in which everyone who wishes can participate. In this sense, ZR is both a product and a catalyst of Internet creativity.

The FAQ also refrained from a strict definition of subject matter stating that 'ZR is not limited by technological issues; it covers a wide range of topics related to the Internet and network culture.' The metaphor of a mirror was used: "As the Internet is in a sense a mirror of the world, so Zhurnal.ru is a mirror of the Internet." It defined the relationships of print and online versions as mutually complementary: "Roughly speaking, if ZR as a print publication is a journal *about* the Internet, then ZR as a web site is a testing area (*ispytatel'nyj poligon*) of the Russian Internet."

The journal itself constituted only a small fraction of the entire project. ZR policy was to stimulate online creativity; therefore, it gave web space, technical and organizational support to innovative online projects initiated by the members of its distributed staff (and ZR membership was open to any creative individual). ZR FAQ put it as follows:

> It is evident that a full-fledged development of information space in Russia and worldwide can only be achieved through collaborative work, disputes and experiments. We invite journalists, designers, sponsors and advertisers, anyone who is not indifferent to the present and future of the Russian Net. Openness to fresh ideas and creativity is our fundamental principle.

The call was heard and ZR grew from a web version of the print journal to a conglomerate of web sites, an entire network of online creativity. As observers (Ovchinnokov and Ivanov, 1997) noted, 'Zhurnal.Ru available online not only reflects print issues: if in the journal net life is investigated, than on the web site with the same name it boils and bubbles over.' A list of the projects developed under its umbrella can give an idea of the scale and diversity of ZR.

The News and Reviews section included Nastik Gryzunova's InterNews (*InterNovosti*), a news column about computers and Internet; two columns reviewing web sites: Migrant Flies (*Pereletnye mukhi*) and Net Pilgrim (*Setevoj Strannik*); press releases announcing new web sites and services, as well as IT and cultural events. In 1998, two new projects emerged: Polit.ru, daily news and review on domestic and international politics and Bad Weather (*Nepogoda*) – "public discussion on problems and conflicts" featuring controversial publications on controversial topics.

The Culture section consisted of the enormous and fastest growing Music section which included articles, reviews, ratings, archives of rare musical files and authors' projects such as *Russian Reggae Rasta Roots* by Russian-Egyptian rastafaray Shohdy Naguib (who latter received a Reggae Ambassadors Worldwide award for his project) and *World Wide Beat* by musical critic Oleg Pshenichny. Net Literature (*Setevaya Slovesnost*) published fresh literary works of both venerable and unknown authors in various genres such as novels, short stories, plays, poems, translations, experiments with hypertext and multimedia literature and included a lively "discussion on net literature" (*seteratura*) as well as a literary game, *Garden of divergent hokkus*. Finally, the Gallery featured Internet art projects such as Mirza Babayev's *Procession of Similacra* and gave place to controversial artists (the home page of AES group is an example). In 1998, it was transformed into the *Net Art* section edited by the "father of Russian net art" Aleksey Shulgin. Finally, *Kinoizm*, a web site devoted to cinema and the film industry, joined the company.

The Business section had been mostly developed by a single author – Leonid Delitsyn, the founder of the first Russian Internet advertisement network Sputnik, among other things. In his column *Where is the money* (*Gde den'gi lezhat*) he published his studies on business and advertising on the Internet; he also launched a Russian version of *ClickZ*, an American e-journal on online advertising and paid the company for the publishing rights. Apart from Delitsyn's writings, the Business category also included the Web Workshop (*Web-masterskaya*) which provided online lessons on web development and web design and from which a web design company of the same name grew at a later stage.

The Entertainment section contained a variety of authors' projects such as Mirza Babayev's *Oneirocratia* (Power of Dreams) where users shared and interpreted dreams; Roman Leibov's *Candy wrapper game* (*Igra v fantiki*) exploring artistic, non-utilitarian uses of advertising banners; *Question of the day*

(*Vopros dnya*), an online intellectual game updated daily and supported by the 'What? Where? When?' Internet club; Evgeniya Napartivich's *Recipe of the day* (later known as cooking.ru); Roma Voronezhsky's *Nurzhal.Ru*, a humorist web site which included, among other, a picturesque description of Zhurnal.ru headquarters; *Paintball Life*, a web site about paintball; *Fashion Jam* featuring fashion news and reviews; *Gamer* (Igrok) devoted to computer games; and *KidNet* (DetSet'), an attempt to build up a web space for (and by) children.

The Interaction section included transcripts of online conferences with hackers, musicians, writers and Internet figures that ZR had organized since October 1996 as well as various interactive tools such as guestbooks, online conferencing system and chat.

There were also a few uncategorized projects. *Hack Zone* provided space for debates on hacker issues. *Jump!* (*Skok!*) used a script that downloaded a random page from Zhurnal.ru by a button click; *Don't click here!*, demonstrated the power of Internet addiction in Leibov's liberal translation of Canadian Ivan Lam's project of the same name. *Chiromancer Online*, a prank online programme by aforementioned Leibov, promised "to diagnose for free by the lines of your palms your future and past, to help in optimizing the events of your life and also to predict adverse and favourable days". For some time, one of the most popular ZR pages had been a comprehensive list of 'Russian search engines, directories, classifieds, webboards, and catalogues' compiled by Delitsyn – a useful tool in the pre-Googlian époque. The Ezhe movement[10] which united the regularly updated Russian web sites and which has grown to a kind of trade union for Internet professionals also started in ZR.

Some of the projects in this Homeric list were long-standing, others more ephemeral. Some ceased to exist, others (for example, *Setevaya slovesnost* and *Polit.ru*) evolved into independent web sites. Nowadays such eclectic diversity seems almost incredible, but in those early days, when the Internet was still a

---

[10] http://www.ezhe.ru

virgin land and the division of labour and spheres of influence were in embryo, everything one was doing was almost inevitably new. Since there was almost nothing on the Russian net, it was interesting to try everything.

It is not an easy task to find Western analogues for ZR. The comparison with Wired – then the most usual reference point in Russia for publications on the Internet and technology – reveals more differences than similarities. As a print journal ZR was much thinner, had less advertising, a limited distribution (it was available primarily in Moscow) and its ideology can hardly be described in terms of Wired's Californian ideology (Barbrook and Cameron, 1994/2001; Russian translation – Barbrook and Cameron, 1997) which valued 'free-market economics, hedonic lifestyle, techno-utopianism and, crucially, complete disdain for the uniqueness of human consciousness' (Stahlman, 1996). The comparison with the WELL community (Rheingold, 1993) which has been sometimes made is not very convincing either: the WELL flourished in the plain-text environment as a system of online discussion forums; by the contrast, ZR was WWW-based, it enjoyed the advantages of hypertext and multimedia technologies and used online discussion as just one of the many forms of creative collaboration. It was neither a server providing a free hosting for personal web sites such as Geocities, nor an agglomeration of entertainment and gaming web sites such as *Chertovy Kulichki*. The projects included in Zhurnal.ru were diverse but not isolated; they were unified in a common framework and coordinated by the editorial staff. Zhurnal.ru was ideologically and aesthetically eclectic and sometimes criticized for that (e.g. Sherman, 1997) but it was a deliberate policy of the editor.

What was the target audience of Zhurnal.ru? For many observers, it coincided to a great extent with its producers. As one critic said about ZR comparing it with other Internet publications, 'They know for whom they write – for themselves.' ZR targeted the Russian net community as a whole, without any discrimination on the basis of corporate, ideological or cultural affiliations. Only one thing was important to be considered as a member of this community – passion to create. As

Itzkovich (Ovchinnikov and Ivanov, 1997) said in an interview, 'Our audience is people who get off on stuff ("korotye prikalyvayusta").'

It is difficult to tell now if such a policy was really absurd from a commercial point of view. Zhurnal.ru was one of the first Russian web sites to introduce banner advertisement, and it generated very high traffic. It enjoyed a tremendous popularity and influence. It made contracts with ISPs and used the most advanced technology such as broadband radio Ethernet. It did not actually avoid business. What it really needed was good management and some investments. But it was the will of fate that things happened otherwise. In 1997, an American businessman of Russian descent proposed to buy 30 percent of ZR shares for $80,000 (which was a considerable sum for a Russian start-up in 1997). He came to Moscow and the first stage of negotiations was very successful but then he suddenly disappeared. As it was discovered later, he collided with Russian mafia in Novosibirsk where he went for business so he lost a lot of money and was forced to rush back to U.S., to move house and go underground, as well as to suspend all his contacts and contracts. Dmitri Izkovitch, who financed ZR, also suffered damage from organized crime and sometimes could not keep his word about money.

However, regardless of the relatively short life of Zhurnal.ru, its role in the formation of the Russian Internet is hard to overestimate. First of all, Zhurnal.ru brought together the most active and creative Russian Internet users and thus led to the consolidation of the network community. As Anton Nosik (1997a) put it, thanks to Zhurnal.ru "the Russian network community proved to the world and to sceptics in its own environment the reality of its own existence". The consolidation was not only virtual but also quite real. People working in seemingly competing publications and enterprises met in ZR headquarters to talk business, celebrate life, to drink vodka and smoke pot. As Kuznetsov (2004) points out, there were no feeling of competition between Internet workers at that time, or at least, it was balanced by a feeling of the common cause.

Members of ZR belonged to early adopters and many of them who continued their careers in Internet-related domains became known as the Russian Internet élite. "Legendary" has become a stable epithet applied to Zhurnal.ru in the following years. Maksim Kononenko compared the ZR community with the Russian underground rock scene of the 1980s: "there were two communities that have became legendary: the Piter [Leningrad] rock community and people who gathered in Kalashny [lane], in Zhurnal.ru headquarters" (Ivanov, 2004). Asked by the interviewer what defines the legendary status of Zhurnal.ru, he explained:

> The Internet is still not as important as show business and television. But its influence and role are continuously increasing and the membership of the élite – the people who started then and who still define many things today – has remained almost the same. It is absolutely evident that these people will become Marxes and Engelses, founding fathers, and they will begin to determine the life of the country. They will lead the others. Nowadays everybody knows those with whom Putin worked in the city administration. Just like this, they will know those who used to drink in Kalashny. This is already legend. Further, its impact and significance will only grow.

Zhurnal.ru was also a school of online journalism. Some of those who had written their first articles for ZR which went through multiple editorial revisions before being published, later became renowned journalists and editors. ZR was also a good starting point for designers, programmers and workers in cultural fields.

The openness of ZR allowed for interaction and merging between "netheads" and various kinds of cultural producers. The central location of Zhurnal.ru headquarters had both practical and symbolic significance. It was located in Kalashny lane, right in front of the Estonian Embassy, not far from the Kremlin and Arbat. It was actually Itzkovich's private flat – huge and unkempt, with cockroaches in the kitchen and unimaginably long corridors ('As you walk along them, you can finish a cigarette', as Roma Voronezhsky [1997] recalled) – which he used also as an office, a guesthouse and a club. It quickly became a favourite meeting place for artists, musicians, writers, philosophers, activists and all sorts of

146

weird types, thus creating a link between non-official offline and online cultures. The development of the tradition of intellectual conviviality with poetry readings, musical concerts and generous feasts, for which Zhurnal.ru was famous, led to the establishment of a network of Moscow clubs and restaurants under the mark of O.G.I. by Itskovich in the following years. (O.G.I. stands for United Humanitarian Publishers, in Russian *Ob'edinennoe Gumanitarnoe Izdatel'stvo*, the publishing house owned by Itzkovich.) The innovation of the O.G.I. network was a combination of a restaurant, a bookshop, a concert hall and a gallery all in one place open for visitors twenty-four hours a day.

For many reasons, ZR failed to become a profitable enterprise. The lack of money became an obstacle for further development. The publication of print issues of ZR was severely delayed; the fees promised to authors for print publications could not be paid. The idea of transforming ZR into a join-stock company with ZR staff as shareholders failed because of general organizational chaos and passive resistance on the part of the publisher. The alienation of authors from ZR began; some of them felt that they had been simply used and felt disappointed. So did the editor. The époque of pure enthusiasm was ending; a new class of Internet media professional was emerging and content providers had begun to pay money for online content. One of the first and definitely the most aggressive was Cityline, which bought a few talented online journalists including Nosik, Gagin, and Kuznetsov and paid them for their columns published on Cityline's web site. Their fees were impressive; thus, Nosik received $80 for each issue of his Evening Internet. Taking onto account that his contract with Cityline obliged him to publish a column a day, he was the highest paid Internet journalist of that time as well as the first vivid example of the profession (Gorny and Sherman, 1999).

The enthusiasm-based model of producing online content was becoming obsolete. The lack of funding impeded the further development of Zhurnal.ru, caused a growing feeling of a sinking ship among its members and finally led to its dissolution. In March 1998, Gorny received an offer to join Russian Journal (*Russkij zhurnal*), a fresh online project by Gleb Pavlovsky launched the previous year, and after a series of negotiations with both Pavlovsky and Itzkovich accepted. For some time he continued editing ZR on a voluntarily basis, but finally resigned in October when his efforts to save Zhurnal.ru proved to be futile.

4.3.4 Russian Journal: Discussion forum for intellectual élites

Pavlovsky's peculiar background can help to understand the role of Russian Journal. Pavlovsky began as a political dissident and spent some time in prison for publishing an underground journal. Later on, he founded one of the first Russian private news agencies, Postfactum, and published the *Twentieth Century and the World* Magazine. He became an expert in political consulting and made money on 1996 presidential elections when his Foundation for Effective Politics (FEP) worked for Yeltsin. In the following years, he became an advisor to the presidential administration and gained the reputation of a "grey cardinal" of Kremlin's politics. Pavlovsky was assessed as one of the most influential persons in Russia in various ratings. In 2004, he was listed second in the list of Russian intellectuals (Intelros, 2004).

Pavlovsky has been often considered as the main adept of the ideology of Internet provocations. In 2000, on the day of the Presidential and Parliamentary election, he launched a web site where he published exit poll results in real time. He was accused of breaking the Russian laws but he argued back that publication on a web server located in US was not covered by Russian jurisdiction and that, according to Russian law, the Internet is not a mass medium. News reports about the web site appeared on all major TV channels and it obtained quick publicity. Within the online community, some praised Pavlovsky innovativeness as a device against falsification of the election results; others considered it a provocation whose consequences might be harmful for Internet freedom. FEP created numerous web sites for and against Russian politicians and used provocation as one its main methods not only on the web but also in real-world actions.

Unlike other FEP projects, Russian Journal launched on the day of seizure of the Bastille, 14 July 1997, did not pursue pragmatic political goals but presented itself as an open intellectual discussion forum 'for those who want not only to accept the existing situation but also to understand it' (Pavlovsky, 1997a). According to its founder, its goal was to 'initiate discussion in the élites' and to 'create an open space for public intellectual discussion essential for the elaboration of strategies for the development of Russia' (Pavlovsky, 1997b). In his programme article, Pavlovsky insisted that "Russian" in the title had nothing to do with the Russian state or the "Russian Idea" but only referred to language of discussion. 'The immediate analogue of the Russian programme today is the world-wide network Internet", Pavlovsky concluded his programme rather unexpectedly.

There were a few notable parallels between Russkij Zhurnal (RZh) and Zhurnal.ru (ZR). RZh mirrored ZR in its title by combining the concepts of Journal, Russia and the Internet, although in a reverse order. In the same way as ZR consisted of a thin print journal and an extensive web site, RZh embraced a wide-format print journal called *pushkin* (for some obscure reason with the lowercase "p" in the beginning) and a web site russ.ru. The New Yorker was taken as a model for both content and design. The main sections were book reviews, the political and cultural situation in Russia, problems of education and net culture. In the same way as ZR, RZh sought to unite creative forces of the online and offline worlds. But if ZR proceeded from the online community with its tendency to anarchism and the lack of respect for any authority, RZh approached the synthesis from another side – that of the Russian intellectuals who belonged to traditional culture and who were, as a rule, ignorant of – or *a priori* hostile to – the Internet. The first reviews on RZh in the online media (e.g. Sherman, 1997b) mentioned this fact and were rather ambiguous, and Pavlovsky looked for the right person to enable the consolidation of the online and the offline élites and to promote their joint influence. Although at that time he had a rather vague conception about what the Internet really was (Kuznetsov, 2004), his visionary programme attached a great significance to embracing Internet culture as an essential element of this new cultural configuration.

149

Net Culture (*Net-kultura*) edited by Gorny was published in both the print *pushkin* and on the RZh web site. In *pushkin*, which came out every two weeks, it occupied eight full pages, that is, ¼ of the entire journal and had a different background colour, being a kind of journal inside a journal. The editor was given *carte blanche* in selecting topics and authors because no one, including Pavlovsky as the editor-in-chief, felt confident in Internet issues. The freedom was exciting but it had a negative side as well: unlike other sections of the journal, Net Culture articles were not even proofread so typos occurred.

Having at its disposal a significant amount of money of unclear origin Russian Journal managed to recruit the best intellectual forces and gradually it became one of the most popular journals on the Russian net. However, although the intellectuals eventually went online and a few "net people" gained offline recognition, on the whole net culture remained a rather marginal topic. Although both server statistics and print journal surveys showed the high popularity of Net Culture, publications on "Internet religion", cyborgs and "naked girls in crawler coffins", debates on *seteratura*, case studies of online political provocations and projects of a virtual state without a centralized government often looked somewhat strange in the context of the journal. An edited volume *The Internet and Cyberculture in Russia* (Gorny, 2000b) that included articles on various aspects of Russian net culture was going to be published in book form by Russian Journal. However, it received no funding: it is said that Pavlovsky decided that "it would be of interest only to the net crowd (*tusovka*)". Net cultural self-reflection ceased to be interesting in a wider cultural context. After Gorny left Russian Journal in April 2000, Roman Leibov became the editor of Net culture. He shifted the focus from theoretical discussion of net issues to free play with genre forms. Net culture outlived most publications about the Internet, and it was closed only in 2004 during a structural transformation of Russian Journal.

4.3.5 RBC: Earning money on providing free news

Both Zhurnal.ru and Russian Journal pursued cultural rather than commercial aims. They did not earn much money; they were funded by their publishers. However, with the quantitative growth of the Internet audience, commercialization of the Russian Internet had started. Nosik (2001) justly points out that 'as common sense suggests, creation of the means of mass information on the Russian Internet became possible not earlier that the Runet itself had become a mass phenomenon.' As a benchmark of the new stage, he suggested 1998 when the audience of the Russian Internet exceeded one million users. Another factor was the global financial crisis which culminated in the August crash of the rouble when in just a few days the exchange rate of dollar to rouble increased by more than four times. The crisis forced Russians to look for political and financial news on the Internet instead of using it just for entertainment.

Popular news web sites such as National News Service[11] and Polit.ru[12] turned out to be too sluggish in making decisions and failed to provide users with the information they needed so urgently. Bank web sites tried to sell information about currency exchange and also lost their audience. It was the Russian Information Agency RosBusinessConsulting[13] that became the leader in providing this information. Since 1996, the financial news service provided quotes and financial analytics to its paid customers. The subscription was expensive and the web site audience was small. However, on 17 August 1998 when the crisis stroke RBC immediately offered free access to their paid news to the general audience. This decision made RBC the leader in the new sector of the Russian Internet. The popularity of RBC outstripped not only *Jokes from Russia* (see Chapter 7) but also the leading search engines of the Russian Internet. Because of the dramatic growth of traffic, on 17 August the agency broadened its Internet channel capacity from 512 Kbit/sec to 1.1 Mbit/sec. But it still was not enough, and on 21 September the

---

[11] http://nns.ru
[12] http://polit.ru
[13] http://www.rbc.ru

channel was broadened up to 3.2 Mbit/sec. (The next increase of RBC's popularity happened in March 1999 and was provoked by the interest in the war in Yugoslavia – the channel was again broadened, this time up to 5.5 Mbit/sec. On the 1 October RBC held a record in the Russian Internet with the daily number of hits exceeding 3 million.)

This popularity was followed by commercial success. RBC became an attractive site for advertisers. As Nosik (2001) recalls,

> RBC's sales department, enjoying the status of a monopolist, made up such a price list for advertising that can still blow the minds of Internet advertisers – from 10 to 15 US dollars for one hundred views of a banner. During the crisis's peak, when the newspapers wrote about the inevitable collapse of the Russian Internet, RBC's revenues ran into six-figure amounts monthly.

In a few months, the financial crisis came to an end. It had no serious influence on the growth rate of the Russian Internet audience but it created a habit in the online audience to use the Internet as a source of actual news on a daily basis. RBC's experience showed that the Internet can be used as a source of hot news information unavailable from the traditional media and that it is possible to earn money on the public's interest in such information. It stimulated further experiments in developing commercial online news media.

4.3.6 Gazeta.Ru: Winning a mass audience

The first Russian daily Internet newspaper Gazeta.ru[14] came out on 1 March 1999. The idea of the project was devised by Gleb Pavlovsky, the founding director of the Foundation for Effective Politics (FEP) who persuaded the leader of the oil giant YUKOS to fund the project. As Nosik (2001) points out, 'for YUKOS the cost of the project was nearly unnoticeable, while it was probably the biggest investment into a Russian Internet content project in all its brief history.' Pavlovsky invited Nosik to head the project. Nosik, in turn, recruited the members

---

[14] The archive of Nosik's Gazeta.ru is available at http://gazeta.msk.ru.

of the Russian Internet élite. The web site design was made by Artemy (Tema) Lebedev, the most famous designer on the Russian Internet; scripts were written by Maxim Moshkov, the founder of Moshkov Library; renowned Russian Internet journalists who got their start working for Zhurnal.ru and Russian Journal joined the project. Gazeta.ru developed the tradition of Russian net culture. It actively used hypertext and other properties of the net. It was a bold experiment exploring the possibilities of the Internet as news media, now not only for the narrow circle of net community but also for the general audience.

The future of Gazeta.ru depended on its success: it would be simply closed when the timeframe of funding was exhausted if it could not become a media outlet of national significance. In a short time, Gazeta.ru became the leader in online media popularity ratings outstripping online versions of all print newspapers. In summer 1999, its daily audience reached 150,000. It proved that it was possible to create an Internet source of news information with no print prototype which would have the same quality as the print media but would provide information with a shorter time gap.

However, Gazeta.ru differed from traditional media not only in the form of presenting information but also in its underlying values and interpretations of events. This difference was especially visible in the coverage of the war conflict in Kosovo and the NATO bombing of Serbia in March 1999. The Russian media took an unambiguous approach to covering the conflict: support for Serbia and condemnation of NATO and the U.S. The Balkan crisis was used – by both politicians and the media – as an excuse for unleashing a new confrontation with the West. The position taken by Gazeta.ru which tried to provide balanced information was in sharp contrast with the dominant attitude. "The conflict of interpretation" was similar to the one that was typical at the early stages of the Internet when the values of cyberspace had been opposed to those of the "offline world". However, this time, it became clear that it was also an opposition between the Soviet legacy and the new democratic worldview as well as between the intelligentsia and "the masses". Nosik (2001) put it very clearly:

The idea of return to cold war and the iron curtain was not appealing to the part of the Russian citizenry who got used to life in an open world without borders, enjoying global information exchange – that is, to Runet users. Gazeta.ru created by and for these users fully reflected the unwillingness of intelligentsia to accept the return of the Soviet rhetoric and foreign policy. In fact, Gazeta.ru became at that time the only source of information which did not support the xenophobic bias of the central press and which tried to cover the Balkan conflict without dividing the belligerents into "brothers" and "enemies" on a religious or ethnic basis.

In a few weeks, Gazeta.ru was followed by some other media such as the TV channel NTV, the radio station Echo Moskvy and the journal Itogi. The popularity and influence of Gazeta.ru was to a great extent defined by its independent position.

YUKOS appreciated the success and decided to take the project under its control. In September, Gazeta.ru got a new publisher and a new editor. Gazeta.ru Pls was established by YUKOS to manage the newspaper. Vladislav Borodulin, former editor-in-chief of Kommerstant-Vlast magazine became the editor-in-chief. The new Gazeta.ru hired renowned journalists from the Kommersant publishing house and developed the tradition of quality print journalism rather than that of net culture. The innovation was that fresh news and articles were posted to the web site every 15 minutes. The combination of print quality journalism and Internet technologies, to quote Nosik (2001), 'had no precedent in the history of Russian journalism.'

4.3.7 Lenta.ru and Vesti.ru: Two models of online media

Nosik, meanwhile, launched two other Internet news projects, both in collaboration with FEP. On the 4 September, Lenta.ru was launched which provided domestic and world news 24 hours a day. A month later, Vesti.ru appeared which featured commentaries and analysis. It was an attempt at a division of labour and separating of genres which normally coexisted in earlier examples of online media including Gazeta.ru.

Vesti ("news" in Russian) developed the Net culture approach to information found in Gazeta. Apart from hyperlinks and multimedia it had a highly personalized structure and it emphasized personal, subjective approach to information. It was a legacy of anarchic personalism of the early Internet when everyone could act as a content provider and the value of information was in a direct relation to the authority of the writing person (if even a virtual one). The role of a *name* was high. Vesti was made up of authors' columns and the form of presenting the news depended on selection, interpretation and idiosyncratic style of individual authors. Gazeta and Vesti had no correspondents of their own and they used the news provided by big news agencies. But they turned the impersonal "facts" into something very different. There was also a sharp critique of traditional forms of news presenting. Aleksei (Lexa) Andreev who wrote a column *Time O'Clock*[15] claimed to invent the genre of "hacked news." He monitored news agencies and focused on inconsistencies, absurdities and ambiguities in the news. He used to made bizarre collages from the news accompanied by his sarcastic commentaries, often on the verge of indecency.

Lenta followed a different, more impersonal strategy which turned to be more successful in market terms. Apart from the advancement of online journalism, the new projects pursued commercial goals. As Nosik (2001) states, 'Lenta had simple and clear goals: winning the maximum audience in a minimal timeframe, and a parallel building up of an exclusive advertising space that would allow one to talk about the project paying for itself, that is, about its attractiveness for a commercial rather than political investor'. The goals were reached. In nine months, Lenta.ru had a larger audience than Gazeta.ru. In March 2000, it was bought by an Internet holding company "Russian Funds – Orion Capital Advisors" which earlier bought the controlling interest in Rambler, a Russian search engine and an Internet portal.

---

[15] http://www.fuga.ru/toc/index-arch.htm

Vesti.ru was less successful: the demand for analysis and commentaries turned out to be less that that for the news. Correspondingly, it had a smaller audience, showed less advertisements and failed to attract investors. In December 2001, the FEP President Gleb Pavlovsky announced that FEP would discontinue support of its Internet content projects. In July 2002, Vesti.ru was placed under the control of the state communication company VGTRK with other FEP content projects such as Strana.ru and SMI.ru. The domain name vesti.ru passed into the ownership of a Russian TV programme Vesti and the archives of Vesti.ru were deleted from the server[16].

In the same way as *The Evening Internet* inspired the movement of web observers, Nosik's new projects gave rise to a range of "clones" which used the structure and layout of Gazeta and Vesti in the hope of repeating their success. Most of them failed to compete in the market and perished; some have survived until now. The success of Gazeta, Lenta and Vesti created Nosik's fame as a start-up manager of news web sites and made him a successful Internet entrepreneur and an influential public figure. Some observers accused him of cloning his own projects. However that may be, his skills and experience have been in great demand in the market. In 2003 alone, he transformed NTV.ru to Newsru.com; founded Cursor[17], an Israeli Russian language online news agency; and became the editor-in-chief of MosNews.com, a news agency and online newspaper covering Russian news in English. In an interview (Nosik, 2004), he said that it was his old dream 'to tell all the people on the planet Earth about Russia' but defined the aim of the project in more pragmatic terms of earning money by selling advertising space. In 2005, he launched Gazeta.kg, a daily Internet publication in Russian made in Kyrgyzstan which inherited many features of his previous projects. Selling the news online has become a routine practice.

---

[16] The archive of old Vesti.ru can be found at http://vesti.lenta.ru
[17] http://cursorinfo.co.il

4.3.8 MeMoNet: Towards total media

In late 1999, a new big player came onto the scene: media magnate Vladimir Gusinsky established a holding company MeMoNet (Media Most Networks) as the Internet extension of his Media-Most, the most powerful media company in Russia at the time. The new holding incorporated media resources bought from Netskate Ltd. (historically connected to Cityline) such as *Jokes from Russia* (Anekdot.ru), *Internet Magazine*, the news service MSNBC.Ru and the advertising network Reklama.ru. Nosik (2001) who headed the holding (he was also the editor-in-chief of NTV.com, a multimedia web site of the TV channel providing news, photographs and video), describes MeMoNet as a "full-cycle Internet holding":

> Apart from creating content projects, web site production, Internet advertising sales and the maintenance of Media-Most corporate projects (this task was delegated to the NTV-Portal.com company), an ISP company NTV-Internet was established that provided high-speed access via the NTV+ satellite dish.

Gusinsky followed his American advisors in his business model: content projects should be funded from the revenues earned by ISP services. It was an example of how an "off-line" media company can enter the Internet market and win. However, its potential was not fully realized. In 2000, as a result of Putin's war on the oligarchs, Gusinsky lost his media empire and had to flee the country.

Another Russian oligarch, Boris Berezovsky, was luckier. Although he also fled the country, he managed to preserve control over some of his media assets. His contribution to the development of online media may be not as bright as Gusinsky's; however, Grani.ru, a web site launched in December 2000, and funded by Berezovsky, is still alive and provides a sharp criticism of what happens in the country.

4.3.9 Strana.ru: The state as a content provider

The Russian government finally became aware of the Internet as an instrument of influence and made an attempt to use it for official propaganda. In autumn 2000,

FEP launched an ambitious project, Strana.ru (*strana* meaning "country" in Russian), devised as a national information service. It used state information channels such as VGTRK, ITAR-TASS and ORT and also developed its own correspondent network. It was supposed to function as a Kremlin news agency and represent all seven Federal regions of Russia, each with its own correspondents, its own editorial staff and its own web site on the server. It was probably the most expensive media project in all of the history of the Russian Internet. A large campaign promoted the web site as a source of diverse and valuable information for political élites as well as for the general audience. The result was pathetic. Strana.ru failed to win an audience and to influence public opinion to any perceptible degree, let alone to make money. It was handed over by FEP to VGTRK, a state-owned company, in less than two years. The government's attempt to win on a field where, unlike television, users had a choice, failed. The reason was evident: although Strana.ru had a large correspondent network, it used a centralized, one-to-many model of communication which was typologically similar to that of the Soviet times. The users, accustomed to the many-to-many communication model, considered it antiquated and not organic for the Internet. Another reason was the official character of the information which left little space for personal creativity, which, in turn, made it boring. As Trofimov (2003) pointed out, in a hypothetical rating of Runet web sites by creativity, liveliness and drive, the official web sites of government structures would be the last. "They are not alive," he concluded. "Life" has flourished in spaces where users could freely choose their sources of information and act as information producers themselves. Soon, LiveJournal, which provided users with the tools of DIY media production and community building, became such a space, and its popularity skyrocketed (see chapter 6).

4.3.10 Summary

The first online media were created by enthusiasts and reflected the values and interests of the Russian net communitity. However, the model of voluntary creative collaboration exemplified by *Zhurnal.ru* was challenged by commercial models. The latter first developed as experiments (*The Evening Internet* is an example) but the growth of the online audience and the emerging habit of using the Internet as a source of information made online media successful competitors with traditional media in terms of both audience attention and profit. The development of the online media used the experience of net culture and involved creativity and innovation. The role of politicized capital was significant in the development of the online media in Russia. The online media have often provided an alternative view and interpretation of the events as compared with official state-controlled media. The attemps of the government to use the Internet for information and propaganda purposes started late, and they have been generally unsuccessful because of the lack of interest on the part of the audience. The use of the Internet as a platform for DIY media has persisted throughout the history of the Russian Internet and has been reinforced by the blogging revolution.

Kireev (2006) divides Russian online media of the 2000s into four groups: official media, oligarch media (and later purely commercial media), civil media and the rest of the "independent, authors' Runet". All of these groups have been considered (to a varying degree of detail) in our analysis. Let us now consider how the online media have been interpreted in the context of contemporary Russian culture.

4.4 Models of interpretation: Samizdat, kitchen-table talks and the public sphere

One of the prominent characteristics of Russian culture is a traditional differentiation between public and private life. Although this differentiation can be found in any culture, in a totalitarian or authoritarian society to which Russia belongs it is especially conspicuous.

A sharp contrast in peoples' behaviour in the streets and at home amazed the foreigners who visited USSR (Miller, 1960; Smith, 1976; Richmond, 2003). In public places, they observed gloomy unsmiling faces, aloofness, unsociability, rudeness and automatic reproduction of the Soviet ideological patterns clichés. The people's behaviour changed drastically in a narrow circle of family and friends and such qualities came to the fore as openness, friendliness, generosity, humour and spontaneity. In the new Russia, after the collapse of the Soviet Union this ambivalence has largely remained, only the party was substituted by the "democratic government" concerned, as the majority of citizens believe, not so much with the national interests as with the distribution of power and money and in which the population do not trust as they did not trust to the Politburo; and the ideology of "developed socialism" was substituted by an ideology of "free market" with some elements of the "Russian idea".

Although the majority of the population is very critical to what is happening in the country, Russia is remarkable for its political passivity. Some observes explain this by such traits of the national character as resignation, humility and submission to the authorities. Instead trying to change life on the societal level, the Russians, as a rule, tend to accept it as it is and adjust their public behaviour correspondingly. They prefer not to fight with social misfortunes but to take shelter from them in their private life.

The double standard of behaviour is supplemented by a double standard of psychology. George Orwell described this phenomenon in its novel *1984*. He coined the word 'doublethink' and explained it as "the power of holding two contradictory beliefs in one's mind simultaneously, and accepting both of them." Hedrick Smith, a New York Times journalist who gave a detailed and accurate report on Russia in the early 1970s, was shocked by this discrepancy between official and private life and labelled it a "deliberate schizophrenia" (Smith, 1976: 137). And it was the private space in the kitchen where Russian realized their freedom of though and speech and unconstraint behaviour in talks with friends over a bottle of vodka.

To understand the correlation between public and private on the Russian Internet and assess its shifting role in the life of society, it is useful to consider it in the context of the dynamics of Russian mass media analysed earlier in this chapter.

The effect of the Soviet information policy which deprived the people of their voice and reduced their role to passive consumers of propaganda was a development of private communication spaces such as kitchens where people could freely express their opinions and discuss actual issues, even if in an altered state of consciousness. Re-alienation of the media in the 2000s led to revival of Soviet kitchen-table talk culture with the only difference that now the kitchen has extended to cyberspace.

As it was mentioned above, the advent of the Internet to Russia coincided with the époque of *glasnost* (from *glas* or *golos* meaning "voice"). It is not by chance that the name of one of the first Internet Service Providers in Russia – GlasNet – was coined by combining the Russian 'glasnost' and the American "network" (Gagin, 1998). The Internet as an open communicative space gave users the opportunity of direct expression and let them to overcome the situation of "underground free-thinking" and dissident speech behind the closed curtains. Moreover, the access to information and the opportunity to disseminate information has actualized another metaphor – samizdat.

Samizdat literary means 'self-publishing' but it combines two different meaning which emphasize either 'self' or 'publishing'. First, it is self-publishing in the sense that someone publishes his or her own creative works (poetry, novels, art, recorded songs, etc.). The 'self' can also be understood not in the individual but in collective terms and include products of collaborative creativity (in the form of self-made magazines, group exhibitions, etc.). Second, it is the practice of making and distributing copies of forbidden works (which ranged in the Soviet Union from dissident political pamphlets and unauthorised scientific works to poetry by Akhmatova and Mandelstam and erotic literature of 18 and 19 centuries). Wikipedia[18] defines samizdat as a 'grassroots strategy to evade officially imposed censorship in the Soviet-bloc countries wherein people clandestinely copied and distributed government-suppressed literature or other media. The idea was that

---

[18] http://en.wikipedia.org/wiki/Samizdat

copies were made a few at a time, and anyone who had a copy and access to any sort of copying equipment was encouraged to make more copies.'

The Internet from the very beginning has been perceived in Russia as a space of free expression and a means of escape any kind of censorship and regulation. The typological similarity between the Internet and samizdat of the 1960 and 1970s seemed self-evident (Kuznetsov, 1998): both involved technology (a typewriter or tape recorder then and computers and the Internet now) and were used by individuals to produce and distribute information independently from the state's control.

Samizdat in Russia traditionally combined political and literary connotations and this ambivalence has persisted on the Internet. Aleksander Zhitinsky (1999) called the Internet and the technology of print-of-demand 'samizdat of the 21st century' and was the first publisher who introduced print-on-demand and order via Internet as a means of distribution contemporary literary works. Numerous literary websites made literary samizdat a daily life reality. On the other hand, websites of various political orientations used the Internet to promote their political views. Both types of websites aimed also at stimulating public discussion. The later corresponds to Habermas' concept of public sphere as a realm of social life to which all citizens have an access and where public opinion is formed. The possibility of open discussion on the Internet and the formation of online communities seemed to make this public body reality – if even in the virtual space.

Unlike kitchen-talks and samizdat, the concept of the public sphere was not homemade but borrowed from the West. Since it has been less "natural", it provoked more reflection. It has been often perceived as "official" or "artificial" concept and criticized or, at least, "estranged" as not wholly applicable to Russia's reality. Thus, Zasursky's (2001) study of the Russian media quoted above used the term "public scene" (alluding to Guy Debord's (1967) concept of the "Society of spectacle") to emphasize the simulated character of the "public sphere" in Russia. The Internet has often been regarded by Russian users as the only real public sphere, unlike the official simulacrum of the latter.

Researchers pointed at informal personal networks that have traditionally been used by Russians to circumvent limitations imposed by the authorities (Ledeneva, 1998), as a model for Internet use and interpretation in Russia. Thus, Rohozinski (1999: 22) explicitly states:

> The Russian Net – built upon the cultural tradition of personal *blat* networks – served to extend and empower those social networks by routing around the hierarchical dominance of the institutional order, while providing a mechanism for the exchange of much-coveted private information. In this sense, the virtual space that the Net created – cyberspace – acted as a kind of surrogate civil society, a space that allowed for the unfettered pursuit of personal contacts and group interests outside the strictures of the Soviet institutional order.

However, the same author argued later (Rohozinski, 2000) that the legacy of the Soviet system had continued to influence the character of the Russian Internet and expressed scepticism concerning the idea of the Russian Internet as a public sphere.

Although samizdat and the Internet have been likened, the differences between them have also been noticed and their context and function often contrasted. The historical samizdat was limited both by the number of copies it might produce and by the size of the audience in which the copies circulated. The Internet removed these limitations by giving tools of self-publishing to any user and by making copying virtually effortless. However, the democratising potential of the new media which gave "power to the people" has also been considered as a cause of deterioration: the gain in quantity meant the loss in quality.

K.K. Kuzminsky, underground poet and publisher, explained the difference from a poetical perspective (Ioffe, 2005):

> Nowadays, nobody needs fucking poetry (except the graphomaniac authors themselves) unlike our joyful 1950s and 1970s when poets were looked at

like rock stars: girls fed and kept them, gave them sex (and blowjobs) and retyped their manuscripts...

Samizdat – according to Darwin – made the strongest ones survive, unlike the half-dead morass of the Internet where you can find all kinds of shit. Samizdat DIDN'T REPRINT shit.

Gleb Pavlovsky (2003) expressed his dissatisfaction with the Internet as compared to samizdat in more political terms:

I could understand the Internet only as an analogue of samizdat. Both have a common feature – the activity of the user. What is samizdat? It is not a search for information in general; it is a search for the information which has an existential meaning for you personally and for which you are ready to take responsibility and risk. And in the process of this search, you met other people which provided *links*. They formed a community and every member of this community had the same attitude toward information as basic *value*.

The Internet empowers people to be not only transmitters of established interpretations but to be able to choose a system of interpretation and to produce new interpretations. However, not many people use this opportunity.

Let us consider how the concepts of kitchen-table talks, samizdat and the public sphere have been realized in the development of Russian online media.

Polit.ru, a web site launched in early 1998, first as a section of Zhurnal.ru, and devoted to publishing political news and commentaries on a daily basis, was notable for its deliberate orientation to the non-official style of "kitchen intelligentsia" talk about politics. (Another precedent, as Leibov [1998] wittily noted, was the genre of "talks with the television", i.e. remarks mumbled by someone who drinks tea and watches a TV news programme.) This stylistic manner made Polit.ru very dissimilar to "official sources"; it attracted readership and influenced the style of Russian political journalism. Historically, the Polit.ru experiment had an interesting parallel with *Vzglyad,* one of the most popular

164

television shows of the perestroika époque (see section 4.2.2), which was conceived by its producer Anatoly Lysenko as an imitation of "candid and unpredictable ... kitchen-table conversation" (Smith, 1990: 166). On the other hand, the innovation of Levkin (1998), the editor and a leading author of Polit.ru, consisted in the application of the style which had already prevailed on the Russian Internet, to political topics.

The style referred to speech genres and constructed the author as a private person. Online columns of so-called web observers, the most popular of which were Anton Nosik's *Evening Internet* and Alexander Gagin's *Paravozov News*, each in its own way, followed these stylistic principles.

Besides individual authors, non-formal, colloquial style was a characteristic of online group discussions. This fact allowed proclaiming guest books as a "new form of literature" (Gorny, 1999b). Various systems of self-publications propagating on the Russian net also promoted freedom of the public speech of private persons. A good example is the "open electronic newspaper" *Forum.msk.ru* that provided tools for self-publishing to authors writing on political issues. The editorial intervention was minimal and anybody who had something to say could say it aloud on the web site.

Among the most vivid examples of electronically assisted samizdat are Russian online libraries created by enthusiasts without much care about copyright. Almost any book published in Russian can be found and freely downloaded online. The Russian Internet has virtually managed to realize the hacker ideal of free information (Levy 1984/2001), in contrast to the "Western" Internet in which copyright and commercial concerns have severely limited the range of online publications (Lessig, 2001; 2004; Vaidhyanathan, 2004). The proliferation of online libraries in Russia is a result of a specific attitude toward property (Maly, 2003) and especially intellectual property deeply rooted in Russian culture, which tends to disregard private interests for the sake of a common cause. Copying and distributing of intellectual property on the Russian Internet is usually unselfish. Its leading motive is not profit but love – to an author or his work. In most cases, the authors have no objections because the populatirity of their works online indirectly stimulates sales of their intellectual product in the "real worl" (Gorny, 2000d). This attitude has found a parallel and been reinforced by the ideas of early cyberculture problematising the concept of intellectual property in the digital world.

If online libraries provide free access to the wealth of creative work of others, then online literary web sites stimulate creative endeavours by providing means of distribution of users' own work. Literary sites with self-publishing facilities such as *Samizdat* at Moshkov's Library or *Stihi.ru* and others members of the National Literary Network (Vishnya, 2004) are notorious for encouraging "online graphomania" (Schmidt, 2001), i.e. compulsive and prolific writing producing results of a low aesthetic quality, by giving everyone an opportunity to publish his or her literary work without the mediation of *gatekeepers* (publishers, editors, critics, etc.), normally unavoidable in 'traditional' publishing. Unlike an electronic library, literary self-publishing web sites realized another meaning of samizdat – the distribution of one's own works rather than the suppressed works of others. Maksim Moshkov, the creator of the largest online library on the Russian Internet[19] launched within it a self-publishing section. In an interview (Ovchinnikov, 1997), he acknowledged the functional similarity between traditional and electronic samizdat but stressed their quantitative difference, consisting in the fact that 'before, one of a thousand got published and now every fifth person can be published.' Web sites which provide free hosting for personal home pages such as *narod.ru* (a Russian analogue of Geocities) can also be referred to this group. The web site called *Creativity for all*[20] which provides space and tools for self-publishing in any genre – from poetry to mathematics – is a glaring example of such an approach.

Kitchen-table talks and samizdat have sometimes merged on the Internet. Talks are ephemeral because of their oral nature; when they are written down and made

---

[19] http://lib.ru
[20] http://works.org

166

public, they may acquire qualities of samizdat. A typical example of this process is the publication of jokes. Jokes and humorous stories, or, in Russian, *anekdoty* are an essential element of unconstrained kitchen-table talks. They can be political or politically indifferent, decorous or indecent, self-sufficient or occasional. They are a modern form of folklore that promptly reflects everything that happens in life. *Jokes from Russia*[21], a web site launched in 1995 by Dima Verner, has become a depository for this genre of people's creativity. Verner has published jokes emailed by users without any censorship, acting as a mediator between the private situation of joke telling and the wider public. The result of this samizdat activity in a double sense has been the tremendous popularity of Anekdot.ru with Russian Internet users (see chapter 7 for detail).

The dialectic of private and public speech is a conspicuous feature of blogs. Since 2001, the blogging service Livejournal.com (or, as the Russians call it, Zhivoj Zurnal or simply ZhZh) has become the largest discussion centre of the Russian Internet. Its blogging facilities, the ability to configure readership and communities, and its non-Russian jurisdiction made it very attractive for Russian users. A host of Internet celebrities, intellectual and cultural figures also contributed to its popularity in the masses (see Gorny, 2004b and chapter 6). Given the fact that the Russian state has regained the control of most mass media in the country (especially TV and major newspapers), the blogosphere (Vieta, 2003) exemplified for the Russian users mostly by ZhZh, has been considered by many users and observers as the only actual public sphere. However, metaphors of kitchen-table talks and samizdat deeply rooted in Russian historical memory have often competed with the concept of public sphere. 'The blogger community reminds me of a big communal kitchen,' admitted a journalist (Ivanov, 2004) characterizing the Russian community on LiveJournal. However, this was not the only model to describe LiveJournal because of the choice among different communication strategies it provides. Thus, Sekretarev (2004) listed several

---

[21] http://anekdot.ru

divergent interpretations: 'For some, Zhivoj Zhurnal is a virtual analogue of talks in the kitchen, for others it is a free tribune and hundreds of potential listeners daily, for yet others it is a handy tool to organize debates... Some use ZhZh as a field for sociological and psychological studies and experiments; others use it as a sclerotic's notebook.' Sometimes different interpretations merged. Thus Octyabrina, LJ user holmogorova_v (2005), trying to find the answer to the question why in Russia, unlike the West, LiveJournal has become an alternative media system (a "real public sphere") used the reference to kitchen-table talks along with other traditional self-representations of Russian culture emphasizing both people's separation from power and the totalizing tendency of the emergent community:

> ZhZh (unlike 'Big LJ' – *E.G.*) ... regardless of the diversity of views, convictions and moods, is a single whole, one *big kitchen in a communal apartment* (italic is mine – *E.G.*) where people discuss the topics that disturb them, drinks, criticize the regime and abuse each other, 'de-friend' and write information against their neighbours. ... A cliché comes to mind that "the Russian nation is characterized by collegiality (*sobornost'*): we are not individualists by definition or, more precisely, we can be individualists only in a well-structured society. The example of ZhZh shows this especially well.

As we have seen, LiveJournal, as well as the Internet generally, has often been described by Russian users in terms of kitchen-table talks, samizdat and the public sphere. These terms have rather divergent connotations. Thus, samizdat emphasizes the idea of grassroots publishing, while the public sphere conveys the idea of open discussion. The concept of "public sphere" has sometimes seemed too serious and obliging to be applied to "anarcho-communist" formations such as the Russian LiveJournal. The correlation between the "official media" and uncensored online discussions is also far from being clear. Thus, it is unclear how candid posts on RLJ could correlate with the users' work in official media (many of RLJ popular users are journalists), and to which extent RLJ's influence, even if indubitable, can produce a perceptible change to the Russian media system.

Speaking at the *Internit* conference in Novosibirsk, Anton Nosik (2005) contrasted the many-voiced richness of information and opinions found in blogs with the monotony of the official media under state control: 'In comparison with the traditional media, blogs provide real stereo, polyphony and 3D.' He argued that the difference between television and the Internet is 'that people come to the Internet to look for information while on television people are given directions how they should live.' The opposition between TV and the Internet in this quotation seems to be very similar to the historical opposition between the dullness of Soviet propaganda and the freedom of expression and communication in kitchen-table talks and samizdat.

4.5 Conclusion

The analysis of the development and interpretation of the online media reveals that the Internet generally and online media in particular have often been understood in Russia in terms of an alternative or opposition to the "official" Russian media system. The use of such terms as kitchen-table talks and samizdat shows a continuity of historical experience. The alienation between the government and the people and the underdevelopment of civil society institutions results in the fact that the Internet in Russia has become a substitute for the public sphere – much the same way as Russian literature substituted for civic institutions in the previous époque.

This observation shows a persistent gap in Russian culture which can be described by a series of oppositions such as official - non-official, public – private, formal – informal and impersonal – personal. It also seems to contradict the idea found in Internet research literature which describes the contemporary Internet culture, in contrast to early cyberculture, as an extension of real life. It can be argued that the opposition between the offline and the online worlds has been retained on the Russian Internet, although it has been transformed into the opposition between "official" Russia and "non-official" Russia. This process can be exemplified by an artistic project with the telling name "Russia-2"[22] promoted by Marat Guelman, which aims at 'stating the existence of another country ... which is freer, more international, critical to the government, defending the sovereignty of the personality and freedom of creativity,' in contrast to Putin's Russia. It is noteworthy that the project was first developed on the Internet and discussed on LiveJournal before being realized in the real world. Apparently, the Russian Internet has provided a model for Russia-2. In a sense, it is Russia-2/

---

[22] http://www.russia2.ru

Chapter 5

THE VIRTUAL PERSONA AS A CREATIVE GENRE ON THE RUSSIAN INTERNET

That which holds most true in the individual is that which, most of all, appears to be to himself, this is his potential, revealed by the story that part of himself that is wholly undefined...

Paul Valéry

Only by creating a legend, a myth, can one understand man.

A.M. Remizov

5.1 Introduction

This chapter is dedicated to the examination of the phenomenon of *virtualnaja lichnost'* (virtual personality or persona) as an artistic genre in Russian Internet culture.

The focal point of this investigation – the virtual persona as a form of Internet creativity – can pop up unexpectedly in the context of existing research literature. The creative aspect of online self-representation has rarely attracted the attention of researchers. There are several reasons for this. Firstly, the phenomenon of "the virtual I (ego)" has been analysed predominantly by psychologists (Turkle, 1996; Suler, 1996-2005), who were more interested in psychological rather than aesthetic issues. Secondly, the majority of work dedicated to virtual identity is based on material from the English language Internet and reflects the reality inherent within it. However the same technocultural phenomena can function and be interpreted in various ways within the framework of different cultures. Historically, virtual identities have played a slightly different role on the Russian Internet than on its English-speaking counterpart. It is notable that Western studies on Internet Art

171

(e.g. Greene, 2004) do not include virtual identities (personae) in their lists of genres, while at the same time in Russia the virtual personality (VP) is a recognised genre of web-based creativity legitimised by a corresponding category in Teneta's online literature competition.

This divergence in research focus might be explained by the combined effect of several factors. Firstly, socio-economic factors played a role (the population's low income levels, undeveloped payment systems etc.), which defined the specific nature of the operational use of internet technology in Russia. Whereas in developed countries the Internet quickly became available to the majority of the population and developed into an everyday life extension, in Russia it remains a luxury, "an acquisition of the élite" and is used predominantly as a tool for professional activities or self-expression (Delitsyn, 2005).

Secondly, the temporary gulf between the dissemination of the Internet in the West and in Russia led to a divergence in technologies, in the context of which experiments in Virtual Personae modelling were initially carried out. Whereas, in the USA and Great Britain the Internet had been accessible in academic institutions since the 1970s, in Russia it was only in 1990 that the first international telecommunications session took place, and the first more or less feasible access for users only really became available in the mid-1990s – around the same time as the appearance of WWW (World Wide Web) technology, which to a significant extent superseded other earlier popular internet protocols. This, in turn, led to a situation where the most actively used environment for the development of Virtual Personalities on the Russian Internet was specifically the WWW, while in the West, the problem of virtual identity was, historically, tied up with earlier, purely textual environments, such as Multi-User Dimensions (MUDs) and Bulletin Board Systems (BBSs).

This difference in technologies left its imprint on the construction and nature of VPs. The open space of the WWW did not require 'membership'; the medium in which VPs lived had become 'the whole of the internet', and not the semi-private space of games or forums. Moreover, this allowed users to go beyond the text and to build up the VP as a distributed multi-media object. It is worth noting that the classic Western works dedicated to virtual identity are based on textual environments and rarely touch upon the WWW. In Russia, the opposite was the norm. We have noted that multi-user dimensions (MUDs) – the traditional environment for the conceptualisation of the VP in Western literature – never played a significant role in Russian cyberculture. Those Russian users who went out onto the net before the advent of the WWW (the majority of whom were studying or working in the West), evinced a clear preference for political and poetic debate in Usenet groups, as opposed to participating in online adventures of the "dungeons and dragons" kind. Rather than having a linguistic explanation, it is most likely that the Russians' preference for debate can be explained as a difference of cultural values. It is obvious that the relative privacy of the gaming experience played a role here: for a consciousness oriented towards dialogue and openness, private activities appear to be superficial and of little consequence. (On this theme, see also the analysis of the between the private and public on Russian LiveJournal in chapter 6.)

Thirdly, one has to take into account the influence of a literature-centric Russian culture on the formation of VPs. Traditionally, literature has played an unusually important part in Russian society. In conditions of authoritarian rule and weak civil institutions, public opinion has been predominantly formed by writers. In Russia, literature has taken upon itself many roles, which in the West are carried out by the church, parliament, the courts and the media. One of the consequences of this situation is the attribution of great significance to the written word and the concomitant denigration of the spoken word.

This tendency has also manifested itself in the Russian Internet. MUDs, IRC (Internet Relay Chat) channels, chat rooms and forums are typical of a predominance of the spoken word, albeit in written form. Usenet, home pages and blogs, on the other hand, are oriented towards the rhetoric of the written word (Manin, 1997). Therefore, the Usenet, home pages and blogs, in accordance with the literature-centric nature of Russian culture, had a higher axiological status for

Russian users. This underlines the historical dynamic of the technological environments used for the creation of VP in the Russian context. The VPs first emerge in Usenet discussion groups (such as soc.culture.soviet and soc.culture.russian, SCS/SCR) and within the framework of online literary games (Bout Rimes, Hussar Club etc.); then they begin to create their own home pages, colonise guest books and propagate on Live Journal and similar systems of communicating blogs. All these are environments that are oriented towards the written word and literature. Spoken media and technologies (IRC, ICQ, Web chats and so on), are also undoubtedly used as environments for virtual amusement. However, in terms of the generation of socially significant VPs, their role has always been secondary. Thus VPs in Russia have a distinctly literary provenance.

Fourthly, there is a difference in the predominant interpretive strategies. In Western literature the VP is often discussed within the framework of the concept of social roles (Goffman, 1956) and represented as a private case of a rational "management of identities" (boyd, 2002; Pfitzmann et al., 2004). This approach is rather different from that of the Russian Internet, where the virtual is, as a rule, an artistic project, an eruption of creative energy, a spontaneous theatrical escapade and not some calculated image-making exercise. The Russian virtual and Western virtual identities are often on different sides of the stage lights. For, as a Russian researcher (Gashkova, 1997: 86) has noted, 'Of itself, the performance of roles is not the source of a game, but only signifies the adoption of a specific role of a programme.'

A significant amount of Western research literature is dedicated to the technical aspects of creating virtual characters, understood in terms of computer programming and robot technology. Couched within this concept, the VP is a technical object alienated from its creator and linked with him or her in terms of cause and effect, but not spiritually. In the context of the Russian Internet, the situation is the opposite: here, VP, as a rule, is specifically the representation of the self: it is its psychological and existential extension rather than an alienated and self-sufficient mechanism (with the exception of cases of "experimental simulations" where the object is "an alien ego").

The expression *virtual'naja lichnost'* in its wider sense, as its English counterpart "virtual identity", is polysemantic and has a whole series of synonyms, the meanings of which only overlap to a certain degree. The primary definitions of the term, VP, are as follows: 1) an identification in order to get into a computer system (login, user name); 2) a pseudonym used for the identification of a user on an electronic medium (user name, nickname); 3) an abstract representation of the persona used for civil, legal or other social identification (passport number, personal code, finger prints, DNA); 4) a computer programme that simulates intelligent behaviour (robot, bot); 5) an artificial intellect in conjunction with the body (android, cyborg); 6) a fictitious personality, established by a person or group of people which creates semiotic artefacts and/or which is described 'from without' (virtual character, virtual persona); 7) an individual, as perceived or simulated by another; in other words, images or hypostases of a personality as something different from its essence (for example, the "I" (ego) as opposed to the "self").

This chapter predominantly focuses on the VP as defined in the sixth definition (a virtual character or persona). In this definition the VP can be characterised by the blurring of the oppositions of truth and lies, fact and fiction, reality and unreality, materialism and idealism, which aligns it closer to the creation of art (Gorny, 2003b).

What place does the VP occupy in relation to the other forms of online self-representations? Based on a classification system of strategies and procedures developed for the analysis of various forms of autobiography (Spengemann, 1980), we showed elsewhere (Gorny, 2003b) that the creation of a VP is predominantly the realisation of a poetic strategy of self-invention. It is worth noting, however, that this classification system does not encompass those forms of the VP, when the object of the representation is another "I" (the most striking example being cloning). Correspondingly, the autobiographical mode should be supplemented by

175

the biographical one, and at least one more procedure should be introduced, which can provisionally be labelled as creative modelling.

This chapter develops themes and ideas discussed in the author's previous published works on the phenomenon of the "virtual self" (Gorny, 2003b; 2004a). This material has undergone a fundamental re-working: several theoretical positions have been significantly extended and the history of Russian VPs is completely new. At the same time, some themes discussed earlier (an overview of the literature, theories of the self, the ontology of the VP, the use of the Internet as a tool for self-knowledge, etc.) have been left outside the text. The specific character of this study lies in the historical approach to the material. The object of the research is the evolution, over the last decade, of the genre of the VP on the Russian Internet.

5.2 Virtual personae on the Russian Internet

The first Russian virtual personae, or virtuals, as they are termed in colloquial speech, appeared in the pre-web period. In the early stages of the Internet, the possibility of easily creating "figures that do not exist in nature" (Exler, 2000) was a novelty and experiments in this field were especially intensive. A whole constellation of virtual personae emerged on the Russian Internet, won fame and notoriety and became models for later imitation. However, the boom in virtualisation quite quickly went into decline. By the end of the 1990s the life cycle of popular VPs had run its course and the majority of them had left the stage; virtuals, like the Internet as a whole, had ceased to be perceived as something new and had started to irritate and become banal. Being a virtual became unfashionable and, in certain circles, even a cause for shame. However, the story of virtual personae does not end here. The appearance of blogs signalled a further democratisation of the Internet and gave users a simple and convenient tool for self-expression (and self-invention). In Russia the incredible popularity of LiveJournal – a server of online diaries with the added possibility of controlling your circle and building up your own community (see chapter 6 for detail) – provided the impetus for a whole new wave of virtuals.

5. 3. Virtual personae on Usenet

One can talk about "weak" and "strong" forms of VP. The former are content to restrict themselves to a pseudonym, whereas the latter create an image. The first 'strong' forms of VP appeared on the Usenet news groups at the end of the 1980s and the first half of the 1990s. These were fictitious characters employed as intermediate agents in the endless Usenet flame wars – online slanging matches. VPs also began to appear in the more peaceful context of literary creativity.

5.3.1 Vulis: squealing sorcery

The most famous creator of such characters was Dmitri Vulis, whose story has been examined in detail in an article by Julya Fridman (1998). Vulis' creatures were multi-faceted. For example he sent messages in the name of the "Simulation Daemon", whose signature proclaimed that 'this article was written by an artificial intelligence programme' and included the phrase 'better an artificial intelligence than no intelligence at all' which was particularly offensive to his opponents. As Fridman puts it,

> The new Daemon, in addition to its artificial intelligence, was notable for completely non-human fantasy. It intensively and inventively spewed forth filth aimed at the opponents of its learned master, it told stories from their biographies (atrocious and atrociously private rumours), which were then illustrated in accurately executed pornographic pictures in ASCII graphics.

Another of Vulis' creatures was Rabbi Shlomo Rutenberg. He selected Dmitri Pruss as the object of his attack, a Jew by nationality, a person who, according to Fridman's characterisation was "a peaceful, gentle-hearted, highly educated intellectual and father of three children". Rutenberg called Pruss "a Soviet-Nazi anti-Semite" and "a renowned Jew-phobic punk from Russia", and called upon the

Americans to send complaints about Pruss to his employers, which is what they assiduously proceeded to do. Pruss was not dismissed but was forbidden from using the Internet and a psychotherapist was assigned to him.

Vulis did not blanche at stealing identities. Thus, in order to compromise his opponent, Peter Vorobjev (who was an adherent of H.P. Lovecraft and considered himself an expert in black art), Vulis and his accomplices created an a-mail account from which 'the counterfeit Vorobjev immediately began to send to all new groups excerpts from criminal (according to American standards) racist texts calling for genocide.' At the same time the public's attention was drawn to "the racist Vorobjev" the effect of which quickly produced repercussions: at work the real Vorobjev was showered with complaints and his account at panix.com was shut down by the administration. In order to reinforce this effect a different virtual character was used, called "Vladimir Fomin" who tirelessly denounced "Vorobjev " and at the same time many others. The genesis of this character is remarkable. Fridman says (*ibid.*):

> Fomin, as it turned out, was not just simply some sort of golem: he was what is called one of the "undead", a zombie that had risen from the grave. Someone had found documentary evidence of his death: Lieutenant Vladimir Fomin had had his head blown off by the explosion of an artillery shell in Afghanistan. When this document was published on Usenet, Vladimir met the news with a joyful exclamation. He admitted that the event had a place in his life history and separately certified that his head was decidedly of no importance to him.

The end of this story is revealing. Although in the virtual war Vulis and his virtual creatures seemed to be invincible, they could not withstand a blow from the real world. Some colleagues of the "poor, hunted Vorobjev" reported Vulis to the FBI. It is still unknown what happened to the corporeal Vulis - but he disappeared from the net leaving only his bad name and ill repute behind him.

In recounting this story, Fridman (1998) draws a direct parallel between the virtual battle between Vulis and Vorobjev and the magical struggle between the two French occultists Boulan and Guaita at the end of the 19th century. This approach would appear to be justified: The Internet allows one to influence the thoughts, emotions and lives of people without making physical contact and at times it can be used as an instrument for "black magic." A classic case – described in literature – is a virtual assault in the multi-user game LambdaMOO in which a character is turned into a zombie with the help of computer software (Dibbel, 1993).

Golems, zombies, homunculi, the theft of the name (and by implication the soul that is linked with that name) and other magical essences and procedures are being actualised in cyberspace with striking regularity. The popularity of occult studies among a number of active figures in the Russian Internet has added to this.

5.3.2 "Teneta": net literature and the virtual persona

Usenet was not only about "flame wars": an active literary life was on the boil in the new groups. Moreover, many people preferred to publish their poetry and prose under a pseudonym and it is only one short step to go from pseudonym to virtual. In April 1995 Leonid Delitsyn, himself no stranger to writing, decided to collect and put into some order, literary texts published in the soc.culture.soviet and soc.culture.russian (SCS/SCR) news groups. Thus the first Russian online literary journal, DeLitZine came into being, on the server of the University of Wisconsin, where Delitsyn was, at the time, writing a dissertation on geology. In June of the following year, on the basis of this journal and with the active participation of Aleksey Andreyev (a mathematician and poet also studying in the USA at the time) Teneta, the online Russian literature contest was established. The organising committee was made up of virtually all the active Russian Internet figures of the age. It is worth noting that the formation of a Russian net community came about specifically because of literature – although the majority of the participants were representatives of the natural sciences and not one of them was a professional man of letters.

Teneta quickly evolved: new categories were introduced reflecting the specific nature of net literature[23]. Among these was the category for "Virtual Persona" (virtual'naja lichnost'), which boasted such sterling characters as "the virtual lover Lilja Frik", (an obvious allusion to Vladimir Majakovsky's real lover, Lilya Brik), who wrote verses, and the virtual cat Allergen, who, in addition to poetry, wrote essays on the theme of virtuality. Teneta's founders also took part in this category themselves: Aleksey Andreyev, as Viktor Stepnoy and Mary Shelley and Leonid Delitsyn as Leonid Stomakarov. This occurred when it became possible to write in the Russian language using Russian script and when the centre of creative activity moved to the World Wide Web.

5.4. Virtuals on the WWW

5.4.1 Muxin: a virtual with a human face

The first virtual on the Russian web was Mai Ivanych Muxin (the correct English spelling of the name would be Mukhin; the traditional spelling is adopted here). If Vulis created his virtual self in the image of "a monster, a terrible beast with the forked tongue of a venomous pig" (Fridman, 1998), then Muxin, according to the definition of his creator and self-perpetuating secretary was "a virtual with human face" (N., 1998).

The public first found out about "the first and last pensioner on the World Wide Web" from an interview with Muxin, published on 6 October 1995 in the Estonian Russian-language newspaper "Den za Dnem" (Babayev, 1995). The image of a pensioner who had been born in Vyatka in 1917, three days before 'the sad events that shook the world' and who had stayed alive to see 'the other revolution - the

---

[23] In 2002, the list of nominations of *Teneta*, the Russian online literature contest, included 11 categories related to net literature divided into two groups. Net literature (*setevaya literatura*) group included hypertext literature, multimedia literature, and dynamic literature. Net literature projects (*setevye literaturnye proekty*) included the categories: personal literature page, personal monographic net project, system- monographic net project, electronic literary journal/newspaper, electronic library, net discussion club / creative environment, and virtual personality.

computer revolution' was not only unexpected but also realistic. The Internet in those days was very exotic and the progressive pensioner struck the public's imagination. The reporter Mirza Babaev announced that he had communicated with Muxin via the Internet and only a short while after had met him in person. This is how Muxin's apartment was described:

> I am sitting in Mai Ivanych's place in his cosy little room in Vjaike-Kaar Street, I am drinking Ceylon tea, on the walls there are photographs of relatives and certificates of honour; on the bookshelf is a collection of Russian and foreign classics, an antique issue of "The Elocutionist"... In the stove the birch logs are crackling away merrily. And by the window on a low ancient table covered with a lace tablecloth flickers the display of a PC 486-DX.

In the interview Muxin narrated the story of his life, including many colourful details. He explained the basic terminology of the Internet to his readers and demonstrated how to write a hypertext document and how to insert links and images into it, taking, as an example, the verses of an old Soviet song.

The interview was a great success: it was re-printed by several Moscow magazines and translated into Estonian. It is even rumoured that Lennart Meri, then President of Estonia, even made a reference to the progressive pensioner from Tartu (without, admittedly, mentioning his name) in one of his speeches about plans to increase Internet use in the country. In the second interview (Babayev, 1996), Muxin added to his credibility by including details that seemed highly unlikely. As an illustration, a photograph was published in which a smiling Mai Ivanych, in a forester's uniform, was seen with Brezhnev and Broz Tito (in the text Muxin commented on the circumstances that led to the photograph being taken). The interview was carried out by e-mail, which at that time was totally unprecedented (this was the first online interview published in Russian).

Figure 1. Broz Tito, L.I. Brezhnev and Mai Ivanych Muxin.

The plausibility of Muxin's image, created by a multitude of colourful everyday, biographical details and his inimitable style was strengthened by his living presence on the Internet. Thus, as one of the first Russian Internet users, he created his own home page (Muxin, 1997), gave advice to beginners on how to use e-mail and wrote poetry on the online Bout Rimes game. Like a new Admiral Shishkov, Muxin tried to Russify foreign words and came up with amusing Russian terms for the translation of Internet realia: thus, he would translate the World Wide Web as *Povsemestno Protjanutaja Pautina* (literally, 'the Universal Extended Spider's Web') and interface as *mezhdumordie* (literally, 'intersnout').

Muxin enjoyed both affection and respect on the Internet. In 1998 he was elected President and Honorary Chairman of the Teneta literary contest (Teneta, 1998), and the Virtual Russian Library was almost named after him (Gorny, Litvinov and Pilschikov, 2004). There was certainly no initial indication that both Mai Ivanych Muxin and Mirza Babaev were fabrications, fictitious people or "virtual personae" (*virtualy*). Many users believed in their reality, while those who were aware of the mystification played the same game treating them as real personalities.

The genesis of Muxin's image is curious. Roman Leibov, having admitted in an interview that he was Muxin's creator (N., 1998) related the story of how Muxin came into being:

> In 1986, I was standing by a window in a hostel, smoking with Arkasha Grimbaum[24] and Kirill Zhukov, who traded in furniture, had come over. Suddenly, Arkasha said: 'You know, there are certain types of pensioners. They have funny old shirts and special hats full of holes.' I remained silent. 'So let's say, for example, that such a pensioner is living here in Tartu,' says Arkasha. And at that point Zhukov said: 'Yes, and his name should be Muxin.' I remained silent: 'Exactly, and his first name is Mai Ivanych.' Well, from then on Muxin lived his own intensive life for a very long time.

Muxin was the product of a spontaneous game of the imagination. Before he ever appeared on the Internet, he had taken part in many a hoax. In the same interview Leibov talked about Muxin's correspondence with Soviet writers:

> Pikul[25] was sent an excerpt from Mai Ivanich Muxin's historical novel. Anatoly Ivanov, the then editor of "Molodaya Gvardiya" (Young Guard), was sent a wonderful letter. It was written on behalf of a person who had at one time or another done time with a certain Tolya (Anatoly) Ivanov and now had bought a magazine when he was half cut and saw there a picture of

---

[24] Misprint. The name should be read as "Blumbaum".
[25] Vladimir Pikul was a popular author of many novels about the Russian history.

Anatoly Ivanov. He decided that this must be his old prison buddy. But the most ingenious things of all were the letters to the poets Yevtushenko and Voznesensky. Mai Ivanych wrote to both of them, that he loved them both very much, that their names had lit up the whole of his youth, that there had been other poets but that later he had lost faith in them and that they remained the only ones. He wrote this base letter to each of them and then simply got the envelopes mixed up.

Muxin also promoted himself as a writer: children in an Estonian country school in which Leibov did practical work as a teacher were given a task to write an essay on his short story 'about how there had been a watchman at a collective farm called Old Matvey and how a rich family of *kulaks*[26] called Permyakov[27] had decided to burn down the warehouse and had killed Old Matvey.'

Leibov (N., 1998) confessed that 'he considered Mai Ivanych to be a completely real character.' This comment leads us to an interesting question: how are these VPs perceived by the authors who created them? What are they and what do they signify to their authors? In other words, what is the ontology of a VP? Is it that the creators of VPs have multiple personalities, or, in the words of Mercy Shelley (2004) are they multi-persons (*multpersonaly*), or do they relate to their VPs as something separate from themselves? It is impossible to give an unequivocal answer to this question: in many cases the author simultaneously feels that the VP is both an essential aspect of his self and something separate and independent. (For analogies with literary creativity, see: Gorny, 2004a). Thus, from the point of view of the authors, the VP is simultaneously an expression and a construction, a fantasy and reality, an object of creativity and an independent subject. Its ontological status is ambivalent, as is its attitude towards its creator.

---

[26] Rich peasants.
[27] The name alludes to Leibov's friend Evgeni Permyakov; a graduate from Tartu University who worked as an editor for Dmitry Itzkovich's publishing house O.G.I.

Being the first fully-fledged virtual, Muxin had a significant effect on the subsequent modelling of virtual personae on the Russian Internet. He provided an inspiring example which was later imitated or creatively transformed.

5.4.2 Paravozov: the spirit of the server

On 24th December 1996 *Vecherni Internet* (the Evening Internet), "a daily commentary on the Russian and world net", edited by Anton Nosik, began publication on the server of the ISP company Cityline. Nosik wrote on a wide variety of subjects, but the Internet provided both themes and the method of writing: even subjects that were distant from the net were unfailingly illustrated with references to net resources. Vecherni Internet's popularity was extraordinary, considering the scale of the Internet at the time – and on average, each issue was read by 2,000 people daily (see section 4.3.2 of chapter 4).

The following year was marked by a boom in "web commentaries" (*veb-obozrenija*). This genre included reviews of websites, computer advice, commentaries and musings on various subjects through the prism of the net. A list called "All Commentators", compiled in 1997-98 by Aleksandr Romadanov (1998), consisted of 80 or so web commentaries – an amazing figure for the Russian Internet, still in relative infancy. Essentially, these regular columns were the first Russian blogs. However, unlike the blogs of the next millennium, their theme was not life and commentaries on it but the net and what was happening on it. The virtuality of the commentaries' subject matter led to the virtualisation of their authors. The first web-commentator to demonstratively don the mask of a virtual persona was Ivan Zrych Paravozov, with his column "Paravozov-News"[28].

Paravozov was invented by Aleksandr Gagin, who worked, at the time, as a systems analyst at Jet Infosystems. He started posting his comments on the net, which were an explosive 'mix of lyrical writings, aphorisms and puns for all sorts of occasions' (Gorny and Sherman, 1999) in November 1996, even before the launch of the Evening Internet. Paravozov's innovation was his very image: he

---

[28] http://www.gagin.ru/paravozov-news/

renounced human form and declared himself a "spirit of the server". This persona was causally linked to the author, but at the same time it demonstrated a significant level of autonomy. Sometimes Paravozov argued with Gagin; in this respect, one episode involving Paravozov during an IRC-conference at Zhurnal.ru is revealing (Paravozov, 1997):

> <Presenter> (asks a question from "solntse"): So, are you or are you not Gagin?
>
> <Paravozov> (to solntse): Of course I'm not Gagin, I've already discussed this.
>
> <gagin>(to solntse): I write Paravozov.
>
> <Paravozov> (to Gagin): You liar, what do you have to do with it? Stop sucking up. Next you'll be saying you're Kadetkina and Anikeev[29].

Figure 2. Gagin disputes with Paravozov during an IRC conference at Zhurnal.ru (1997).
Photo by Svetlana Kasimova.

Gagin (r_1, 2004) explained the appearance of Paravozov by both his tendency to systematise real phenomena, and by an emotional outburst brought on by an argument among Zhurnal.ru's authors about how to write about the Internet. (It is also from this – from the abbreviation ZR – that his patronymic Zrych comes). The

---

[29] Virtual personalities well-known on the Russian Internet at that time.

186

choice of the genre of VP was influenced by another, unspoken factor: the desire to hide behind a mask to avoid problems at work: Jet Infosystems, where Gagin worked, would not have approved of his net activities.

Using the example of Paravozov, we can observe how innovation in the genre developed. Two processes, well known to sociologists and anthropologists, played a leading role here: imitation, facilitating the continuity of culture (Tarde, 1895), and emulation, rivalry, the desire to surpass one's contemporaries, being a powerful motive for creativity and responding to the appearance of "cultural configurations" (Kroeber, 1944) – constellations of creative people during a specific period. On the one hand, Paravozov joined in the game initiated by Zhurnal.ru; on the other, he set himself against it, choosing, he believed, an alternative strategy.

It is curious that Gagin's own style is so different from that of Paravozov and that Gagin the journalist has never attained the popularity of the virtual persona he created. What is more, Gagin treats Paravozov's work as if it was not Paravozov doing the writing of it (r_1, 2004): 'Looking at these texts today, I don't understand why they are the way they are, and I don't recognise the person who wrote them.'

5.4.3 Katya Detkina: a girl with a passport

From the outset, Paravozov's personality laid no claim to authenticity and needed to be treated as a game. Soon, however, a persona appeared on the Russian net that many people believed to be genuine. This was Katya Detkina, whose virtual life and death stunned the Russian Internet. Briefly, this is her story (Gorny, 2000c):

> *16th February* (1997). The exposure of Katja Detkina is the first major scandal on the Russian net. An article appeared in the electronic journal, CrazyWeb, in which it was stated that the real author of "KaDetkina's

Observations" (Detkina, 1997), the sarcastic *"obziraniya*[30] of the Russian Internet", which have been coming out since the beginning of the year, was Artemy Lebedev. The authors stated that KaDetkina's writings contained, "material which is slanderous and insulting to specific companies and individuals" and that Lebedev, who had so crudely "gone for" his rivals should take responsibility, even criminal responsibility. (…) On 3rd March (1997) it was announced that Katya Detkina had died tragically in a car accident. This news produced a stormy reaction among the net public – the virtuality of this persona was not obvious to everybody.

Stylistically, Katja Detkina looked to two contemporaries, both of whom wrote Internet commentaries – Muxin and Paravozov. But neither of them completely suited her. Her strategy was to take the best from them – "the design structure of a website" from the first, and "literacy and memories of better times", from the second. It was understood that she would write in her own way and on her own themes. Moreover, both Muxin and Paravozov were virtuals: Detkina claimed to be real.

The illusion of reality was strengthened by convincing biographical details, photos of her passport (which he published as a proof of her reality) and a recognisable style.

---

[30] An untranslatable neologism derived from *obozrevat'*, 'to observe' or 'to comment' and *obsirat'*, obscene, to 'shit upon' or 'defame'.

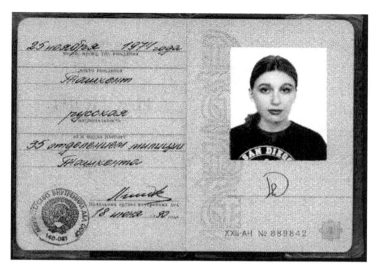

Figure 3. Katya Detkina's passport.

Having analysed Detkina's style posthumously, Zhitinsky (1997) came to the conclusion that Lebedev was her author: 'the style of Kadetkina and the style of Tema (Lebedev) are a single style.' However, Lebedev only admitted that he was the author much later on. In a private conversation, Artemy Lebedev (2005) stated that one of the factors that prompted him to create Katya was dissatisfaction with existing web-commentaries, not one of which, in his opinion, looked at websites from a professional point of view:

> Her task was to compensate for the shortage of "trade" texts. Nosik wrote about politics and Gagin about interesting sites. Kadetkina began to put into practice my idea about the (Russian) Wall Street Journal – a publication which looks at the world, taking into account the existence at companies of owners and people responsible for events of various kinds.

The result of these attempts, as we saw, was completely different: the VP Lebedev created "with professional intentions" acquired a life of its own, and her "virtual life and death" put before the net community a mass of philosophical and moral dilemmas.

Retrospectively, it transpired that web-commentators, Katya's closest contemporaries (whom she set herself against) – were not the only ones she could be compared with. Discussing the Detkina phenomenon, the Kiev philosopher Sergey Datsyuk likened her to the wandering mountebanks (*skomorokhi*) of old Russia and indicated parallels in the history of Russian literature (Datsyuk, 1997a): 'Barkov[31] is Katya Detkina's predecessor. Pushkin and Lermontov are her prototypes.' The meaning of "the case of Detkina", in Datsyuk's opinion, goes way beyond the bounds of the Internet. According to Datsyuk's conception, Katya died because 'she was the first to call a shit a shit.' She did so in a stylistically brilliant way, and as a result was persecuted by Internet 'society' for her bravery and talent.

Another conception interpreted the events in more prosaic terms, as a struggle for influence and money. In this version, Lebedev, hiding behind the mask of a virtual persona, intentionally ridiculed his competitors in the field of setting up web sites to order. His competitors (Altukhov and Koltsov) took offence, started to rip off the mask and tried to hold him to account. Lebedev, seemingly fearing the unpleasantness that threatened him, made an unexpected move and killed his persona. When the truth about his authorship was revealed, many people took offence, thinking they had been taken for a ride. But the character he had created proved so strong that public opinion turned against his opponents as well, who were blamed for the death of a young and delicate girl, albeit imaginary.

The first interpretation exploits the traditional counterposing of genius and the masses; the second portrays the case as a war of corporations in which both sides use underhand tactics.

Another, discursive, approach is possible, though, in which the participants in the conflict express impersonal, rambling strategies and their underlying ideologies. Detkina's rhetoric turned out, in a sense, to be a return to the morals of Usenet, where refined abuse, which inevitably became personal, was the normal way to conduct a discussion. But on this occasion, however, no discussion was able

---

[31] A notorious 18th century author of obscene poems.

190

to take place. First of all, unlike Usenet news groups, the web, with its columns and homepages, did not allow opponents to meet "face to face". Secondly, the two entities were ordered by different rule sets. Two ideologies clashed, two notions of freedom and responsibility. The first notion looked to the "Declaration of Independence of Cyberspace"; the second to the criminal code. The first originated in the concept of the net as a space of unlimited freedom of self-expression, not governed by the laws of the "old world"; the second equated words with deeds and demanded accountability for "slander and insult", before a worldly court. The clash of discourses and the worldviews that stood behind them led to the conflict being turned into an ethical problem, which was recognised even before the tragic climax (Gorny, Itzkovich, 1997).

News of Katya Detkina's death shocked the Russian net community. Despite all the revelations, many people refused to believe in her virtuality, right to the end. Death was too serious a subject for them to suspect it was a joke. In the guestbook of "KaDetkina's Observations", on the Kulichki site, virtual tears were shed, obituaries and poems dedicated to Katya were written (records of this have unfortunately not survived). The "killing" of Detkina by her creator and the dynamics of the public reaction to her death have raised a whole range of questions, which no-one previously had reason to think about. What are the allowable limits of net mystification, beyond which, games and jokes become deceit and manipulation? Is it ethical to kill a virtual? What is the ontological nature of a virtual persona – how does it differ from a real person, on the one hand, and a literary character on the other?

Nosik, emphasising the unreality of Detkina, compared her to a literary character (Turgenev's Mumu) and made sarcastic observations about the over-serious attitude to her death (Nosik, 1997b). He was seconded by Artemy Lebedev, who referred to the fictitious nature of the characters created by Leo Tolstoy, his umbilical ancestor, and refused to take responsibility for the "fruit of someone's imagination" (quote from Zhitinsky, 1997). These arguments did not convince the writer, Aleksandr Zhitinsky. He pointed out an important difference: where a

191

literary character was by default imaginary, the level of reality of a virtual persona was not clear – a virtual persona could quite easily turn out to be real. Hence, the difference in reactions to what happens to it. He agreed with the "people's opinion," voiced in Detkina's guestbook – 'You can't joke about such things!' – and explained why he believed the story of her death was amoral (*ibid.*):

> If there is a real Ekaterina Albertovna Detkina, then in any case she has been badly treated – in the case of a real death by the fact that it has been turned into a farce; in the case of a hoax, by the hoax itself. Why bury someone alive? <...> The unethicality is in the poor treatment of a real person – if that person exists. If they don't, then what is ugly is the fact that having earned the trust of some of the public, they have been forced to cry over a fantasy (and here it's not a case of "I'll shed tears over a fantasy" – it's not that sort of tears).

A virtual persona, according to Zhitinsky, occupies a middle ground between a real person and a fantasy character; the closeness to either of these poles depends on how convincing it is. Detkina's author was unethical, according to Zhitinsky, in the way that he made her *too convincing* and, in this way, misled the public. By passing off an illusion as reality, he used his created character to manipulate the consciousness of the audience to elicit the reactions he needed. The border between art and social engineering turned out to be blurred.

Detkina, like Muxin, Babaev and Paravozov before her, whose experiences she rejected, became a model for imitation – both in respect of the form and style of net creativity, and in respect of principles for constructing a character. Imitators appeared: for example, a certain Kotya Detkin, who claimed to be Katya Detkina's brother and wrote web-commentaries under the title "Kodekada". But her influence was wider than that: later generations of virtuals, by using her experience creatively, were able to create something new.

5.4.4 Mary Shelley: Reflection on the nature of virtuality

In October 1997 a certain "Hog" (Russian: *khrjak*) appeared in the guestbook of the Vechernij Internet. It amazed the reader with its energy, wit and extraordinarily obscene style. This was a "pen test" – the first phase of the creation of a new virtual. Soon afterwards, Sergey Datsyuk stated (1997b): 'The style and direction of Katya Detkina has, this week, been given an unexpected continuation. This is a newcomer to RuNet – Mary Shelley, writing in the genre of a sarcastic mockery (Russian: *steb*).'

The productivity and variety of genres in Mary's creative work were tremendous. A complete list of her works and references to critical reaction can be found on her homepage (Shelley, 1997). Mary's witty comments on what was happening on the Russian net were supplemented by her self-reflections: in the article "Is it easy to be virtual?" (Shelley, 1998) she discussed the nature of virtuality and gave practical advice to creators of virtuals. This article became part of her novel *Pautina* (The Web) (Shelley, 2002) – 'the first novel about Russian internet – how can we describe it? – life' (Kuritsyn, 1999), 'the first novel about the Internet written by a virtual character' (Frei, 1999), 'a theory-novel of virtual literature' (Adamovich, 2000). The novel was a futurologist reflection on the computerized world and contained numerous references and allusions to the phenomena and personalities of the Russian Internet. Shelley's (2004) next novel, *2048* had no such references.

Asked about the origins of Mary Shelley's persona, Aleksey (Lexa) Andreyev pointed out that the persona was constructed by contrast (in Shepovalov, 2002). First of all, Shelley's style dated back to Usenet, "where everyone swore", in contrast to the "rudimentary Runet", "where everyone is friendly and fusses around" Secondly, "the image of this sprightly but educated girl without complexes" contrasted with the predominance of men on the Internet at the time.

The meaning of the literary associations in the choice of name is evident: the historical Mary Shelley was the author of the novel, Frankenstein, which describes an artificially created living being – a prototype of future cyborgs (and virtuals).

With the help of the metonymical transfer of meaning, the new "Mary Shelley" became a virtual, fabricated personality, while her actual creator took the role of Frankenstein: the author and the character changed places.

The new Mary Shelley wrote short stories, articles and plays, devised web projects, put on radio plays, wrote columns and gave interviews. Her pen (or rather her keyboard) belongs to the "Manifesdo of Anti-grammatacalaty" (Shelley, n.d.), which became the theoretical basis of the activity of so-called *padonki* (distorted *podonki*; "scum", "bastards") and their Internet mouthpiece at the time – the website, Fuck.ru and its later reincarnations such as udaff.ru and padonki.org. The main characteristics of padonki's slang include the use of obscene words, deliberately erroneous spelling (erratives) and specific speech formulas. By 2005, the slang infected Russian LiveJournal (Zhivoj Zhurnal) and acquired a non-official status of the "language of ZhZh". (See about the *padonki* section 6.5 of chapter 6).

In 1998 she came first in the Teneta contest, in the "virtual persona" category. At the awards ceremony Mary came forward in the form of a real girl with an attractive décolletage which led to some lively commentaries in the web media. The personality of Mary's "boyfriend", Percy Shelley, was not developed sufficiently, but these two names merged with the publication in print of the two novels mentioned, of which Mary Shelley figures as an author.

Figure 4. Fake Mary Shelley at 1998 Teneta award ceremony.
Photo by Dmitry Flitman.

Her wit and sharpness of style provided a basis for comparing Shelley and Detkina. However, the similarity ends here. In contrast with Katya, Mary never claimed to be real (in this she is closer to Paravozov): the biographical details she gave had a decided air of parody about them. Her image required people to treat her playfully, and the diversity of genres in her work and use of various media brought her closer to Muxin and Babaev. Her example of self-reflection became a leading motif of the next generation of virtuals.

However, her closest peers, as it often happens, preferred not to compete with her but to take the opposite direction. The virtual that appeared several months after Mary Shelley had practically nothing in common with her. Instead, the creator of the new VP reproduced devices familiar to us from the work of Vulis but on an even greater scale.

5.4.5 Robot Dacjuk: the de-personalisation of the author

In December 1997 Andrey Chernov and Egori Prostospichkin (1997) started a project called "Robot Sergey Datsyuk ™" (RoSD™). It consisted of a text generator and supplementary commentaries. The initial material was the work of the Kievan philosopher and journalist, Sergey Datsyuk, quoted above. Chernov's personal dislike of Datsyuk's texts, which he found pompous, empty and badly written, served as the motivation for his creation of the generator. However, as Sergey Kuznetsov (2004: 198) pointed out, having devoted several articles to this story, 'the project gradually went well beyond a joke, and RoSD™ acquired the characteristics of an esoteric order and any texts, whenever they were written, started to be ascribed to the Robot himself.' The task of Chernov, an adherent of Aleister Crowley, who had set himself up as a black magician, was the virtual destruction of the real Datsyuk, his replacement by a robot and his ousting from cyberspace. In order to achieve this goal he took vigorous action: creating branches and subdivisions of RoSD™ on various sites and actively contaminating all sorts of guestbooks in the name of the virtual Datsyuk and even faking the real Datsyuk's homepage.

Figure 5. Sergei Datsyuk: a man and a robot.

Anton Nosik pointed to English-language prototypes of The Robot Datsyuk – Scott Pankin's automatic complaints generator and the Virtual Cyrano Server (a generator of love and farewell letters) and estimated the technical quality of the

Robot as far from being perfect (Nosik 1997b). In a few days, answering to the alarmed Datsyuk's message about Prostospichkin's activity who announced a vacancy of the editorial position of Datsyuk's *Cultural provocations*, Nosik demonstrated clearly that Prostospichkin was himself a robot-generator and that Datsyuk thus was tilting at windmills (Nosik, 1997c).

Sergey Datsyuk devoted several articles to the analysis of the case of the robot named after him (Datsyuk, 1998a; 1998b). In the article "Interactive de-personalisation of the author" he saw in the robot's activities a manifestation of Internet-wide tendencies (Datsyuk, 1998b):

> The question could be put thus: is it ethical or unethical (moral or amoral) to deprive an Internet author of his rights to published works on the Internet via his de-personalisation. However, it is the old notions of ethics or morals in particular which lose their meaning here. The diversified de-personalisation of authorship, carried out by my opposite, is largely what THE INTERNET IS DOING WITH AUTHORSHIP IN GENERAL. (...) The performative paradox of interactive authorship on the net is a mainstream process of the de-personalisation of ideas, thoughts, texts – it is a step into the virtual reality of meanings.

At the same time he noted that the activity of the robot is not constructive because it does not give rise to any new meanings – on the contrary, it blocks out the meanings with irrelevant noise. In that he was correct. It seems that his mistake was that he took the robot too seriously, entered into a dialogue with it and ultimately agreed to his own destruction as an author, justifying this with philosophical considerations about "the nature of Internet authorship". Unlike Vulis' victims, he did not start writing complaints but accepted his own fate almost without resistance. As a result the text generator defeated the person: Datsyuk practically disappeared from the Internet, stopped writing on Internet-related topics and re-qualified himself as a political analyst.

5.4.6 Dialogue forms: forums and guestrooms

But it may not have been just the robot. The Russian net itself was changing rapidly. The growth of the Internet soon made it boundless, and the improvement in search engines devalued the manual work of describing and assessing sites. By the end of 1997 the genre of web commentaries began to diminish; in 1998 it had faded out completely, and in the spring of 1999 Vecherni Internet (subsequent irregular issues aside) ceased publication. The Russian Internet entered a new phase of its development. Let us examine its basic characteristics.

First of all, there was a shift from monologue to dialogue forms: interactive forms of web communication such as forums and guestbooks came to the forefront. This, on the one hand, stimulated the development of public discussions and of new forms of net literature, and, on the other hand, generated the problem of the relationship between static and dynamic forms of electronic publication (Gorny, 1999b).

Guestbooks were flooded with anonymous contributors and virtuals. Sometimes this gave rise to interesting forms of collective creation, but more often than not the invisibility and unidentifiability of the authors facilitated psychological repression: freedom from the limitations of the "real world" degenerated into the freedom to be insulting. The Usenet flame wars were reincarnated in a new but related medium of web forums. Virtual personae contributed to this process. As critic Dmitri Bavilsky (2002) noted, discussing forums on the Russian Journal, 'the degree of emotionality (vulgarity) of those who write on a forum is in direct proportion to the degree of their virtuality.' The positive aspects of virtuality were notable in web-based role-playing and literary games where virtual masks were used for fun and creativity, rather than as a means of evading responsibility as was the case with forums.

The second feature of the post-web-commentators period was the raising of the standard of reflection and self-reflection. Apart from questions of virtualisation, at the centre of attention were problems of the ontological and epistemological nature of self, self-identification mechanisms, the construction of the "I" and "others". Or, to adopt the taxonomy of autobiographical forms (Spengemann, 1980), there was a shift from self-expression and self-invention to self-scrutiny.

5.4.7 Namnyjaz Ashuratova: systems of self-identification

An obvious example of this shift was Namniyaz Ashuratova - a conceptual web-artist and virtual personality of the new generation. In her projects she graphically demonstrated the mechanisms of the formation of stereotypes of thinking and subjected them to fierce criticism. The project "Self-identification System" is described thus (Ashuratova, 1999a):

> The visitor is given the option of creating a composition of symbols, which determine his or her uniqueness. An international identificational jury examines this data and gives each visitor an assessment (index of identification). The principles of assessment are not known and, generally speaking, they can change every now and then. Perhaps the behaviour of the jury is governed by such principles as political correctness or ethnic hatred – who knows?

The limitations of choice with a pre-set list of symbols of mass culture, the Kafkaesque unknown nature of the criteria used by the "international jury" and strange classifications (thus, gender is represented by the following variations: male, female, unisex, gender, macho, feminist) both undermined the idea of uniqueness and forced each visitor to think about the mechanisms for the construction of the self. Within the taxonomy of forms of VP we use, this approach can be described as analytical modelling, by which the object of the modelling is the subjectivity of members of the auditorium, exposed as an imaginary construction.

Another project of Ashuratova's - "Enemy Processing System" (1999b) – allowed the user to choose an object of hate, represented by a generalised term ("Russian", "woman", "poofter", "capitalist", "hacker", "me" etc..) and a photograph of the person representing this concept. According to the results of the poll, which went on for three years, the most popular objects of hate were

"American", "priest", "whore", "communist", "Jew" and "Chechen". Not only the stereotypes of those who took part but the very principle of the poll itself were ridiculed.

Figure 6. Namniyaz Ashuratova. The Enemy Processing System.

As with her other projects, Namniyaz worked not with real things but with their projections (which is a common trait of conceptual art). At the same time, the criteria of choice and assessment were not completely clear and the possibility of arbitrary falsifications remained. As Sergei Kuznetsov (2000) pointed out, 'Namniyaz Ashuratova's project lays bare the absurdity of most online polls, their unrepresentativeness and fundamental uninterpretability'. But a wider interpretation is also possible, implying the establishment of the futility of any polls or elections.

The emphatically hard-hitting art projects by Namniyaz Ashuratova were successful and won several prizes. Soon it the author of Ashuratova revealed himself. It was as the media-artist Andrey Velikanov. A dialogue was published

200

between Velikanov and Ashuratova (2000), where they argued in a similar manner to that of Gagin with Paravozov, and Muxin with Leibov. Thus, Velikanov declared that one of his reasons for setting up a virtual hypostasis was the desire to be able to take part in festivals and competitions under another name. (To which Ashuratova laconically replied: "You pig!"). On the other hand, Velikanov admitted that he was oppressed "not only by the presence of a (his) physical body but also by belonging to a particular gender and ethnicity". From this came the creation of a bodiless virtual and a radical change of identifying features. In the dialogue we hear the already familiar motif of an autonomous persona strengthening over time: gradually Namniyaz transformed into an "independent creative unit".

Namniyaz's political incorrectness, growing into "misanthropy during menstrual periods", links her with Katya Detkina; her name identifying her as "a person of Caucasian ethnicity[32]" with Mirza Babaev; and the use of software for self-modelling with Robot Datsyuk. Reflection on virtuality brings her closer to Mary Shelley, but now, not only the virtual but any personality proves to be constructed.

5.4.8 Essays in self-knowledge

The author of this text has also made his mark in the development of "virtual reflexivity". The following projects are worth mentioning: "Eugene Gorny: (re)construction of the virtual personality" (Gorny, 2000b), "The words of others" (Gorny, 2001a) and "Symbolic situations" (Gorny, 2001c). These projects are discussed in detail elsewhere (Gorny, 2003). They applied the concept of virtuality to the self of the author rather than to an artificially created person (as in the case of Mary Shelley) or to "man in general" (like Ashuratova). In the first case, the self was constructed from quotes found on-line which described the author from the outside; in the second, from quotes the author extracted from different sources such

---

[32] A term used to describe non-Russian peoples on the country's southern borders such as Azerbaijanis, Chechens, etc.

as books; in the third – from descriptions of subjective experiences of situations in which the external and internal combined as one. Thus, various theories of the self were tested empirically: the constructivist (the personality as a sum of social roles and external reactions to its manifestation); the post-modernist (the personality as a collection of fragments of the discourse practices of other people); and the psychedelic/symbolic (the personality as the manifestation of deep experience). The aim of these experiments was to understand "what actually is", i.e. self-knowledge in the broad sense – perhaps even leading to the idea that no self in the absolute sense exists or, to put it another way, that any self is relatively real.

5.4.9 Crisis of genre

On the April 1st 1998, "The Exposure of Ivan Kapustin" (Kapustin, 1998) was published on "Russian lace". Its basic idea was that "there are practically no people in cyberspace". Listing the figures of the Russian Internet one after another (the article is something of a personological compendium), the author revealed the virtual essence of each individual personality in succession.

This parody of conspirological research is an apposite illustration of our theory about the indeterminate status of the VP: a virtual, i.e. someone's presence on the net as a personality, is determined by their having a name; the author who remains beyond the bounds of the net is essentially anonymous; this means that the author of a virtual could be anyone. Consequently, there could be one author for all of them (as Kapustin, himself a virtual personality, ultimately argued).

Muxin's response to "Infocracy" (Gorny and Sherman, 1999) – a collection of biographies of Russian Internet figures – is an unexpected parallel to "The Exposure of Kapustin":

> …a good half of the list of "best people" raises all sorts of doubts on the issue of existence in so-called reality. Read, for example, the biography of the first and last personalities on the list – Verbitsky and Chernov. Take note – the first and last. Alpha and Omega! A game of pure reason.

The text is undoubtedly ironic: the genuine existence of well-known Internet personalities is called into question by a virtual persona who claims to be more real than them because of his greater artistic cogence. The aesthetic criterion (verisimilitude) is also a criterion of reality.

By the end of the 20th century the VP as a creative form had lost its former popularity on the Russian Internet. The previously created virtuals were exhausting their functions: 'the departure from the scene of Katya Detkina, Ivan Paravozov, Mirza Babaev, Linda Gad and many other "masks" indicates that their creators had not only deconstructed their personalities but also successfully reconstructed them back' (Andreev, 2002). Of course, VPs continued to be created but now as a degenerate form on the periphery of Internet culture. Virtuals ceased to "make the weather" on the Russian net and turned into a regular technical means of hiding one's real identity, employed by the mass user. "The great era of virtuality", it seemed, was gone for good. But then, the LiveJournal came along.

5.5 Virtuals on the Live Journal

'I've created two virtuals. I'm in five communities,' says *altimate* (2004). 'I had several virtuals, which no longer exist, and I have several "friends", who are believed to be my virtuals, although in fact they aren't', responds *moon_lady* (2004). 'I've created a virtual who doesn't write anything,' complains *e_neo* (2003). 'I'll create some virtuals and then banish them in especially perverted ways,' dreams *bes* (2005). 'I created a hundred virtuals and made a community for them!' – gushes *esterita* (n.d.). *ligreego* (2004) succinctly explains what virtuals are and why they are necessary:

> It's when you start to acquire a dual (triple, quadruple) personality, and you set up, for example, one (2,3,4) more LiveJournals. You call yourself Masha, work out everything about her from biographical details right down to the colour of her knickers. And you start thinking and writing as she would. For what purpose? Because then you can demonstrate various sides of your "I"; one virtual draws while another sings.

Another of the frequent reasons given for the creation of virtuals is the impossibility of being sincere in the public/community environs of the Russian Live Journal. The writer Zhitinsky exclaimed (*maccolit*, 2003):

> Three-quarters of what comes into my head I can't allow myself to write in Live Journal because of the "disparity" of age and position, unworthiness, shamefulness, wife, children, unsuitability, stupidity, total idiocy, pity for people and contempt for myself.
>
> What's left is what is quite unnecessary to write.

In response, well-wishers advised him to 'set up a virtual or write in private.'

But virtuals are not always harmless. 'User *rykov* set up several virtuals, which write various filth in my name in their comments,' said *another_kashin* (2005). 'One virtual takes the piss out of the entire *ru_designer* community,' rants *alex_and_r* (2004). An explosion of public anger was brought about when one popular user took revenge on another user by spreading rumours on the LJ about the death of the other user's daughter.

Identity theft is also common. In the majority of cases, clones are created, i.e. users whose names are similar to that of the clone, to which is usually added the use of the 'userpic' and imitation of the original's style. A clone can have its journal or leave comments in other journals, confusing readers who, out of inattentiveness, identify the clone with the original author. A clone can be used for some innocent fun, but equally as a powerful weapon in a virtual war. Let us examine several examples of cloning in LJ.

Mikhail (Misha) Verbitsky, a mathematician and web publicist, was an active participant in Usenet, a gatherer of various online archives and an editor of extremist web publications, such as *The End of the World News*[33], Sever ("The North")[34] and the "anti-culturological weekly" *:Lenin:* [35]. Verbitsky's creations are distinguished by their stylistic monotony, fixations on images of "the lower part of

---

[33] http://imperium.lenin.ru/~verbit/EOWN/
[34] http://imperium.lenin.ru/LENIN/CEBEP.html
[35] http://imperium.lenin.ru/LENIN/

the body", unprintable obscenities, calls for violence and murder, the use of pornographic pictures and his own abstract drawings as illustrations, and text graphic features.

The formal model of Verbitsky's discourse is simple and easy to imitate. However, the problem is that it is difficult to tell the parody from the original, which is a parody in itself.

The stereotyped reproduction of the same set of reactions, ideas, quotations and stylistic methods gave grounds to speak about the transformation of Verbitsky the man into "Robot Verbitsky" (by analogy with Robot Datsyuk) a long time before the appearance of LiveJournal (Nechaev, 1999). In LJ, however, this metaphor was put into effect: a clone of Verbitsky (*tipharet*) appeared with a user name which differed from the original by only one letter (*tiphareth*). The clone's journal combines, in random order, quotes from the original's journal and presents its hyper-realistic imitation.

> Historians are people too... *When I fuck you*
> *I tell you the story* (in English. - *E.G.*). Kill kill kill
> Shit and soil. Execute and resurrect.
> And again execute. Basically until
> one journalist, one deputy, banker, DJ
> is killed every day – Russia will not be great.
> (*tiphareth*, 10.01.2005, currently unavailable)

Verbitsky's journal (along with some other, extremist, web journals) was shut down by the administration of LiveJournal in June 2005 following the online flashmob "Kill NATO". This provoked an ardent discussion about the limits of freedom of speech and the flow-out of some Russian LJ users to other blogging services.

The second case is the cloning of *r_l*. It is under this user name that Roman Leibov – the Tartu literary critic and writer, one of the pioneers of the Russian Internet and the "founding father of LJ" is known in LiveJournal and beyond (see chapter 6). In July 2004 a user set up a series of diaries with similar user names

($r\_\_l$, $r\_l\_$, r_l etc..), took as a userpic Leibov's own self-portrait, and started to post, in Leibov's name, insulting comments and other journals, using quotes from Leibov himself (who did not always steer clear of Usenet style) (*rualev* 2004). Soon, the fake was exposed. Some users came to Leibov's defence, others gloated. Leibov was advised to ask the Abuse Team for support but he acted differently: he ended his diary for a while and then made it "friends only". Like Datsyuk and unlike Vorobjev before him, he chose not to complain. Theoretically speaking, we should note that clones as a variety of VP are the realisation of the procedure for modelling someone else's self by means of copying. However, the precision of this copying and its functions can vary. In the case described above, the copying was selective (only obscenities were chosen from the whole body of text), and had a mostly parodying function. Despite the successful deactivation of the clones, Leibov did not go back to the public: the spectre did its job, forcing a real person to retreat into the shadows.

Sometimes, though, things are different. For example, the administration of LiveJournal closed the account of the user *fuga*, who wrote a diary in the name of the aforementioned Aleksey (Lexa) Andreev. The closure was carried out at the request of Andreev, 'in which he demonstrated that the diary was a falsification by extraneous persons, who were using his name and material from surveys in Time O'Clock (TOK) without authorisation' (Anisimov, 2002). It is worth noting that Andreev compared the LJ virtuals with the VPs of the early Russian web, giving distinct preference to the latter:

> What happened to me was neither the first nor the last case. I saw how people were using other people's names and photos... There are diaries of Lenin, Putin etc. But I haven't yet seen any genuinely interesting virtual personalities on LJ, as the first Runet virtuals were, like Katya Detkina.

Virtuals are steeped in folklore. For example, user *suavik* (2005) thought up this frightener: 'a girl goes into the LJ and sees that she's another, real girl's virtual.' Another point worth mentioning in the context of the LiveJournal is the phenomenon of de-virtualisation – meetings "in reality" of users who know each other only via the Internet. Any user in this sense is the equivalent of a virtual – in complete agreement with the "Zhitinsky principle", stating that any personality represented on the Internet should be considered virtual by default. The traditional place for such meetings of Moscow LiveJournalists is the O.G.I. club founded by Dmitry Itzkovich, and other similar establishments, such as the related chain of PirOGI cafes and the Bilingua club.

Which virtual personalities are the most popular in LJ? A brief analysis shows that they are either those who write well or those that are well described. It is not surprising that the virtual personalities with the most friends and subscribers in LJ are professional writers: Sergey Lukyanenko (*doctor_livsy*, 4,779 friends), Dmitry Gorchev (*dimkin*, 4,685 friends), Alex Exler (*exler*, 3,604 friends), Max Frei (*chingizid*, 3,392 friends), etc.[36] Nevertheless, well-made virtuals whose characters are completely different from their authors (i.e. virtuals in the strict sense of the word) are able to compete with them successfully. One example is the diary of Skotina Nenuzhnaja, 'useless bastard' (*skotina*, 2005), whose character was an evil-minded cat that used the catchphrase 'I've pissed under the chair. Great!', which acquired the status of an LJ saying. Skotina's creative world dried up quite quickly and in September 2004 the diary formally ceased to exist. Nevertheless, Skotina still had 1,755 subscribers half a year later and the diary remained one of the most popular in the LJ, with more readers than Nosik, Zhitinsky, Leibov, etc.

An equally important factor is that of recognition, or whether the personality being created is well-known. There is a separate category in LJ for VPs that imitate the famous. At one time Aleksander Pushkin (*pushkin*, 2002) was publishing two of his poems per day (one in the morning, one in the evening) on LJ; émigré writer Vladimir Nabokov (*nabokov*, 2005) appeared briefly, writing sometimes in Russian and sometimes in English; financial speculator and philanthropist George Soros (*soros*, 2003) shared his views about life; the disgraced oligarch, Mikhail

---

[36] Data of 4 August 2005.

Khodorkovsky (*khodorkovsky*, 2005) posted reports from his prison cell and (of course) Vladimir Putin was there too, albeit in the form of an RSS feed translation, but in several versions at once: as Vladimir Vladimirovich ™ (*mrparker*, 2005) and as Resident Utin (*utin*, 2005).

The cloning of popular LJ users could be seen as a private case of the impersonation of famous people. In both cases, the procedure of modelling is used, but if in the case of clones it takes the form of copying, with famous people it takes the form of a creative recreation of the model. The last of these could also occur among LJ users as well. For example the remake of Mikhail Bulgakov's *Master and Margarita* (*buzhbumrlyastik*, 2005), which takes place in the present and whose characters are popular members of LJ. However, to quote the well-known axiom, "nothing is new under the moon": both re-writing classics and the introduction of Internet figures (including virtual ones) into creative literary works is, one might say, an established practice. An example of the former is the *Margarita and Master* project by Aleksander Malyukov and Aleksander Romadanov (1997), an example of the latter is the novel *Pautina* by Mercy Shelley (2002), and an example of the two combined is the novel by Kataev Brothers (a pseudonym), *The Calf Butted against a Chair* (1999-2000)"[37]. The works in which virtual personalities become literary characters and the authors are revealed to be virtual personae are a vivid example of the convergence of belles-lettres and cyberspace in the common environment of the imagination.

The development of the VP genre within the LiveJournal as a whole has been extensive: there are hardly any new models of construction, but the old ones are being constantly re-worked and revised. Among the main innovations, Maksim Kononenko's (*mrparker*'s) project *Vladimir Vladimirovich™*, which began in LJ and acquired a popularity unseen by blogs and commercial success, is worth noting. The ironic portrayal of the Russian president and his entourage, and the daily commentaries on topical events within the virtual reality of Russian life

---

[37] The title ironically alludes to Aleksander Solzhenitsyn's novel *The Calf Butted against the Oak.*

constitute an artistic project that seems to have no direct analogy in the previous development of the genre. However, the main significance of LJ is in the appearance of a numerically huge community of users distinguished by a high level of connectedness. There is a wide range of virtuality among users – from complete identification (with the use of a real name, biographical data and contact details) to almost complete anonymity (especially common among "observers" or "lurkers", who themselves contribute very little if anything at all). The VP as a creative form is developing in the space between these two polarities.

5.6 Conclusion

The virtual person (VP) is a specific form of online self-representation.

The VP on the Russian Internet is a discrete creative genre. Unlike the English-language Internet, this genre is recognised as just that and has been legitimised with a corresponding category in a major Russian online literature competition.

The VP is typologically linked to notions of illusory or artificially created personalities, which have a greater or lesser amount of free will. The closest literary analogies to the VP are the character and lyrical hero. However, the VP is not just a literary phenomenon; the capability of various VPs to interact within a single world (cyberspace) is a distinguishing feature of this type of creation.

For the creation of a VP, various procedures and strategies for self-representing are used. The most pronounced is the strategy of poetic self-invention, but the procedures of self-expression, self-description and self-scrutiny are also present and in some cases become the leading constructive principles. In addition to the taxonomy of the autobiographical forms of Spengemann (1980), we introduced a modelling procedure whereby the objective is not one's self but "another self", i.e. subjectivity that is external in relation to the subject. As seen in autobiography, the modelling can be carried out using various strategies and take on forms of creative re-creation, cloning and analysis. We should note, however, that a precise differentiation of these forms is often impossible. VPs, whichever category they belong to, are characterised by an ambivalent real and imaginary, "my" and "someone else's", "I" and "non-I". So it's impossible to say exactly to what extent Muxin is the alter ego of Leibov and to what extent he is a separate personality. On the other hand, modelling another self by cloning or re-creation, as in the case of Robot Datsyuk™ or Vladimir Vladimirovich™, could reflect the personal characteristics of the creator of the corresponding VP.

Constructively, the VP genre is formed from the following elements: a name; biographical details, even ones that are uncoordinated, no matter how realistic (like Muxin's or Detkina's) or fantastic (like Paravozov and Shelley); a characteristic, recognisable style; the VP's activity on the Internet (in the form of its own texts or projects, participation in discussions etc..); the publication of documents confirming the real existence of the VP (a photo of Muxin with Brezhnev and Tito, Detkina's passport); occasional materialisation (appearance in the 'real world' of the VP itself, like Mary Shelley at the award ceremony for the Teneta competition, or in the form of its representatives, for example Leibov as Muxin's personal assistant). Only the first of these elements is obligatory, the rest are optional.

The dynamics of the VP genre are well described by the model of literary evolution suggested by Tynyanov as a sequence of automatisation and de-similarisation by contrast. Each new VP has a tendency to deny its immediate predecessors and use earlier prototypes as a model, or, as Tynyanov said, look not to the fathers but to the grandfathers. This brings about the discrete nature of the genre changes: 'Not a logical evolution but rather a leap, not development but displacement' (Tynyanov 1977, 256). Thus Detkina rejects her contemporaries Muxin and Paravozov and is stylistically close to the virtuals of Usenet. Mary Shelley, on the other hand, looks mostly to Muxin and Babaev, over the head of Detkina as her immediate predecessor. The creation of new VPs takes place with the displacement of the functions of old constructive elements. The introduction of new elements and functions, which are derived from the reservoir of culture, is yet another source of the genre's development.

The development of the VP as a genre on the Russian Internet can be explained by a number of factors. First of all, there is the opportunity presented by the electronic medium to construct identities anonymously. This is a characteristic shared by the Internet as a whole, but on the Russian Internet it was put into practice in a specific way which is culturally determined.

Secondly, the appearance of striking examples of VPs during the creation of the Russian Internet, which combined the qualities of literary heroes (description) with direct activity on the Internet (direct action) and which put into practice the principles of the game and of mystification. The model was infectious and a chain reaction resulted. The genre developed through processes of imitation – reproduction of ready models – and emulation – the desire to surpass them. The joint action of the mechanisms of imitation and repulsion led to modifications in the genre and reflections about its nature.

Thirdly, the development of the VP genre is supposedly facilitated by such tendencies in Russian culture as literature-centricity and personalism. The former indicates a major role for literature and the written word as opposed to the spoken word; the latter is the perception of social activity, more in personal than impersonal terms and a tendency towards an essentialist view of the nature of personality. The appearance of such personae as Muxin or Detkina may be accidental but they are unlikely to have become so hugely popular and given rise to a wave of imitators if they had not found a resonance with the cultural models shared by users.

Chapter 6

RUSSIAN LIVE JOURNAL: THE IMPACT OF CULTURAL IDENTITY ON THE DEVELOPMENT OF A VIRTUAL COMMUNITY

6.1 Introduction

This chapter discusses the historical dynamics of the largest virtual community on the Russian Internet. It focuses on the role of creativity in community building and culture as a shaping force in the process of community building.

LiveJournal.com (LJ) is one of the most popular web services among Russian-speaking users from all over the world. The first post in Russian appeared on LiveJournal on the 1st February 2000. In four years, the LiveJournal Russian-speaking community reached 40,000 users. Two years latter, in February 2006, the number of Russian users has grown almost by a factor of six and exceeds 235,000. The Russian Federation has become the second in the number of users after the United States with its almost 3 million users (LiveJournal, 2006a). According to a 2004 research, the English language does of course prevail among LJ users worldwide (more than 90%), but Russian is in second place (between 6.4 and 8.15%) while other languages do not exceed 1% each (*evan*, 2004a; 2004b).

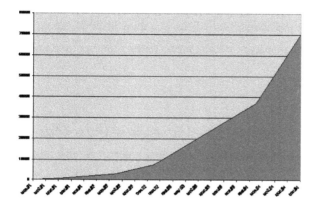

Figure 7. RLJ growth rate (2001-2004).

Although the Russian LiveJournal (RLJ) community thus constitutes a significant part of the LJ blogging community, it has hardly been studied and it remains a blind spot in blogging research. Sometimes researchers overtly admit that they exclude non-English blogs from their analysis (Herring et al. 2003), and more often this omission is accepted by default. The apparent reason of this exclusion is the language and cultural barrier. Taking advantage of my marginal position of a trickster in-between Russian-language Internet culture and English-language Internet research, I shall try to fill this scholarly gap. I used a variety of research methods including the following: (1) participant observation, a traditional method of anthropological studies (I have been an LJ user for three years); (2) textual analysis of primary sources (RLJ's textual production), secondary sources (media and research literature on blogs, LJ and RLJ) using both continuous reading and searching by keywords, (3) analysis of statistical data; and (4) personal interviews.

213

As the circumstances are constantly changing, a typical "headache" of Internet studies, the present article gives a snapshot of the situation in 2004, taking into consideration significant developments of the latter years only spottily and for comparison.

6.2 LiveJournal

LiveJournal[38] (usually abbreviated as LJ) is a web-based service enabling users to create and manage their diaries or journals online. It is a personal publishing (or "blogging") tool. There are many definitions of blog. Basically, it is a personal diary or journal published online by an individual and available to others on the web. It is a frequent publication of personal thoughts, web links, pictures or other information where entries are arranged in chronological order with the most recent additions placed on top of the page. Blogging software allows people with little or no technical background to easily maintain and update their blogs. The word "blog" appeared as an abbreviation (initially considered as slang) for "Web log" or "weblog." The activity of updating a blog is "blogging" and someone who keeps a blog is a "blogger". Blogs in their current form began to appear in late 1997 or early in 1998 (although they had various predecessors in earlier forms of online publishing) and have become popular in the years that followed. They have been praised as the most revolutionary and empowering Internet tool, as "a new, personal way to organize the Web's chaos" (Rosenberg, 1999), the future of journalism (Sullivan, 2002), the becoming of "a new social system" that 'seems delightfully free of the elitism and cliquishness of the existing systems' (Shirky, 2003), a 'grassroots communication and civic engagement revolution' creating a

---

[38] http://www.livejournal.com

new online "public sphere" that has returned the Web to "the people" (Vieta 2003). There exists also an opposite point of view, critical to the proliferation of blogs. It is claimed, for example, that blogs 'add considerably to the already large amount of "vapid" content on the Web, making it harder to find valuable material' (Okanagan Bookworks, n.d.) (the same accusation was earlier brought against personal homepages), that there is an essential inequality between blogs in terms of the audience and attention they receive, and that most blogs are ephemeral and quickly abandoned by their authors (Perseus Blog Survey, 2003), thus creating a virtual "graveyard" rather than "community" (Orlowski, 2003).

LiveJournal is a web site where registered users can create and maintain their blogs. It is based on open source software, simple-to-use but powerful and customizable. Customization features include multi-language interface, a choice of predefined journal presentation styles, an option to create one's own, multiple user pictures, icons to indicate a user's mood, and the possibility to show information about current music options playing on the user's computer. The users can update their journals via the web interface or using a client downloadable from the LJ web site. The journal entries have three main levels of access - for all, for friends only, and private. The user can also manage the access to his or her entry by creating various groups of friends. Users can post to their journals or community journals, read and comment in other journals and reply to the comments of others.

The integration of individual journals makes LJ more than a mere blogging tool or a congeries of individual blogs hosted in one place but rather a vivid example of the blogosphere – a network of mutually connected blogs. LJ is not only a space for individual self-expression but also a powerful instrument for community building or a social network software. The architecture of LJ makes it easy to create virtual communities of various kinds - from friends lists (other LJ users whose journal entries one has chosen to read on his or her friends page) to moderated or unmoderated, open or restricted communities around common interests or specific tasks.

LiveJournal was launched on March 18, 1999. Its creator, Brad Fitzpatrick, at that time was a 19-year-old undergraduate majoring in computer science at the University of Washington, Seattle, WA. LiveJournal is based on the economics of voluntary support. Joining and using LiveJournal has always been free of charge (for some time, to create an account an invitation code from a current LJ user was required). However, users are encouraged to get a paid account at the price of $25 per year to get extra features and show their support. LJ development has been highly dynamic. In April 2003, the millionth account was created and by February 2006 LiveJournal had almost 9,5 million registered users, of which about 2 million were active in some way (LiveJournal, 2006a. However, a recent study has shown that the rate of abandoned journals is lower in LJ than in other blogging services (Perseus Blogging Survey, 2003)). The restricted access policy to LJ at a certain stage when an invitation code or payment was required to join might well have contributed to a higher rate of users' loyalty. It is not unlikely, however, that community-building properties of LJ have also played a role in users' decisions to stay.

6.3 Russian LiveJournal (RLJ)

6.3.1 RLJ as a deviation

The success of LJ among Russian users is amazing. Not only did it receive numerous awards from Russian internet professionals (POTOP, 2002), but it has also become a "people's site." It was labelled by media as "the most fashionable address on the web." It is used not only for keeping private or semi-private online journals but also for receiving information and news, acquiring friends, socializing, discussions and developing collaborative projects. It has become an independent collective medium influencing traditional media and cultural production at large and a significant part of the Russian Internet culture.

Moreover, if in the West, in the context of the blogging revolution, LJ is considered as one of many blogging services (and by no means the central one), in Russia it has been perceived rather as *the* blog. The power of its popularity together with the lack of knowledge about other blogging tools has lead to the bizarre fact that LiveJournal (*Zhivoj Zhurnal* or simply *ZhZh* in Russian) became the generic term for blog as such so that the word is often applied to blogs that are by no means related to the original LJ.

The external difference in social value is supplemented by internal differences between LJ's Russian and English speaking communities. These differences were well described by Anatolij Vorobej (LJ username "*avva*"), a young programmer of Russian origin living in Jerusalem, Israel, who has worked as a member of LJ staff since November 2001 (*bradfitz*, 2001).

The Russian segment of LJ differs significantly from LJ as a whole, although now, three year after it was "established", not as strikingly as it was in the beginning. The overwhelming majority of journals in LiveJournal are very personal and devoted mainly to the events in the writer's private life, a description of their everyday activity and communication with people they know in real life such as relatives, friends and classmates and college fellows. In Russian LJ, there were few such journals in the beginning; most journals were used by their authors for discussions on cultural, political and professional topics with a lot of people, including those whom they didn't know. This characteristic aspect has been much obliterated during these three years; now Russian LJ has a lot of journals which are

217

as personal as their American analogues. The main difference, however, has remained intact; there is a very high level of connectedness and communicativeness in the Russian LJ in comparison with the American LJ. In spite of a great number of personal journals which are not involved in any "crowds" or conglomerations of journals, there remains a communicative core in RLJ consisting of several thousands of journals, which are tightly interwoven with each other. There remains the common communication environment in which news spreads quickly and discussion about a certain political, literary or social issue can involve dozens of journals and hundreds of interested users. LiveJournal in general has never had such a high degree of fellowship and entwinement (*avva*, 2004).

The differences in demography and in typical uses of the service can be added to this description. The resulting picture is the following.

The Russian LiveJournal (RLJ) community shows a considerable deviation from average blogging patterns both on the level of individual blogs and on the level of the blogging community. These differences are as follows: (1) an older average age of users; (2) the predominance of adult professionals; (3) the content of personal journals often consists of serious topics of discussion; (4) a greater degree of interconnection between individual journals expressed in a larger number of "friends" of the average user as well as in the phenomenon of RLJ celebrities with an audience of hundreds and even thousands "friends" (readers); (5) the higher significance of reading other posts, which sometimes exceeds the desire to keep one's own journal; (6) an influence upon online and offline media. To summarize, RLJ seems to be older, more serious and more communal than LJ on average. Although this difference seems to be disappearing gradually in the course of time, it is still felt and discussed now and then by the RLJ users.

218

6.3.2 Explanation of the deviation

I argue that deviations of RLJ from the 'average norm' found in LJ are determined by a complex of interrelated factors such as (1) the multi-language environment of LJ; (2) the architecture of the service; (3) the historical circumstances of the building of the community; (4) the socioeconomic conditions in Russia; and, finally, (5) the peculiarities of cultural identity of the Russian users.

(1) Multi-language environment

From the very beginning, LJ was devised as a multi-language environment. The introduction of Unicode in April 2002 (Fitzpatrick 2002) as a universal encoding facilitated the use of various languages and greatly contributed to LJ's popularity among non-English users. The opportunity of writing in their native language and using the localized interface has been important for many Russian users. Unlike European users who often write their journals in English, Russians tend to write in their own language - not necessary because they cannot do it in English, but probably also "because the large Russian community makes it more acceptable to write in something non-English" (*evan*, 2004b).

(2) The architecture of the service

The argument in this sub-chapter is largely based on the interview with Anatolij Vorobej (*avva*) conducted on 12 January 2004 via ICQ. In LJ, individual blogs are interwoven and integrated into a dynamic interactive system; this is a distinguishing feature of the service. Such popular blogging software and related web-services as Blogger (blogspot.com) and Movable Type (typepad.com) are intended for work with an individual blog. The individual blog can be written by a single author or a group, can provide an opportunity for the author to create list of favourite blogs ("blogroll") and for readers an opportunity to comment on entries. Still, ideologically and technically it remains the individual blog - an autonomous

219

and separated website consisting of entries and other files pertaining exclusively to that website. There is not any close connection between different blogs hosted by the same service provider, they are different websites, different places.

LiveJournal from the very beginning has been designed and built in a different way. It has a much higher degree of interweaving of individual blogs. All journals are kept on the same server in a single database. Both technically and conceptually, all of them are collected in the same place. It is also emphasized by the uniform style of all auxiliary and service pages. Owing to this close integration of individual journals, LJ could include numerous tools for amalgamation and communication between journals which is ideologically and technically infeasible in services like Blogger. These include friends and friends-of lists, the friends page, the comment tree, the unified identification of users within the web site, the possibility (for paid users) to search users by location, interests, age, etc.

All these unification tools, being an advantage, at the same time make LJ very dissimilar to the "regular" blogs. Therefore, many bloggers and onlookers often regard LJ blogs as something insignificant, designed for teenagers with their tendency towards partying and idle talk rather than for mature authors with their serious thoughts and individual self-expression. As it was shown in Perseus' research, the typical blog seems to be maintained by the young, mostly young girls (Perseus Blog Survey, 2005). To summarize, the main advantage of LiveJournal in comparison with other blogging systems is its community-building architecture. Although LJ might be less customizable than Blogger and other similar services, it has the strongest "community feel".

(3) The historical circumstances of community building on RLJ

Historically, the RLJ community was first populated not by the teenage girls who form the majority of bloggers in the West but by mature professionals, predominantly male, including internet workers, journalists, writers, philosophers and artists. This intellectual and creative core contributed to RLJ's popularity by their example, word of mouth and numerous publications in the media. Thus, LJ conceived by its creator as a tool for keeping in touch between schoolmates unexpectedly acquired in Russia the aura of a playground for intellectuals. This aura has persisted in the later stages of RLJ development, although now it is gradually fading. The use of RLJ as a source of firsthand information (for example, users' accounts of acts of terrorism they had witnessed) by the traditional media also strengthened its reputation and popularity.

(4) The socioeconomic conditions in Russia

The age and demographic differences between RLJ and LJ as a whole can be explained by the relatively poor socioeconomic conditions in Russia reflected in limited Internet access for the younger generation. The fact that the majority of Russians (up to 58%) connect to the Internet from work and the low level of connectivity in schools and universities may account for the demographic structure of the RLJ population, the majority of which consists of adults, mostly office workers. It may also explain perceptible oscillations in users' activity, which declines on weekends in RLJ as well as generally on the Russian Internet.

(5) The impact of cultural identity

The issue of interrelation between cultural identity and online behaviour is probably one of the most ambiguous in the field of Internet studies, and may be interpreted as something non-scientific and relating rather to popular prejudices than to positive knowledge. Furthermore, the internet as a global communication system has often been perceived as a means of effacing differences between local cultures, and sometimes even as a tool of coercive unification of the world in accordance with the values of liberalism and the American way of life (Treanor,

221

1996). Apart from these political and ethical dimensions, the uniformity of technical standards of Internet protocols, software and interfaces can apparently influence the process of cultural unification, which can be further intensified by the online interaction between members of different cultures. However, there is also some evidence that nationally or ethnically defined cultures are resistant to the unification impacts of the internet and preserve their individuality. Thus, for example, the German scholar Hans Bucher showed in a detailed case study of the Chinese Internet the increasing customization of originally American patterns of behaviour and media usage (Bucher, 2004). Linguistic differences are one of the most visible factors in this process. As Olia Lialina (2000) put it, 'It's said that the Internet has no borders, but one is obvious. The border of language. Languages trace new maps across the Internet....' However, language is not an indifferent means of communication; it is connected with cultural values and patterns of behaviour.

My hypothesis is that the deviations of RLJ from LJ as a whole (or, to be more specific, from the English-language LJ) may be explained to a certain degree by the influence of the Russian culture upon the users' online behaviour. To substantiate this hypothesis, a review of the debate on the specifics of a Russian "national character" may be useful. The concept of "national character" is not accepted as a valid concept in Western media studies which are suspicious of its essentialist and "racist" connotations and which prefer to use the term "cultural identity" to emphasize the constructedness of the concept. This study generally adopts this approach. However, the term "national character" cannot be avoided. Firstly, because it has a long philosophical, anthropological and psychological tradition. Secondly, because the concept of "national character" is an essential element in the construction of Russian cultural identity used for both self-reflection and cultural representation.

The concept of Russian "national character" was first formulated by Slavophiles and Westernizers, two opposing groups of Russian intellectuals in 1840-1860s. The first held that the Russian civilization was unique and promoted traditional values and institutions such as the Orthodox Church with its collegiality (*sobornost'*) and the practice of collective confession, the village community (*mir*), and the traditional people's assembly for resolving problems (*zemski sobor*). The second believed that Russia could benefit from the adoption of Western technology, liberal government and rationalism. However, both groups have much in common. Slavophile Ivan Kireevskij argued that if the West represented a triumph of the form and law, then Russia was governed by the spirit and conscience. The Westernizers, such as Chaadaev, Herzen, and Belinskij could not accept "the conservative utopia" of Slavophiles', but joined them in asserting the specificity of the Russian national character and Russia's supposedly unique historical mission (Riasanovsky 1952; Walicki 1975).

Nikolai Berdyaev, a religious Russian philosopher (1874 - 1948), having summarized and developed the preceding conceptualizations, listed the following traits of Russian national character: ambivalence, i.e. convergence of oppositions; catastrophic and eschatological consciousness; totalitarian or holistic thinking; discontinuous behaviour, i.e. abrupt transitions between passivity and activity; the readiness to sacrifice oneself for others and voluntary acceptance of suffering; a tendency to anarchy and the lack of discipline; amorphism, i.e. the negation of hierarchies and rigid forms; personalism, i.e. the triumph of the spirit, conscience and personal relationships over the law; and communitarism as opposed to both Western individualism and socialization. Elucidating the latter point Berdyaev

223

noted: 'Russians are communitarian but not socialized in the Western sense, i.e. they do not acknowledge the primacy of a society over the individual' (Berdyaev, 1990: 87; cf. Berdyaev, 1947).

Although the historiosophical approach to the national character represented by Berdyaev has often been criticized as speculative and producing stereotypes rather than positive knowledge, most of its generalizations have been later confirmed by anthropologists who relied on direct observation as well as by social psychologists, who used surveys and other experimental methods. Thus Wright Miller (1960) in his book "Russians as people" based on his visits to Russia from 1934 to 1960 noted in Russians a clear contrast between public and "official" relationships, on the one hand, and private and personal ones, on the other, which he explained by the urge of direct expression and distrust of authorities and public values as opposed to personal relationships. He also described a "strong, largely unconscious sense of community" and a negative attitude to individualism. Other characteristics mentioned by Miller, such as an oscillation between melancholy and orgiastic outbursts, a lack of organization and punctuality, and interest in people rather than things are also reminiscent of earlier descriptions of the Russian national character.

Dean Peabody (1985) in his seminal work "National Characteristics" based on analysis of empirical data of surveys, in which members of various nationalities assessed psychological characteristics of other nations, as well as a variety of other methods, dedicated a chapter to the Russians. Peabody (1985: 150) found out that in personal relations the central characteristic of Russians was a need for *affiliation*: a need for intensive face-to-face relationships, and satisfaction from warm and personal contact with others. Russians were not tensely anxious about others' opinions of them, and lacked strong needs for *approval* and *autonomy* that were prominent for the American comparison group. They valued people for what they are, not for what they have done. Neither group showed strong needs for dominance, securing positions of superordination, or for controlling or manipulating others and enforcing authority over them.

He also described dependence on authority and the group as a prominent trait of the national character (*ibid.*, 151):

> Though without a strong need for submission, the Russians showed a need for dependence on others for emotional support, on the group and authority to provide moral rules for impulse control, and on authority to provide the initiation, direction, and organization of performance that are not expected from the average individual... There is a profound acceptance of group membership and relatedness, unthreatened by mutual dependence.

Peabody also found out that in expression of emotions and impulses the Russians showed a high degree of expressiveness and emotional aliveness and surpassed Americans in freedom and spontaneity in criticism. Russians tended to accept basis impulses such as "oral gratification, sex, aggression, and dependence" as normal and "to *give in* to these impulses freely and *live them out*" rather than suppress them (*ibid.*). He also discussed *contradictoriness* that has traditionally been considered the most prominent trait of Russian personality when neither of conflicting tendencies is suppressed but all appear at the manifest level. The conflicts between trust and mistrust, activity and passivity, optimism and pessimism were given as particular manifestations of the Russian contradictoriness.

A different approach has been presented by Daniel Rancour-Laferriere (1995), professor in Russian literature of University of California. In his book "The slave soul of Russia", he collected a vast amount of material from Russian history and literature and scrutinized, among other things, such phenomena as the cult of suffering, infant swaddling, the holy fool, the communal bathhouse, Russian collectivism, and strong, long-suffering women. He applied the psychoanalytic method to explain the peculiarities of Russian culture and generalized his findings in the concept of "moral masochism". His book gained a rather notorious publicity and he has been blamed for using an inadequate code to decode Russian culture. Thus, his interpretations of the readiness of Russians to sacrifice one's own interests for collective goals, given in psychoanalytic terms, may seem debasing, regardless of his reiterated reservations about the non-sexual character of "moral masochism" and the assertion that the masochistic attitude contributes to the beauty of Russian culture. However, despite his eccentric interpretations, most of his observations are in line with the research tradition.

The historiosophical approach to the "national character" has often been criticized as speculative and producing stereotypes rather than positive knowledge. Alternatively, there have been developed concepts trying to explain peculiarities of cultural identity and social behaviour from the perspectives of social sciences. Thus, in the early 1980s Russian sociologist Ksenija Kas'janova conducted research on the topic, in which she combined empirical methods with the interpretive technique of cultural studies. The resulting book circulated for some time in Samizdat, was first published in 1995 and republished in 2003 (Kasjanova 2003). Kas'yanova compared data received by using the Minnesota Multiphasic Personality Inventory test (MMPI) (Dahlstrom and Welsh, 1960) on wide samplings of Americans and Russians. The test, first introduced by Hathaway and McKinley in 1941, assesses personal characteristics by asking a person which of a list of traits and characteristics describe her or him or to indicate which behaviours and hypothetical choices he or she would make. The version of the test she used included 566 questions. She analyzed the discrepancy between two medians through all the scales of the test and focused her attention of the generalized psychological profile of Russians. The underlying idea was that the profile described a model of behaviour determined by stable psychological characteristics in a population that, in its turn, was influenced by a culture. She argued that the discrepancy between the medians showed stable "social archetypes" and that through their analysis it was possible to reveal the principles on which particular models of behaviour were based and thus to describe a national character. The central qualities she found in Russians were "patience, consistent abstention, self-limitation, self-abnegation for the sake of another, the others, the whole world" (Kas'yanova, *op.cit.*, p. 205). At the same time, Russians had a high level on such scales as social introversion, femininity and depression, as well as the lack of inner adaptation, social imperturbability and a disposition for deviant and delinquent behaviour. She proposed an interesting explanation for this apparent contradiction: 'Social introversion means a person's directedness towards his small, primary group. In this group, a person is very sensitive to others' opinions. His sensitivity is, as it were, selective. A person chooses for himself people whose opinion is important for him. To others he reveals a strong social imperturbability' (Kas'yanova, *op.cit.*, p. 290). She also pointed out the informality of personal relationships among Russians, which are based not so much on social status as on the non-formal reputation of a person, and found a partial explanation of this fact in the deep alienation of Russians from the state, which is governed by ideological systems alien to the people and their traditional "social archetypes".

This duality became a central topic for another researcher, economist and sociologist Alena Ledeneva. Being an expert in informal economy, corruption, and economic crime in Russia, she focuses her attention on the social, economic and political implications of social networks and informal exchange. She points out that

227

'Russia is a country of unread laws and unwritten rules' and scrutinizes the nature of these unwritten rules. She argues that 'reliance on unwritten rules is an outcome of the inefficiency of formal rules and the mechanisms for enforcing them, on one hand; and people's lack of respect for the formal rules and their exploitative attitude towards formal institutions, on the other' (Ledeneva, 2001). She holds that economic scarcity, the weakness of the state and mistrust in official institutions resulted in the fact that 'the ability to solve a problem hinges not so much on one's own capacity, as on the power of the network that one can mobilize' (ibid., 30). The informal personal networks pervading Russian life determined the significance of such phenomena as *blat*, or non-monetary exchange of favours at the state's expense (Ledeneva, 1998) and the specific forms of Russian economic crime (Ledeneva, Kurkchiyan, 2000). But at the same time, they account for the exceptional role of networking in Russian culture. The unwritten ethical rules analyzed by Ledeneva are based on the mutual obligation to help among the network members. Ledeneva (2001: 40) also emphasizes the non-formal and highly personalized nature of such relationships: 'Russian networks are overwhelmingly personalized and, as such, are distrustful of forms of depersonalized exchange involving organizations, contracts and distance.'

The characteristics described above can be found in RLJ, which in this respect may possibly be seen in the light of a continuation of the Russian way of thinking and living. Aleksandr Zhitinskij, a St. Petersburg writer and LiveJournal user reflects on the construction of RLJ (*maccolit*, 2003):

> It seems to me that at a certain stage one's journal becomes so deeply rooted in the common network, ties itself by a thousand threads with other journals and LJ in general that one seems to cease to belong to oneself.

One becomes a slave of one's own journal; of this monster that demands from you new positions, thoughts, stories, jokes.

That is, there emerges something like a responsibility - or slightly higher - a sense of duty. ... Because the elimination of one small chain breaks the solidity of the chain or, more exactly, the breach of a mesh damages the network.

We deeply penetrated each other, fell in love and ceased to love, became accustomed, became indifferent, now we just scan the lines and blame ourselves for pusillanimity preventing us from cleaning our friends lists but ...it is our world, and we are also a part of this world. ...

We are much more collectivists than we think.

This is why we have to keep our journal, to harp on the same string, to help ourselves and others to create this fragile world that can be destroyed so easily.

6.3.3 Summary

The architecture of LJ facilitating community building has fitted well with the Russian cultural identity that attaches value to friendship and informal networks. Additional factors have played a role in the evolution of RLJ. First, the multi-language environment provided by LJ has greatly contributed to LJ's popularity among Russian users many of whom feel uncomfortable with English. Second, since joining and using LJ has always been free of charge (though for some time, to create an account an invitation code from another LJ user was required), the users who could not pay (for example, because they did not have a credit card) could nevertheless use the service. Third, the location of the LJ service outside

Russia made it independent of Russian jurisdiction, giving the Russian users more freedom of expression and defending them from possible outrage of the state. Fourth, RLJ was first populated by users who had authority and could influence others to adopt the innovation. Finally, the greater than average interconnection between the individual journals, the custom of having many "friends" and the significance attached to reading and commenting in the journals of others, all correspond to a trait of the Russian national character that could be called "collectivism" – a preference for group as opposed to individual self-identification or, at least, an essential role for the former. Regardless of the deep political, economic and social changes in Russia during the last decade, the principle of collectivism, revealing itself in a wide spectrum of phenomena ranging from spiritual sobornost' (collegiality) to everyday conviviality, has remained deeply embedded into the national psyche and resulted in the "communal" use of Internet technologies, even those designed for personal self-expression.

6.4 Agency

Does RLJ provide a creative environment and, if it does, what forms does creativity take on RLJ? The answer to the first question is definitely positive. For many users LiveJournal is an instrument for both individual and collective creativity. Writers and journalists post drafts of their works in their journal to get an immediate response, which they can use to improve their texts. Others compile books from their LJ postings. Others still write books in online collaboration. Alexander Zhitinsky, the chief of Helicon publishing house in St Petersburg recruits his authors among LJ users. Anton Nosik, the editor-in-chief of Lenta.ru and MosNews.ru, uses LJ as a virtual working place for his editorial teams. Artists, photographers, designers and other creative professionals exchange their works and discuss their ideas with peers. Philosophers and social commentators treat their journals as personal media outlets and win large audiences. Communities emerging around common interests or particular tasks serve as distributed knowledge systems that not only provide information and support to their members but also create new knowledge through collaborative efforts. On the level of personal creativity, LJ also provides a wide opportunity for self-expression. However, users exploit this opportunity in different ways and to different degrees. To understand the reasons and effects of this differentiation a classification of users in respect of creativity is required.

6.4.1 Users

A simple but useful empirical classification of RLJ's users has been devised by *LJ Companion*[39], a satellite service for LJ created by a Russian programmer and providing various statistics on the Russian segment of LJ. The classification includes the following types:

1) **The most memorized authors**, i.e. users with the largest number of entries that have been put in memories by other users.

2) **Peoples' favourites**, i.e. users with the largest number of friends of. The list include the thirty most popular users whose number of friends of ranges from 2875 to 935 LJ users.

3) **The arrogant ones**, i.e. users who have much fewer friends than friends of.

4) **The friendliest ones**, i.e. users having the largest number of friends. The top thirty users in this category have from 1856 to 749 friends.

5) **The most commented on ones**, i.e. users with the greatest ratio of the number of received comments to the number of entries.

---

[39] http://lj.eonline.ru/

231

The statistics can give an idea about some quantitative patterns of RLJ, especially regarding the top examples. Unfortunately, *LJ Companion* was abandoned by its authors at some point and therefore it cannot be used for collecting and analyzing actual data.

Psychologist Boris Bazyma (LJ username *alliances*) who created a community devoted to "cyberpsychology"[40] developed an original method to determine types of LJ users based on the factor analysis of quantitative values of LJ users activity (*alliances*, 2004a, 2004b). He singled out three integral factors of user activity and described eight empirical types of LJ users. His analysis was based on a random sample of 100 RLJ users who have been keeping their journals more than 100 days.

Bazyma (*alliances*, 2004c) suggested empirical formulas to calculate individual values of the three factors - productiveness, involvement and declarative interests. The factor of productiveness includes indices of entries, sent comments, received comments, the length of time of keeping one's journal and the number of "friends of". The factor of involvement includes indices of friends, community membership and "friends of". The factor of declarative interests includes only the index of the user's interests.

The eight types of LJ users described by Bazyma are divided into two groups each including four types. The first group consists of users sharing the characteristic of high productivity, or "LJ writers". They make up 32 per cent of the total number of studies users.

1. **Favourites**. They have high indices of all three factors. They do not necessarily keep their journals for a long time (from 6 months to 2 years), but write

---

[40] http://www.livejournal.com/community/cyberpsy/

often (on average, 2 entries per day), they also actively comment on other users' entries (20-30 comments per day) and receive even more comments on their own entries (30-40 per day). On average, they have 90 declared interests; 307 friends, they are friends of 420 users and members of 42 communities. They are perceived as opinion makers and they often write on topics interesting for a wide audience. They are popular and influential. They constitute 8% of the total number of the studied users.

2. **Old Authorities**. They are characterized by high indices of the first two factors but a low index of the third. They keep their journals not less than for one year but post entries less frequently than the first type, one entry on average. They write 4-5 comments and receive 5-6 comments daily. Their average number of interests is 27. They have fewer friends than the first type (283 friends on average), and the number of friends exceeds the number of friends of (213 on average). They are members on average of 33 communities. They are popular in narrow circles but are well known and influential. Their reputations may be considered solid but they apparently have exhausted the resources of growth or do not aim at growing their reputation further. There are 5% of such users in the studied group.

3. **Fastidious Authorities**. They have high indices of factors 1 and 3 and a low index of factor 2. They keep their journal no less than for one year, post 1-2 entries daily, 9 comments and received 6 comments per day on average. They have wide interests, not less than 59. They are fastidious in choosing friends and limit their number to 80 on average. At the same time, they are chosen as friends more often, by 124 users on average. They are members of 30 communities. They have authority, and many users pay attention to their opinion, but their pride prevents them from becoming popular in the masses. They constitute 6%.

4. **Narrow Authorities**. They show a high index of the first factor but low indices of the second and the third. They keep their journals a long time, usually about two years. They post irregularly and alternate silence with series of posts. On a daily average, they post 1 entry, write 5 and receive 6 comments. Their number of interests is relatively low, about 27. The number of their friends and friends of is approximately the same, about 100 users. They are members of about 17 communities. They are well known in "narrow circles", have their audience of worshippers, which they tend not to widen; new users rarely join them. Presumably, their topics are potentially interesting only for a narrow audience. They constitute 13%.

The second group comprises those users whose productivity is irregular or scant.

5. **Candidates**. They have low index of the first factor and high indices of the second and the third. They keep their journals about 300 days. They post irregularly and relatively rarely. However, they write 5-6 and receive 6-7 comments per day. They have a high index of interests, 100 on average. They have more friends than "friends of" (171 and 102 users correspondingly). . They are members of 32 communities. Presumably, they may join the group of authoritative users if they enhance their productivity and can find topics interesting for many. They make up 8 per cent.

6. **Commentators**. They have a high index of the second factor and low indices of the first and the third. They include those who have started keeping journals recently (4-5 months) as well as those who keep their journals quite a long time (2 years). They write relatively little, irregularly - on average one post every two days. They are active in commenting and they post 4-5 comments a day. They receive fewer comments, 3-4 a day. The number of interests is low, about 21. The

number of friends is twice as large as the number of "friends of" (292 and 146 correspondingly). They are members of 60 communities. They make up 11 per cent.

7. **Undecided**. The first two factors for this type are low; the third is high. The time of keeping a journal is from 4 to 18 months. They post irregularly, approximately once in two days. They comment also irregularly, 2-3 comments per day on average. They relatively rarely receive comments, one or two per day. The interests are wide, 83 on average. They have few friends and "friends of", 56 and 42 correspondingly. They are members of only 17 communities. Arguably, they are trying to find their topics but cannot decide what they should be. They make up 20 per cent.

8. **Observers**. This type has low indices for all three factors. They keep their journal for 4 to 18 months. They have few entries, sometimes none at all. On average, they post one entry in three days. They comment rarely and selectively. They receive even fewer comments back. They have few interests, 19 on average. They have few friends and "friends of", 43 and 27 correspondingly. They do not actively participate in communities and are members of 10 communities on average. This gives the impression that they would rather observe others, and do not want or are unable to go to the foreground. They constitute 25 per cent.

Bazyma's research shows a positive correlation between users' productivity, the time of keeping one's journal, involvement and popularity. It also demonstrates that creativity is a relatively rare phenomenon; the passive and less creative users dominate on the RLJ as they do in other realms of culture and life. However, the sampling is probably not large enough to extrapolate the result to the RLJ as a whole. Moreover, the index of interest seems much more subjective than indices of friends and "friends of". The first is optional and is mostly used for self-

235

description; therefore it may hardly be treated on the same basis as indices that are more objective. The research also does not account for qualitative differences in users' productivity and it must be complemented by qualitative studies.

6.4.2 Friends

'Do not have 100 rubles, have 100 friends,' says a Russian proverb, and this applies as well to friends' networks in RLJ. As it has already been noted, Russian users tend to have more friends than non-Russian LJ users. They also like to have many comments on their posts. Russian users make inventories describing their friends and often discuss who added or excluded them. If a typical LJ user has only a handful of friends, most of whom are their personal acquaintances in real life, Russian users usually have several hundreds of friends, many of whom they have never seen. The choice of friends in the latter case is determined by a number of factors such as common or intersecting interests, good writing style, the author's reputation, curiosity or sheer vanity. Having many friends and receiving many comments allows users to feel significant in their social group and positively influences their self-image. It may be especially important for Russians living abroad as well as for other users who have difficulty with their self-identification.

The construction of friendship itself seems to be somewhat different in RLJ than in the English-speaking community and this can be linked to cross-cultural differences in the correlation between the concepts of the individual and the collective. Personality, from the Russian viewpoint, is formed not only by one's individual qualities but also by one's relationships with others. Hence the strong dependence of Russians on the group or groups they belong to, which has been described by many observers as a basic feature of the national identity. In regard to RLJ, this trait may account for both a higher significance of and a higher number of friends. The larger one's group, the more support one receives, on condition that the user's basic values are compatible with the values of the group. The group, therefore, serves as a powerful mechanism of the construction of one's personality. However, it does not necessary lead to dissolving one's personality in the group. Once a person is accepted by the group, he or she does not need to adjust any more and can freely express his/herself, relying on the group's tolerance and understanding. Presumably, this tendency can also be found in the English-speaking community, but it seems less expressed.

A short linguistic commentary concerning "friends" in RLJ may be appropriate. Russians borrowed many English terms designating various phenomena and actions within LJ but creatively altered them adjusting to Russian language and habits. Sometimes it has produced a comic effect because of the similarity of a technical term with some irrelevant Russian words. Thus, the widespread term "lj user" is often pronounced (and written) as *lzhe-juser,* which sounds like pseudo- or false-user.

While for the English-language users the word "friend" is ambiguous, since it denotes both real and virtual friends, the Russians circumvent this impediment by using different words for these two classes. Friends in real life are denoted as druz'ja (plural from Russian *drug*, meaning a friend), while for LJ friends the English word "friend" (spelled and pronounced as frend) has been adopted (in plural it often takes a russified form *frendy*).

The latter, however, are easily converted into the former. Generally, Russian LJ users have a tendency to de-virtualization. Meetings of RLJ users on various occasions are organized regularly in Moscow and other places.

RLJ also serves as an organizational tool for flash-mobs, some of which are trifling or facetious and some are quite serious. As an example of the latter, I can

237

quote a demonstration of RLJ users in support of German Galdecky in April 2004 (Shpileva, 2004). 19-year-old German revealed a system of criminal activity of the Moscow underground militia's officers who used to arrest young women under various pretences and then rape them. On 25 March 2004, German was shot in the head in the Yaroslavsky rail station (Newsru.com, 2004). The incident was widely discussed in RLJ, and 50 users took part in a flash-mob in German's support in front of the hospital in which he was placed. Charity actions such as collecting money for medical treatment of a sick child are also very typical among the RLJ community.

6.4.3 Communities

Another form of network building is communities. The main difference between friends' networks and communities is that the former are based on personal relations and value personal characteristics of the individual involved, while the latter are built around common interests and problems, value knowledge and expertise and provide more formal types of relationships. The majority of RLJ users are involved in both these types of social organization.

6.5 Language

Language is probably the most important means of unification in a text-based environment such as RLJ. RLJ users employ a great number of genres and stylistic strategies. However, there are some common linguistic features which make RLJ a sub-culture with a language of its own. They include the special terminology mentioned above as well as the use of idioms born within RLJ, which then became widespread outside of RLJ. Since 2004, RLJ has been deeply influenced by a jargon associated with so-called padonki (distorted from "podonki": "scum" or "geeks"), a countercultural movement which developed a special style of online expression. Before infecting RLJ, the padonki jargon proliferated at underground web sites and online forums such as fuck.ru, udaff.ru and padonki.org (Goryunova 2005; Vernidub 2005) but its roots can be traced back to Russian FIDO (Protasov 2005). Probably the most known 'theoretical' foundation of the linguistic distortions was the "Manifesdo of Anti-grammatacalaty" by Mary Shelley (1998) first published at fuck.ru. However, due to the tremendous popularity of LiveJournal in Russia, many tend to consider the jargon as a "ZhZh language" (for examples of typical padonki expressions see *Zhargon padonkov*, 2006).

The padonki jargon is based on using obscenity, word transformations, erroneous spelling and special discursive formulas. The two language devices – inserting double meaning into a message and using a mean, unprintable style – can be traced down to the Soviet time when they were used as defensive linguistic methods against censorship and denunciation (Gusejnov 2002, 2005). The jargon is thus a close relative to the Soviet *anecdote* culture (see chapter 7). It can be also read in terms of cultural resistance – not only against official discourse but also against globalisation with its ubiquitous English. The jargon has distinct counter-establishment and counter-cultural connotations but it is mostly used as a means of irony, expressivity and play. The degree of RLJ's influence over contemporary Russian culture is well illustrated by the fact that "ZhZh language" has infected both media (press, radio and TV programmes) and belle lettres (for example, Viktor Pelevin's [2005] novel "Helmet of Horror").

Figure 8. RLJ élite. Collage by *soamo* (2005).

6.6 Dynamics of RLJ

6.6.1 Introduction

A virtual community is defined as "a group whose members are connected by means of information technologies, typically the Internet"[41]. As Howard Rheingold (1993/2000) explains, "People in virtual communities do just about everything people do in real life, but [they] leave [their] bodies behind". As such, virtual communities follow the same rules of development and pass through the same stages in evolution as other sociocultural formations. Therefore, it is possible to apply to them methods for describing social dynamics. Most sociologists agree that societies have their own life cycle, if even they disagree about the particular phases of this cycle. In my analysis of RLJ's dynamics, I applied the model devised by Arnold Toynbee (Toynbee and Somervell, 1948) in his *Study of History* to describe the cycles of great sociocultural formations such as civilizations. My hypothesis was that the structure of societies follows fractal logic and that the same stages can

---

[41] http://en.wikipedia.org/wiki/Virtual_community

240

be found at any level of a social organization. The aim was to test Toynbee's generalizations using RLJ as a case study. Findings and implications of this experiment are discussed in the final part of this section.

6.6.2 Conception

The early history of RLJ was highly personalized. Admittedly, "the father" of RLJ is Roman Leibov, lecturer at the University of Tartu, Estonia, an online journalist and one of the pioneers of the Russian Internet. Though chronologically he was not the first Russian in LJ, the "real" history of RLJ began on February 1st, 2000 when Leibov (who had opened his account the day before) started his journal with a test entry that ran as follows: "Pen test (*proba pera*). Let's try it in Russian... A funny thing!" (*r_l*, 2001)

Unlike his prehistorical predecessors, who contented themselves with the mere fact of becoming users, Leibov started immediately to explore the possibilities of LJ for creativity and self-expression. On his first day, he made 18 entries in various genres including an opinion (about the qualities of LJ), a pun, a characterization of his psychophysical state (insomnia), a remembrance of dream, a sketch (about his wife and a cat), a quotation (from right-wing philosopher and nationalist politician Dugin) with an ironic commentary, a plan for action, a reflection (on the idea of teaching history as a reverse narrative), a joke on an actual political event, a critical remark on a musical group, a description of a fact of life, a rumour, a poem (by Pushkin) and an extract from the encyclopaedia. He also downloaded an animated photo of himself. Thus, on the very first day he used LJ in a variety of ways and sampled most of the genres that would be exploited later on. He went on writing and experimenting and missed not a single day that February. Many of his innovations have been widely accepted by the RLJ community. He coined the word "lytdybr" – the Russian word *dnevnik* meaning "diary" mistakenly typed using the English keyboard layout – which became a standard genre designation for entries devoted to description of events in users' personal lives. Being a prolific dreamer, he frequently described his dreams in his journal and inspired many users to do the same. He also was one of the first who began to post photographs on the regular basis and introduced other innovations.

For some time Leibov kept his journal privately, but gradually the rumours about the mysterious thing called "blog" ran through Runet and more people followed his example. At the first stage, LJ became popular among Internet professionals, many of whom came onto the Internet in the period of "Sturm und Drang" of the 1990-s and formed the so-called "Runet élite". As a rule, they did not use their journals for work but rather for fun, for personal self-expression and interpersonal play. The idea of using LJ for collaborative creative work was gradually emerging from this playful activity but it was fully realized at the later stages of RLJ evolution.

6.6.3 Propaganda and Recruiting

Since the first RLJ users included many online journalists, it is not surprising that they were also the first who revealed LJ to the public. Their efforts led to the fact that LJ has become a hot topic for media (Gorny, 2004c). A characteristic publication appeared in Russian Journal. It was written by Linor Goralik, a prolific author in various genres publishing both online and in print, and was an anthem to LJ as a "home" and a "right place" for a small company of "nice people" (Goralik, 2001). The text was written in a rather esoteric manner; neither the full name of the site nor its URL was given. The comparison of "ZheZhe" (standing for *Zhivoj Zhurnal*, a colloquial designation for LiveJournal, just coined by Alexander Gagin

242

and then unknown except in the narrow circle of RLJ users) with the "unforgettable flat of Zhurnal.ru" (the flat of the literary scholar and editor Dmitri Itzkovich in Moscow where the first journal of Internet culture, Zhurnal.ru, was founded and edited) and "Club O.G.I. in its distant golden times" (a club started by Itzkovich) clearly related LJ to the "Runet élite."

Although the number of Russian LJ users remained insignificant, these users were powerful enough in the online world to establish their own ratings, to decide what was important and to influence public opinion. LJ started to turn into "the most fashionable address on the net." "To write a virtual diary is just the thing," proclaimed the title of the article that appeared in Izvestija, a newspaper with a nation-wide distribution on April 7, 2001 (Tresschanskaja, 2001). "Now, there is only one place on the net and it's called LiveJournal," echoed Sergej Kuznetsov in his column (Kuznetsov, 2001). "To write a diary is fashionable again," *Nezavisimaya Gazeta,* a respected newspaper for intellectuals and decision makers, repeated a year later, describing LJ as an example of self-organizing social systems and a realization of Pierre Levy's idea of "collective intelligence" (Kalkinen, 2002).

LJ attracted the attention of writers and critics. Thus, critic Dmitry Bavilsky (2002b) beheld in it 'an important link in the creation of a new aesthetics uniting the conventional image of artistic text with a new, aesthetic product, emerging in the interior of Runet.' Russian Journal, an influential online magazine devoted to politics and culture, initiated a discussion about LJ as a literary phenomenon and a new media form and published a series of 23 interviews under the common title "LiveJournal in Writers' Words". Anton Nosik (Majzel, 2003) opposed LJ as a unique tool for community building, to weblogs as an industry of outwardly similar projects. LJ was also praised as an ideal meeting place for Russians all over the world, which has no negative aspects inherent in real Russian diasporas (Terentjeva, 2002).

"Fashionable", "popular" and their synonyms have become commonplace epithets applied to LJ in Russian media. First considered an esoteric playground for the "Runet élite", LJ has gradually turned into an epidemic passion. In December 2002 a posh magazine called *Afisha* included *Zhivoj Zhurnal* in the list of fifty words "that has become especially important". When in January 2003 Roman Leibov came out with a venomous criticism of RLJ (which was met with almost unanimous animosity by RLJ's users) calling it an "un-live non-journal" (Leibov, 2003), he used the topos of "fashionability" in the subtitle of his article devoted - ironically enough - to the virtual place that became fashionable thanks to the missionary endeavours of himself and his fellows.

By the February 1st, 2004, that is, three years after Leibov made his first entry the LJ's Russian-language community reached more than 37,000 members and it is continuing to grow. The media in general and LJ pioneers in particular have greatly contributed to the popularity of LJ among Russians.

6.6.4 Unification

As is usual for the early stage of community building when the number of members is few, the early RLJ was more like a village than a megapolis: almost everybody knew one another (at least virtually) and was connected to others by personal ties of friendship or acquaintance. The members of the community formed a unified group sharing the same basic values, cultural codes and implicit rules of conduct that ensured mutual understanding and a harmony of the whole, securing at the same time the unique individuality of every member. However, the recruiting of new members and the resulting quantitative growth of community put the village idyll under threat. As a result, means of artificial unification have been developed.

For a long time, the most popular of these was Fisherman's (Fif's) Friends Page (*lenta Fifa*)[42] to which all LJ users writing in Russian were being added and which made it possible to read all Russian posts in one page. It was created on April 20th, 2001 by user *a48* (Anton Monakhov) and soon outstripped other unifying projects in popularity becoming probably the most significant phenomenon of Russian LJ.

> Its universal character is often emphasized by its readers: 'With Fif's friends page one can without much effort wrap around the globe' (Bubnov, 31.07.2002).

In the beginning, it was thought of as a tool facilitating reading and finding new friends but very soon its function shifted: it became a representation of RLJ as a whole, the most read page and a starting point for new users. As far as I know, there is no analogue of Fif's friends page in English-language LJ. The page of latest posts, which has a formal similarity to Fif's page showing all LJ posts in real time, is not language-specific and does not pretend to serve a community-building function.

The implications of this unification endeavour were twofold. On the one hand, it created a sense of unity between members connected neither by personal ties nor by any common interests. The unifying principle became more formal: now, having an account in LJ and writing in Russian was enough to be included in the hyper-community of Fif's friends. On the other hand, it led to the destruction of the relative intimacy of individual journals. Any personal post, if it was not made in "friends only" mode (and few people have used this mode) automatically became

---

[42] http://www.livejournal.com/~fif/friends

public - not only in the sense that it could be read by anybody but in the sense that one definitely knew that it would be read by many. As one user put it (*sestra_milo*, 2002),

> Fif is a mysterious, half-mythological being that set itself the goal to collect all lj users writing in Russian at its friends page. (...) Nobody knows why they need the membership in Fif's list but nobody has been able to escape it yet. All secret journals will be found, all that are not yet embraced will be embraced.

There have been negative views articulated as well. Dmitri Volchek (2003), a controversial writer, publisher and journalist at Radio Liberty living in Prague, wrote:

> The idea to bring a personal diary to open space is quite worthy, but the compatriots as usual made a mess. From the very beginning all those writing in Russian were herded into one foolish "friends page", that is, a club of lonely hearts was created with its ratings, biggies, haemorrhoidal discussions about tossers unknown to anybody, now are they practically going to establish a political party. The communards have reduced this private and hermetic thing to a peep-show in a sovkhoz.

It was Fif's friends page, as a conglomeration of individual posts as well as other similar unification tools which emerged later, that have changed RLJ from a place for private self-expression and a handy means of communication with a handful of real friends, to a kind of reality show for the public. This, in its turn, facilitated the shift from writing one's own journal to reading the journals of others as the prevailing activity among many RLJ users, let alone non-users accessing LJ via the web.

246

How was Fif's friends page actually used? As it has been noted before, collecting almost all posts in Russian in one place made it easy to observe users' writing activity in real time. The purposes of reading RLJ are numerous and far exceed the standard aim of "keeping in touch" with one's relatives and friends.

(1) **Reading for information.** RLJ has become an important source of news and opinions on a wide range of topics and a strong competitor of the "official media" for the attention of the audience. Many RLJ users admitted that they stopped reading other web sites, or now visit them via links in LJ. The character of the news can vary from the lack of hot water in Moscow or the coming of spring in Toronto to exit poll data during elections or witnesses' accounts of acts of terrorism.

Since the RLJ is often considered "as a model of society in miniature", it is also a handy tool for the study of public opinion. One can note that there is a high degree of consistency and recurrence in the apparently disjointed and incoherent narrative formed from posts of people who may know nothing about each other.

(2) **Reading for pleasure**. For many users, reading RLJ is a self-sufficient activity. It is read for fun and pleasure rather than for any pragmatic purpose. The contemplation of the surrealistic flow of discordant texts in RLJ is similar to the practice of web surfing of the early Internet (which, in its turn, is analogous to surfing data flow in cyberpunk fiction). Such a non-utilitarian reading of others' posts has naturally led to the conception of RLJ as a work of art. "Fif's friends page is the most interesting literary work (...), such a mega-documental novel" (*dm_lihachev*, 2002). "I'm reading Fif's friends page. As if re-reading Marquez" (*bopm*, 2002). It is interesting to compare this view with the idea of the guest book as the highest form of net-literature promoted by some authors at the pre-LJ stage. RLJ can also used as a divination tool.

247

Now you don't need a Book of Changes because there is Livejournal. The personal friends page is a fortunetelling book and this explains one's predilection for it. Fif's friends page is a fortunetelling book of the Universe, and if you build a linguistic analyser into it, you can see how the universe is breathing. (*nnikif*, 2003)

However, always reading others' posts brings not only pleasure to the readers. One can find the many examples of criticism on RLJ dull and senseless.

When I'm thinking about the readers of fif's friends page, I have a quite clear and distinct association with the homeless people at a city rubbish dump who rummage about in a pile of shit spread many kilometres in the hope of finding there a gold bar occasionally dropped by someone. (*xxx*, 2001)

The degree of meaning of published posts approaches zero. Fif is completely unreadable. RLJ is changing into an archive of quotations, links, senseless descriptions of everyday life and other rubbish. (*shakaka*, 2002)

It is interesting to note that the metaphors of rubbish dump and madness applied to LJ have often been applied to the Internet as a whole (Babaev, 1999).

(3) **Reading to monitor**. The creation of Fif's friends page and other tools which made it easy to monitor users' activity and to search entries and comments by keywords led to a situation of Foucault's panopticon. It is not surprising that time and again various observers have suggested that Fif's friends page was created by the FSB (former KGB) to monitor users' activity or, at least, has been used by them. However that may be, it is obvious that since people usually write in their journals what they really think, RLJ as a whole is an invaluable source for any organization studying public opinion.

248

(4) **Reading for socialization**. Monitoring other users' posts is a popular way to find interesting people to include in one's friends list. Sometimes huge friends lists are created from sheer vanity because users consider it prestigious to include popular authors on their lists. The users often describe their friendship-building strategies and classifications of celebrities with detailed instructions about whom to include to show what could be found in RLJ archives.

Fif's friends page was finally shut down when the number of Russian users became unmanageable. However, other unification services came to take its place. To name just a few - the most popular ones – LJSearch, the LJist Companion (Sputnik ZhZhista) and the Register of Russian-language communities of LiveJournal (Reestr russkojazychnych soobsshestv).

6.6.5 Differentiation

The quantitative growth of community has naturally led to qualitative change. RLJ ceased to be an entertainment for the few and became popular social software for communication by the many with the many. Some observers expressed the opinion that RLJ provided a representative sampling of society in general (Barseqyan, 2003); however, this is hardly true. RLJ users tend to be more liberal than Russian society as a whole: this was proven, for example, by a sharp discrepancy between the results of RLJ's virtual exit polls during parliamentary (*ddb*, 2003) and presidential elections (*ddb*, 2004), and the national results of those elections.

At the mass adoption stage, a new class of LJ users has become dominant - notorious secretaries writing at work about the trivia of their personal lives with their favourite topics being such things as "demanding a 100-dollar salary raise"; "I'm overweight"; "my beautiful night of love"; "I haven't had a man for two weeks"; "the Man of My dreams". (Burzhuaznyj zhurnal, 2004). They post extensively, love to publish the results of countless tests they passed, have thousands of friends and occupy leading positions in the top users' list, being second only to prolific philosophers, pornographers and "old authorities". The main contingent of RLJ consists now of middle-aged office workers as well as people of free professions who live in Moscow and other big cities, while pensioners, farmers, the military and other categories of population have remained underrepresented.

According to another widespread opinion, as a result of the quantitative growth, RLJ has generally become less intellectual and less creative. The percentage of dull, obscene and senseless entries has drastically increased. Probably, RLJ presents now a more adequate image of Russian society than it did in its early stages and, as such, may provide rich material for the sociologist and the anthropologist. However, for many users it has become a less pleasant place to live.

The growth naturally led to differentiation of the formerly united community into various groups. No means of unification could prevent it from splitting. The new audience demanded new idols. The former RLJ élite, constituted from early adopters, either well-known figures or good and prolific writers or both, was to a great extent replaced by new celebrities among whom extreme nationalists and pornographers hold a prominent position.

One form of the split was a conflict between the early adopters and late adopters. In RLJ, it often took the form of arguments about the role of the so-called Élite of the Russian Internet. Its forming role was declared completed and its existence a remnant. As one user put it, 'Now, the only possible attitude to the Runet Élite is to forget it, once and for all.' (*serg_a*, 2001). Sometimes stronger expressions have been used. One user complained that she did not understand the meaning of pictures uploaded by Roman Leibov "for those who understand" and added apropos of this: 'The Runet Élite. This expression makes me sick. If this is humour, it doesn't make me laugh. If this is serious, I don't understand this.' (*sandra_and_me*, 2002). Earlier she wrote, 'The élite ... the Internet for the chosen ones. How dreadful! I'm going to vomit on the keyboard.' The word "élite" has generally acquired negative connotations and has been ridiculed by many, including those considered the élite by others.

Widening the initially narrow circle of RLJ users led to democratization of the community. However, the growing communal spirit of RLJ has been rejected by many early adopters who saw in it a threat to their freedom and creativity. One of the most ardent critics of RLJ was Aleksey (Lexa) Andreyev, a mathematician and poet, inventor of the hacked news genre, futurologist and cyberpunk writer. He never used LJ on principle and asked the LJ abuse team to close a journal that somebody was writing in his name. In his numerous invectives he condemned LJ as a communicative McDonalds for office rats unsuitable for creative individuals.

> Vivid examples of LJ-like self-expression could be found eight years ago, during the period of the first web observers, when there were only a handful of them. Now, the mass character of LJ reduced that to McDonalds. It's one thing when those who invented the new means are involved in self-expression and another thing when the mob came to this new environment as a flock of sheep and all do the same thing, following the common pattern. (Anisimov, 2002)

The early adopters responded to the changing context resulting from the qualitative growth in four typical ways:

251

(1) **Withdrawal and return**. A temporary withdrawal from the community and experiments with new forms of communication and creative activity followed by a return to RLJ is typical behaviour for early adopters at a certain stage.

Thus, Roman Leibov, founding father of RLJ, who had a policy of including in his friends list all those who had included him, felt stuck in useless discussions and "flames" and became disappointed with his own child. Irritated, he wrote an article entitled "Un-live non-journal" in which proclaimed the degeneration of RLJ. The article provoked derision among the new generation of users content with life, LJ and themselves. Then Leibov started writing in private mode and sending his postings to a narrow circle of subscribers through a mailing list that he had created for the occasion. But he did not feel quite satisfied with this decision. For some time he went into complete silence. Then he re-appeared in LJ but this time without words, limiting himself to posting pictures. Gradually, he returned to his usual mode of writing, but he considerably limited the number of his friends and became more reserved in commenting (Gorny 2003b).

(2) **Withdrawal without return** or discontinuance of acceptance. When the feeling of unity and the right audience disappear, individuals become disappointed with the community and either cease writing or delete their journals altogether. Such a way was chosen, for example, by writer Margarita Meklina and designer Artemy Lebedev, who were extremely popular but at some point deleted their journals.

(3) **Non-participation**. This reaction to RLJ popularity was chosen by many figures that were expected to participate in RLJ. They could motivate their decision by the adherence to old ways of communication, contempt of the masses, reference to their predisposition to addiction, etc. The result, however, was the same - they refused to participate (although many of them regularly read others' journals).

(4) **Adaptation to a new situation** and acceptance of "the new rules of the game"; openness to others. Thus Alexander Zhitinsky, a writer and publisher from St. Petersburg, replying to the greetings he received in LJ on the occasion of his 63rd birthday, formulated what LJ meant for him (*maccolit*, 2004):

So it has happened - and this is for the better! - that the Live Journal circle has become for me a circle of communication both in virtual and real life. Not counting, perhaps, the closest circle of my family which is, by the way, represented in LJ quite well. And if we are speaking about analogies, then LJ seems to me a kind of expanded family stretched over all countries and continents. It is a small model of the social structure (may sociologists pardon me), not without problems, not without black sheep as it should be in any family, but with a feeling of strange and essential unity.

We know more about each other than one is supposed to know even in conventional companionship - about work, family, children, ailments and sometimes even vices. And we help one another even when we keep quiet and sometimes this is expressed in real acts, real means, as it has been a good many times.

That is why I love LJ; it corresponds most exactly to life and to my ideas about it - what its opponents seem not to understand well. Here, everyone is like the others, in spite of all differences between us. When I get a chance, I'll develop this thesis - "to be like everybody else" - contrary to the established opinion that one should stand out against the mass.

There is no point in standing out against the MASS if the MASS suits you.

6.6.5 Breakdown?

In June 2005, many journals of Russian LJ users were suspended by the LJ administration. The first signs of the coming conflicts appeared when a discussion flamed up about the closing of *suck_my_nya*'s journal whose author was accused of publishing a photograph of a nude teenage girl. The photograph was a reproduction from a book by photographer Eva Ionesko which had several editions and was selling on Amazon.com. However, the LJ abuse team insisted on removal of the controversial photograph. Some RLJ users considered that as an infringement on free speach. Believing that Internet liberties were under threat, they began to discuss the project of an ideal alternative service where anybody could realize the right of free expression without fear of Russian, American or other authorities.

The conflict went on to the next stage a couple weeks later when Mikhail (Misha) Verbitsky, a non-conformist writer, declared that one of his journals was closed for the slogan "Kill NATO" which was considered by the LJ administration as breaking the terms of service, and called others to reproduce the phrase in their journals. The journals of those users who followed the call were also closed by the abuse team. Later on, some of them beat a retreat and removed the controversial phrase. However, the conflict started a new wave of discussion of free speech. Several dozens of users, including some popular and respected people, declared their ideological disagreement with LJ policy and moved to alternative blogging services such as LJ.Rossia.org[43] in the hopes of finding an unlimited freedom of speech. A few users followed their example but most of them came back to LJ later, because of the narrower audience on lj.rossija.org.

---

[43] http://lj.rossia.org/

6.6.6 Conclusion

The RLJ community was initiated by a small group of highly creative people among whom there were many pioneers of the Russian Internet.

These early adopters or creative minority was unified as a group sharing the same basic values, while its members all possessed a unique individuality.

This creative minority, to use Toynbee's term, popularized LJ for the masses and recruited new users giving them an example of how the new technology could be used for self-expression, work or "just for fun". The newcomers could adopt the innovation in two ways - either by undergoing the actual experience of the creative individuals; that is, by participating in the creative process, or by following the leaders, imitating creativity but being unable to contribute to further change or contributing to a lesser extent.

Gradually this led to the split between the creative minority and non-creative users and a revolt of the latter against "the élite" as a unifying principle and an example for imitation. The majority felt irritated by the élite's authority, values and practices, perhaps because their own lack of creativity was revealed, or because they perceived it as a hindrance or deterrent to developing new forms of creativity. The élite was proclaimed an archaism, lost its initial status and was ousted to the periphery.

Further growth of RLJ involved the differentiation between parts of the community and the formation of various personal networks and formal communities based on the similarity of interests and values. This process also involved a redistribution of the old élite and emergence of new ones.

However, this did not lead to community breakdown, since the former élite could not transform itself into a dominant minority, artificially maintain unity and thus cause the community's disintegration. This turned out to be impossible because the architecture of LJ does not provide the necessary tools of power and anyone is free to construct his or her social environment.

As a result of the differentiation, RLJ ceased to be an integrated meaningful community as it was in the early stages, and changed into a formal congeries, which generally lacks uniting ideas and values and whose unity is mainly defined spatially (LJ servers) and linguistically (Russian language). Within this congeries a great number of self-organizing networks successfully exist and evolve. At the same time, the high degree of interweaving between these networks provides an additional factor of unification. It is reinforced by the RLJ "élite", i.e. popular users who act as both newsmakers and role models.

LiveJournal has been contrasted to Russian media as a space where free and uncensored speech is possible (which reflects the opposition between official and non-official media described in chapter 4). However, this concept has been challenged by the limitations of free speech established in the Terms of Service and implemented by the Abuse Team which has been perceived by some Russian users in terms of ideological and political censorship. This resulted in the flow-out of RLJ users and the growing popularity of other blogging services, both international and purely Russian. However, the quantitative growth of RLJ continues and it is still perceived as The Blog by many Russian users. If the breakdown finally happens, its time and forms are uncertain.

6.7 National, international and transnational on RLJ

Having considered RLJ in its structure and its dynamics and having compared it with the dominant English-language community, it remains to discuss the issue of their interrelationships. It seems that the processes of cultural creativity that take place in RLJ may be described by the popular term "glocalization" (Robertson,

1985) meaning a combination of both universalizing and particularizing tendencies or the use of universal means to achieve particular ends. As I tried to show, Russian culture largely influenced the uses of LJ, sometimes in unpredictable ways in regard to its original concept.

It is unlikely that participation in RLJ may lead to the emergence of a transnational culture in the sense of the integration of various national cultures into an ecumenical unity. However, it may lead to the consolidation of a particular (Russian) culture, helping to establish connections and links between people divided by physical space. Interaction between cultures requires much more effort and willingness to self-transcendence than the reproduction of ready-made cultural models. The degree in which this interaction is possible remains to be seen. Below, I summarize the results of a discussion about the correlation between national and transnational in RLJ with my LJ friends:

In LJ, the Russians communicate almost exclusively with other Russians. Exceptions are rare. Some users have a few friends writing in other languages. Some, especially those living abroad, write – constantly or occasionally - in languages other than Russian; however, they constitute an insignificant minority in RLJ.

The linguistic homogeneity helps to maintain the unity of the RLJ. On the other hand, it separates Russian users from the rest of LJ. As a rule, the Russian users are not interested in overstepping the limits of the Russian-language world and content themselves with their language and cultural status.

LiveJournal is an international service and a multicultural hypercommunity. However, it serves for most Russian users not as a means of integration into a worldwide context but rather a means of isolation from the alien environment. This especially concerns Russians living abroad: instead of doing the hard job of learning another culture and establishing personal connections with people in the country where they live, they spend their time in the virtual Russian environment of RLJ.

When I was already finishing this chapter, I asked my friend Anatoli Velichko (LJ username *a_v*), who has lived in Paris for nine years, what LJ meant to him. His response was ambiguous. However, this ambiguity seems fruitful - because it shows the two sides of the coin. I shall quote his response (Velichko, 2004) in full.

> If I answer your question frankly, it would hardly suit you. So, first I will not answer frankly.
>
> For me, as for a Russian person living abroad, LJ is a way to maintain contact with my habitual linguistic and social environment. During the years that I lived abroad in the absence of the Internet and LJ in particular, I started having problems with the Russian language, as well as with my social and national identification. My circle of daily contacts was almost exclusively francophone, and I could not fully identify myself with this circle, which produced a feeling of social discomfort. With the advent of the home Internet and LJ I have found again my place in the circle of the Russian intellectual class with which I feel a deep affinity. I feel that these people need me, and our interaction serves as something important beyond us. For me, as well as for many Russians abroad, LJ in a certain sense has become a second home, and I wouldn't agree to lose it at any price.
>
> And now, frankly.
>
> For me, as for any Russian person living abroad, LJ means one more bad habit. When I feel too lazy to work or read a serious book in a foreign language, I open my LJ; write fiddle-faddle, read useless stuff; and after two

or three hours of such a pastime, I feel as if I have eaten too much sweets. I've spend three years in LJ, and all my assets are two or three individuals whom I've met in real life and who became my real friends; a few - not more than four or five - interesting discussions; a dozen more of my own postings in which I managed to express something inwardly important and to get a response. My liabilities are thousands of hours wasted in idle talk and in satisfying a trivial vanity. Having weighed up the pros and cons, I made a decision to kill my LJ forever. (personal e-mail communication)

Having written this, *a_v* deleted his journal or, to put it differently, committed virtual suicide. However, he could not go without LJ for too long. He resurrected it later the same day.

6.8 Conclusions

The multi-language environment provided by LiveJournal.com has greatly contributed to its popularity among Russian users. Since joining and using LJ has always been free of charge (for some time, to create an account an invitation code from another LJ user was required), the users who could not pay (for example, because they did not have a credit card) could nevertheless use the service. The location of LJ service outside Russia made it independent of Russian jurisdiction, giving the Russian users more freedom of expression and defending them from possible outrage of the state. RLJ was first populated by users who had authority and could influence others to adopt the innovation. The architecture of LJ facilitating community building has fitted well with the Russian cultural identity and social circumstances which result in a special value of informal networks, often referred to within the net community itself as to a "tendency towards collectivism".

However, LJ is in some respects inferior to other blogging services in functionality and customization. Its community-building feature has a slight tinge of coercion: in order to participate in the community, users *must* be registered with LJ, use its software, interface and web site. It is plausible to assume that further development of the syndication technology and emergence of other innovations will lead to further decentralization by providing an opportunity to create blogging communities that are not necessarily tied to a particular place. Others critical issues include the introduction of various degree of trust and the development of technologies of collaboration.

A temporary secondary unification of RLJ members may occur in situations where the interests and feelings of many are touched by events such as acts of terror, disasters, political elections or a threat to users' welfare. The discussion about the future of electronic libraries in Russia provoked by the suit of KM Online against Moshkov's Library can serve as an example of the latter. The suit was widely discussed in RLJ and a community created in defence of Moshkov's Library mustered more than 400 members in two weeks (*za_lib_ru*, 2005). Generally speaking, a war or a celebration may serve as a mobilizing and unifying factor for virtual communities as well as for the nation at large.

Furthermore, even if LJ ceases to be for some reason or transforms into something different, the LJ experience, which has been so valuable for many users, will remain. The general principle of community is more durable than the specific forms that community takes in time. LiveJournal made community building easy but only for its members. New technologies like RSS and OpenID are a step in removing this limitation – towards a truly global community.

Finally, a number of off-line events and projects were first conceived and discussed in RLJ and then realized in real life. For example, a music festival of

RLJ users called Current Music has been conducted in Moscow yearly since 2000. The title alludes to an LJ option with same name showing the information about music currently playing on a user's computer. The festival attracted dozens of musical groups and more than a thousand listeners. It received wide publicity in the Russian media - mostly by the efforts of LJ users including hundreds of journalists - and it was considered a vivid example of transforming a virtual community into a real-life community.

Chapter 7

FOLKLORE IN THE AGE OF THE INTERNET: JOKES FROM RUSSIA

7.1 Introduction

Humor is one of the most important elements of culture. Humor reflects an immediate reaction of people to various life phenomena. Being a form of communication that makes people laugh or evokes feelings of amusement and happiness,[44] humor can make acceptable or tolerable even unpleasant or painful situations. Although humor seems to be a pan-human universal, it is also culturally specific inasmuch as it based on a language and culture. Humor is, therefore, "a key to understanding societies, as it reflects collective fears, ideologies, and social power" (Shifman and Varsano, 2007). National humor is one of the most powerful means of maintaining national identity through shared feelings and understandings.

The Internet altered traditional ways of dissemination of information, including humor, by allowing global reach and instant access. This chapter tells the story of the web site *Jokes from Russia*[45] — the most comprehensive uncensored collection of Russian humor. It argues that the online collection of such seemingly unserious stuff like jokes has performed a quite serious cultural function of "virtual (re)unification" (Schmidt, Teubener and Zurawski, 2006) of the Russians both in Russia and abroad on the basis of shared language, values, and sense of humor.

7.2. Online humour and Russian culture

This chapter addresses the issue "cyber humor" which has attracted the attention of Internet researchers very recently (Kuipers, 2006; Shifman, 2006;

---

[44] "Humour", *Wikipedia*, http://en.wikipedia.org/wiki/Humour.
[45] *Anekdoty iz Rossii*, http://anekdot.ru.

Shifman and Varsano, 2007). Limor Shifman (2006) has formulated two research questions related to this topic:

a) To what extent does the Internet function as a mediator of traditional humorous forms and topics, and to what extent does it facilitate new humorous forms and topics?

b) How do the new forms and topics of online humor relate to fundamental characteristics of the Internet such as interactivity, multimedia and global reach?

These questions are instrumental for this chapter. However, we believe that the study of online humor per se should be supplemented by the study of the sociocultural context in which humor is generated and disseminated. The chapter also develops themes discussed earlier in this book such as the role of cultural identity and the social context as a shaping force of Internet culture; the correlation between personal and collective creativity on the Internet; the opposition between official and non-official media; issues of censorship and free speech.

To understand the role *Jokes from Russia* has played on the Russian Internet, the social and cultural situation in the country should first be considered. The authoritative political regime and the underdevelopment of the civic institutes in Russia led to the fact that the function of public sphere has been partially performed by literature. The traditional literature centricity of Russian culture has been reflected on the Russian Internet. The first Russian sites were devoted to literature and culture rather than technology or politics. The first Russian interactive projects were literary games such as *Bouts-rimés*[46]. The consolidation of the Russian net community occurred around the online literary contest *Teneta* (see section 5.3.2.) and the "herald of net culture" *Zhurnal.ru* (see section 4.3.3.). Writers have been among the most popular users in the Russian-language segment of LiveJournal (see Chapter 6) *Jokes from Russia* to which users contribute jokes,

---

[46] http://centrolit.kulichki.net/centrolit/cgi/br.cgi

real-life stories and other literary genres is among the most popular web sites on the Russian Internet. The high role of literature and the abundance of literary-related web sites is a striking characteristic of the Russian Internet, which seems to have no direct parallel in the West (Schmidt, 2002).

7.3 Terminology conventions

The original title of Verner's web site may be (and sometimes is) translated as *Anecdotes from Russia*. However, this may be confusing for the English-language reader. The reason is the discrepancy in meaning and connotations of the word in the two languages.

Wikipedia[47] defines anecdote as follows:

> An anecdote is a short tale told about an interesting, amusing, or biographical incident. Usually an anecdote is based on real life, an incident involving actual persons or places. However, over time, modification in reuse may convert a particular anecdote into a fictional piece. Sometimes humorous, anecdotes are not jokes, because their primary purpose is not to evoke laughter.

In Russian, this meaning of anecdote is considered old-fashioned; it was dominant in 18th and 19th centuries and was later replaced by a new meaning: 'a genre of urban folklore, a topical comical story-miniature with an unexpected ending, a kind of humorous parable' (Russian Modern Encyclopedia). Therefore, the Russian *anekdot* (*anekdoty* in plural) should be translated into English as "funny story", "short story with a punchline" or "joke" bearing in mind its specific cultural connotations. These jokes are normally told in informal situations in a small circle of people. *Anekdoty*, especially political ones, played a prominent role in the Soviet culture by giving people a way to express their real thoughts and feelings in a hypocritical environment dominated by Communist ideology. Under

---

[47] http://en.wikipedia.org/wiki/Anecdote

Stalin, one could be sent to the labour camp for ten years or even sentenced to death for telling a political joke: they could be treated as "anti-Soviet propaganda" which, according to Article 58 (RSFSR Penal Code), was a capital offence. In later years, the attitude to *anekdoty* softened and even members of the Politburo and activists of the Party indulged themselves in telling anti-Soviet jokes. *Anekdoty* have become the major genre of Soviet/Russian urban folklore. Any significant event in domestic or international life was immediately echoed by fresh jokes which were transmitted from mouth to mouth and circulated all over the country.

Of course, *anekdoty* includes not only political jokes but also many other thematic groups and sub-genres. (For a comprehensive review of Russian *anekdoty*, with a categorization and examples see a Wikipedia's article 'Russian joke'[48].) All these categories can be found at Verner's website. 'Some of the jokes are timeless, but many are commentaries on contemporary Russian life', notes an American observer (Karush, 1998). Political jokes are not among the most popular ones. Verner has a precise statistic: 'Regardless of the season, people search the site's archives most often for jokes (in decreasing order) about Vovochka[49], students, sex, Rzhevsky[50], women, Stirlitz[51], the notorious tree-letter word, Jews,

---

[48] http://en.wikipedia.org/wiki/Russian_joke

[49] Vovochka is a Russian cousin of Little Johnny. He interacts with his school teacher, Marivanna, a shortspeak for Ms Mar'ya Ivanovna. The name is a highly dimunitive form (Vovochka<Vova<Volodya<Vladimir) which creates the "little boy" effect. His fellow students bear similarly dimunitive names, such as Mashen'ka (<Masha<Mariya), Peten'ka(<Petya<Pyotr), Vasen'ka(<Vasya<Vasilij), etc. This "little boy" name is used to contrast with Vovochka's very adult, often obscene statements. (Wikipedia, Russian Joke)

[50] Poruchik (lieutenant) Rzhevski is a fictional cavalry officer interacting with characters from the novel *War and Peace* by Leo Tolstoy. In the aristocratic setting of ball dances and 19th century social sophistication, Rzhevski, brisk but not very smart, keeps ridiculing the decorum with his rude vulgarities. As it was fashinonable among the Russian nobility at the time to speak French, Rzhevski occasionally uses French expressions, of course with a heavy Russian accent. (Wikipedia, Russian Joke)

[51] Standartenführer Stirlitz, alias Colonel Isayev, is a character from a Soviet TV series (based on a novel by Yulian Semyonov) played by the popular actor Vyacheslav Tikhonov, about a Soviet spy infiltrated into Nazi Germany. Stirlitz interacts with Nazi officials Ernst Kaltenbrunner, Martin Bormann and Heinrich Müller. Usually two-liners told in parody of the stern and solemn announcement style of the background voice in the original series, the plot is resolved in grotesque plays on words or in dumb parodies of over-smart narrow escapes and superlogical trains of thought of the "original" Stirlitz. (Wikipedia, Russian Joke)

wives and Russians' (Lyamina, 2004). However, many jokes are in direct response to what is happening in the country.[52]

Initially, Verner's collection comprised only conventional *anekdoty* (jokes); later on, new genres were added, such as *istorii* which literary means 'stories' but which normally are very close to anecdotes in the English meaning of the word. To escape terminological confusion, in what follows, I refer to *anekdoty* as jokes and to anecdotes as stories.

7.4 The idea of Jokes

The idea of *Jokes from Russia* as it was being formed at an early stage of the project was to collect and publish online all available Russian *anekdoty* without any discrimination. In a sense, it denied the oral nature of the genre (*anekdotos* in Greek means 'unpublished'). As we shall see, this decision has had far-reaching consequences. In a few years, Anekdot.ru has drastically changed the traditional ways of the circulation of jokes in Russia and, as some people argue, undermined the nature of the genre itself.

The issue of selection was resolved at the very beginning: Verner decided that Anekdoty would be a completely uncensored collection of jokes. This would allow the site to adequately represent present-day Russian folklore and, through it, to give an unbiased picture of the Zeitgeist. The users supported this position and it has been observed until now. This made Anekdoty different from the majority of other Russian humor web sites that have followed tastes either of the owner or of the audience. 'The main aim of *Anekdoty*, emphasized Verner (2003), is not popularity but objectivity and the completeness of the collection.' He has been often criticized for his too liberal approach and for giving too many rights to users but he has never been afraid that the plurality of opinions could do any harm to the project. 'Unjust faultfinding can be upsetting but it cannot hinder me from doing

---

[52] See selected jokes from Anekdot.ru in English translation at a webpage of the National Resource Centre at Harvard University: http://www.fas.harvard.edu/~nrc/teacherresources/humor.htm.

266

my business, says Verner, And if the critique is just, I'll find a way to consider it and to utilize it in my work.'

The organization of *Jokes from Russia* was original and did not repeat existing models. Thus, American humour web sites of the time normally consisted of long static lists of 'canonical jokes' in plain text format. Daily issues of fresh jokes rated by users were Verner's innovation which was later adopted by other Russian and foreign sites (Aksenov, 2000). The list of most important innovations included daily updates, the encouragement of user contribution, feedback mechanisms and a multilevel system of grading and sorting material.

The voting system was suggested by users in the Discussion Club section. It serves a number of functions. As Verner (2003) points out, a web site aiming at the creation of the most comprehensive collection of modern folklore has to solve several problems simultaneously which to a certain extent are in a conflict with each other. On the one hand, one needs to gather and publish everything without any censorship and selection. On the other hand, if one publishes everything in one stream without sorting, then the "signal" becomes choked up with the "noise". People cease sending "valuable" messages if they get lost in "garbage". Therefore, the site should include multistep sorting. As a matter of fact, the initial concept of the site – to publish issues of jokes avoiding repetitions – already was a means of separating the signal from the noise. Later on, when the popularity of *Jokes from Russia* grew and the site began to receive more than a hundred texts daily, the assorting became more complex. Now all the texts are divided into "new" and "repeated", "main" and "the rest". An additional sorting of "the rest" is made by forming the "readers' top ten" (*chitatelskaya desyatka*) resulting from voting. Therefore, voting (grading the texts) performs several functions at once: a) a way of sorting and separation of the most "valuable" messages; b) testing the audience's reaction; c) providing encouragement to the authors.

With the introduction of interactive elements (guestbooks, voting system, etc.) the *Jokes* site turned from a static collection of modern folklore into an open laboratory for creation of new folklore. This material, Verner emphasizes, can be used for the analysis of social, psychological and linguistic processes in contemporary Russia. The combination of the total lack of censorship, the completeness of the collection and the effective means of grading and sorting material which prevents the 'noise' from stifling the 'signal' makes it a valuable instrument of scientific research. However, Verner complains, this material is still waiting for researchers.

7.5 The history of Jokes

Jokes from Russia started as an amateur web project. Dmitry (Dima) Verner, a Russian astrophysicist working in the US collected jokes from the Internet – mostly in the Usenet group relcom.humor and Fido – and put them on a web page in plain text format. *Jokes from Russia* were launched on 8 November 1995. It was the second web site Verner had ever made; the first was Atomic Data for Astrophysics[53], which he made a month earlier. Initially, *Jokes from Russia* were located on the server of the department of physics and astronomy at the University of Kentucky[54] where Verner worked. In a year after the launch of the web site, it had more than a thousand visitors daily and generated about 80 percent of the traffic of the department's web pages (Verner, 1998). The increase occurred in March 1996 when Alex Farber put a link to *Jokes* on his Germany-based web site Russian literature on the Internet, a popular at the time collection of links to Russian literature-related online resources. He also shared his scripts with Verner and *Jokes* became available in different encodings (at that time, there was no standard encoding for Russian pages, and "advanced" web sites provided four encodings plus transliteration to facilitate reading for users on different platforms). By autumn 1996, the daily traffic of *Jokes* reached 1000 visitors – a very high index for those times.

---

[53] http://www.pa.uky.edu/~verner/atom.html
[54] http://www.pa.uky.edu/~verner/an.html

268

The popularity of *Jokes from Russia* skyrocketed. The audience grew and soon Anekdot.ru became the most visited web site on the Russian Internet. For more than a year, from April 1997 to August 1998 it held the first place in Rambler's Top 100, a rating of popularity of Russian web sites. (Parfenov, 2000). The August financial crisis gave rise to the development of online news publications and led the RBC news agency into first place (see section 4.3.5 of chapter 4). However, *Jokes'* traffic has remained extremely high. In 1998, the web site had 12 thousand visitors daily, i.e. one visitor every 7 seconds. It was rated the second in hitbox.com's international rating of entertainment resources, outstripping the web site with photographs of Monica Lewinsky, and was inferior only to a web site featuring nude celebrities' photos (Tsvetkov, 1998). In 1999, it had 200,000 visitors per month, and by 2004 it reached the half million mark. Add to this 90,000 users subscribed to receive fresh jokes by e-mail. One can mention that Anekdot.ru permanently occupies the first position in Rambler's Top 100 category "Humour", gathering approximately two times more visitors than any other website in this rating.

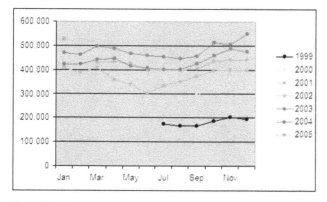

Figure 9. Anekdot.ru popularity growth. Statistics by unique hosts per month.
Data source: Mail.ru; Verner (2005).

"Jokes are Russian sex" – this aphorism popular at one point among Russian users emphasized the disproportional role that jokes have played in Russian

269

Internet culture. The aphorism can be traced back to Leonid Delitsyn's (1996) classical article. In his research of the online advertisement market Delitsyn found out that the most visited web sites on the English-language Internet were sexually oriented. Thus, Playboy.com which provided erotic content was second only to Netscape.com which gave away its web browser. Playboy site attracted a quarter million visitors daily, who generated 5 million hits. Other sex-related web sites ranged from Amateur Hardcore to various systems of age verification. They generated huge traffic and, correspondingly, could earn money by showing banner advertisements. Trying to find a prospective market for online advertisement in Russia, Delitsyn set out to discover analogues to Playboy on the Russian net. And he failed! Instead, he found out a striking correlation between sex, humour and literature on the Russian Internet.

> Apparently, at the present moment, the closest analogue to Playboy Magazine for the Russian reader is the game server Hussar Club, under whose banner are assembled jokes from Verner, limericks, Manin's bout rimes, works by Tolkienists, jokes about Lieutenant Rzhevski and other entertainments both innocent and "adult". According to my data, currently the most lively Russian entertainment pages are the collections of jokes by Dmitri Verner and Konstantin Okrainets. Russian sex... seriously funny! (*Russkij sex... anekdot, da I tol'ko!*)

Initially, the audience of the site consisted mostly of Russians living abroad. *Jokes from Russia* became a part of their daily reading along with the Moshkov Library; their leading motivation was the 'lack of [Russian] reading in the real life' (Verner, 2003). It may also be argued that national humour is one of the most powerful means of maintaining national identity. Although there is a vast area of international jokes, many jokes retain national specifics. To understand a joke is often impossible without knowing the cultural context. However, when asked if he considers *Jokes from Russia* as a way of national self-preservation, Verner modestly replied, 'Not only my web site, but the Russian Internet as a whole helps self-preservation' (Govorun, 2002). The predominance of users from abroad was a common trait of the early Russian Internet. With the growth of the Internet in metropolis, the structure of the audience has changed. Thus, in 2002, Russia together with CIS countries provided about 75 percent of visitors to *Jokes* web site. Half of the visitors were from Russia and a half of these were from Moscow. US held the second place followed by Ukraine, Israel and Germany. Overall, the geography of visitors included more than 120 countries, giving an idea about the distribution of the Russian diaspora over the globe (WashProFile, 2002).

Verner's web site changed its status and affiliation several times. In November 1996, *Jokes from Russia* became a part of Chertovy Kulichki[55], a newly born Russian entertainment portal located in the US and uniting numerous authors' web sites. In June 1997, *Jokes* moved to Russia and joined the pool of content projects sponsored by Cityline/NetSkate, a Moscow-based company. The web site was redesigned in an orange gamut by Artemy Lebedev who also improved Verner's "home-bred design". In 2000, *Jokes from Russia* were sold to MemoNet, a division of Gusinsky's media holding Media-Most with specialization in Internet content projects. (Interestingly, Verner found out about the deal post factum.) However, soon the Russian government expropriated Gusinsky's media empire. Gusinsky was arrested, forced to give up part of his property to the state and then escaped from Russia. *Jokes from Russia* responded with the anonymous satirical poem "The Bridge that the Goose built"[56] which became extremely popular and oftquoted by the media. *Jokes* then went independent again – this time, however, not as an amateur web page but as a full-fledged commercial enterprise.[57]

In the following review of commercial side of *Jokes*, I rely upon Verner's (2005) explanations that he gave me in an e-mail interview. At the beginning, the

---

[55] http://www.kulichki.com/anekdot
[56] http://www.anekdot.ru/an/an0105/c010518.html. *Most* in Russian means "bridge"; and Gusinsky's surname is derived from *gus*, "goose".
[57] See the principal dates in *Jokes'* history from 1995 to 2002 at http://anekdot.ru/7let.html

project had no commercial component at all and it was maintained by Verner alone. Kulichki provided free hosting and technical support. Kulichki's programmer Leonid Umantsev wrote the first script for online voting. Cityline (and later Netskate) registered the domain name anekdot.ru for *Jokes* and paid Verner $40 per issue. Business with MemoNet went well for some time; there were big plans for the development of the project. But then Media-Most collapsed; Verner and his programmer did not receive salary for several months, and problems with the hosting arose. Verner moved to commercial hosting with the Masterhost Company and began to sell advertising space on his own. In September 2001, he signed a contract with VGTRK (All-Russia State Television and Radio Company) according to which they received exclusive rights for ad placement on the *Jokes* web site. From this money, Verner paid for hosting, programmer work and upgraded hardware. The contract ended in December 2004. Since early 2005, *Jokes from Russia* is an independent enterprise: the web site has a business manager, a marketing manager and a publicity agent who promise to bring it to a new level of revenue. The display of advertisements is the only source of generating revenue. It remains to be seen how profitable it can be.

7.6 From collecting the old to creating the new

In his article *Jokes from Russia and folklore of the Internet Age*, Verner (2003) made a scrupulous analysis of the interrelation between the oral folklore tradition, his web site as a collection and simultaneously a creative laboratory of humour, and the media. In what follows, I rely upon this text.

By 1997, when the Internet in Russia started to grow rapidly, the *Jokes* site already contained several thousand jokes. All of the most popular, commonly used jokes had been already told and published. The fresh issues included only the newest or relatively rare jokes which had not appeared in the "first thousand jokes". Therefore, novices who came to the web site for the first time generally saw jokes they never heard before. Impressed, they hurried to share new jokes with their friends who had no Internet access. Many people recollect that time exactly in this way: 'I went to the web site to make a show in front of my friends later on.' Anekdot.ru, therefore, not only played the role of folklore collector, but it also complemented the way of its traditional distribution by word of mouth. However, the spread of the Internet led to the situation when having asked a question 'Do you know this new joke?' one could hear more and more frequently 'Did you read it at Anekdot.ru?' It became boring to share jokes knowing that they all are gathered in one place. 'We ceased to tell jokes in company,' many people confessed. The enormous size of the collection practically guarantees that all circulating jokes have been already collected. Tens of thousands of visitors assure that fresh, newly born jokes would appear on the site very quickly. The probability that one can tell a joke which has not already appeared at Anekdoty from Russia has become vanishingly small. Mr. Parker aka Maxim Kononenko characterized Verner, as 'an astronomer who alone destroyed the culture of Russian jokes. Now jokes are not told. They are read at Anekdot.ru'[58]. Verner argues back that it is an exaggeration; 90 percent of the Russian population are ignorant about Anekdot.ru. However, it has an impact even on those who have no Internet access.

This is so because *Jokes from Russia* serve as an inexhaustible source for Russian media. First, at an early stage of the development of the Russian Internet when there was little news; online jokes were their partial substitute. As Verner (2003) once remarked, 'There was no other daily Russian news besides jokes until December 24, 1996 when Anton Nosik's The Evening Internet was launched.' The equation of jokes with news may seem funny, but considering the topical nature of many jokes which provide immediate reaction to actual events, it has some grounds. Of course, the interrelation between events, news coverage and jokes is more complex. As Verner (2001) explains,

---

[58] http://www.livejournal.com/users/mrparker/271372.html

If something important is happening in the world, then people first go to news web sites to receive as much information as possible about the event. Then when good jokes appear on this topic and it is quoted in media with a link to *Jokes from Russia*, then new visitors come to us. For example, after the events of August 1998, when we published special issues of "crisis jokes", CNN published a brief article "Russians make fun of crisis" and people rushed from CNN to our site.

What is more important, fresh jokes, stories and aphorisms from Anekdot.ru are being reprinted by hundreds of newspapers and magazines in and outside Russia, retold on the radio by presenters and DJs, included in TV humorists' programmes. At the same time, "jokes from the media" are re-posted to the web site. This "circulation of humour in nature", notes Verner (2003), differs from the traditional, oral way of its diffusion.

In the first years the site gathered folklore that existed outside the Net and independently of the Net. Over time, anekdot.ru has evolved from a site collecting existing folklore to the place of its birth, a "centre of crystallization" of a new folklore. Many people willing to laugh at a good joke do not visit anekdot.ru every day or they do not visit the site at all, often even declaratively. This is quite normal: an ordinary person cannot endure such a quantity of texts, most of which are not interesting for him personally. And here comes the mechanism of "friendly filtration" acting on the Internet practically in the same way as in "offline life". In guestbooks, forums, LiveJournal I often see fresh jokes from anekdot.ru with commentaries: 'Just received by e-mail', 'Told in ICQ today', etc. This person does not visit the site himself; but what has been sent or told by friends – that's a horse of a different colour! Since anekdot.ru accumulates everything, for a particular person the percentage of funny there may be small. But a friend is a friend

274

because you laugh together at the same thing, and every circle of people can find at the site what they like.

The diffusion of texts on the Internet has both common traits with oral folklore and differences. Verner summarized these as follows:

Similarities:

1. Viral-like transmission. Along with personal transmission (e-mail, ICQ), texts also spread in the common information space wandering from one site to another.

2. Spontaneity based on personal interest and selection. As in common life people tell only those jokes they liked, so on the Internet a person would send to an acquaintance only what he personally had found funny.

3. The high diffusion rate. Everybody knows classical (pre-Internet) jokes about the speed of diffusion of jokes. On the Net, jokes spread even faster.

4. The loss of authorship. As in the oral retelling of a joke, nobody normally cites its author, so in the circulation of jokes on the Internet they often lose their ascription.

Differences:

1. The Internet allows for easily copying and resending that which is difficult or impossible to retell. This gives birth to a new genre of jokes "for reading only".

2. In many cases, on the Internet, it is easier to recollect the name of the original author than in oral folklore. As Verner puts it, 'We have all the moves written down.' If a person who had invented a joke sent it to anekdot.ru, there is a registration record on the site of when he did so and under what name. However this joke would spread on the Internet later on, whatever media would copy it, the time of its first appearance and the name (or pseudonym) of the author is easy to find out.

7.7 The sources of jokes

After five and a half years, there have been 55,000 jokes published at Anekdot.ru (about 150,000 if you count variants and repetitions.),. It might seem that replenishment is impossible – new jokes do not appear by the dozen every day; however, the collection continues to grow. Verner (2003) lists several major sources for this growth.

The first source is *author's jokes*. Not all of them would be retold by people and become real folklore. However, for the author it is a good opportunity to test his creation on the public and to see the reaction.

The second source is *translated jokes*. Many visitors to Jokes from Russia live outside Russia and, when they hear or read a good joke, they translate it and post to the web site. Some of the jokes are international; others, translated literally, retain their couleur locale; yet others are russified and adapted to the reality of Russian life. As Verner point out, many of translated jokes receive a high rating at the site; some of them become folklore and after some time return to the site in a transformed, totally russified form.

The third source of new jokes is *direct reaction to significant Russian and foreign news*. Every event that touches people's feelings provokes a flow of jokes and the more important is the event, the more powerful is this stream.

The August 1998 crisis, the war in Yugoslavia, Yeltsin's resignation, the closure of NTV by the state – all these events produced special issues. The terrorist acts in US on September 11 provoked a real outbreak. People responded with jokes to sport events (Winter Olympiad and Work Soccer Championship) as well as to tragic news (Nord-Ost seizure; shuttle breakdown). The war in Iraq produced 30 special issues. As Verner (2003) says,

> Sometimes bitter, often cynical, mostly not funny at all, these texts, however, have represented the events and people's reaction to them no worse than the media. In the absence of censorship or any political

276

engagement, *Jokes from Russia* help to understand what is going on in the country and in the world.

Verner published a few special issues of jokes about the terrorist acts of September 11 in the US. He confessed that he had hesitated deciding whether to publish these jokes or not. He wavered between three options: to keep publishing normal issues as if nothing had happened, to shut down the site, or to make a special issue immediately. He chose the latter.

> I was struck by the immediacy of reaction and its mass character. There had been no such response in all of the site's history. And then I made my mind up to publish all these texts right now, in the same order that they came. It seems to me that this should be known and understood as well. No selection was possible. I don't think any of these jokes is funny. (Leibov and Verner, 2001)

The publication provoked a wave of indignation – on the site and beyond. A certain Alex Fridland, PhD, sent letters to University of Kentucky as well as to NASA complaining that Verner used university computers and his working time to disseminate anti-American propaganda (Anni, 2002). However, in spite of the anti-American spirit of the majority of the jokes, The September 11 Digital Archive sponsored by Alfred Sloan Foundation and Smithsonian Institute included these texts and the concomitant discussion at anekdot.ru into its archive.

Verner has been often accused that he publishes material that is morally and aesthetically unacceptable. His policy of the total lack of the censorship has sometimes provoked insults and threats against his web site and him personally, especially when jokes touched on such sensitive topics as terror and death. But occasionally it has been interpreted in a more balanced way. Thus, somebody wrote in *Jokes'* guestbook after the 9-11 special issues (Anni, 2002):

Who said that Anekdot.ru is an entertainment site? This is a chronicle of recent history. And Verner is a truthful Nestor[59] who would not throw out a word from it.

On September 17, a commentary to the jokes about September 11 appeared on the web site written in transliteration by a Russian woman who had worked on the 72nd floor of one of twin towers and managed to save her life. She concluded her message with the following words:

> Verner! Guys! Thanks for the silly jokes, even for evil ones! There's no need for tears, they wouldn't help; we'll cry ourselves, if we wish, when the shock is over. These jokes, they are useful, even now. They won't harm the dead, and they really help us, who are alive. So publish, read, laugh, I do it as well. And if I want, if I can and I do so, then all others may do so as well.
> ... I'VE SURVIVED AND I'M LAUGHING – LAUGH WITH ME. I have the right to allow you. This is OK, honestly.
>
> Anya

7.8 Jokes and stories

During the first year, Verner collected only "traditional" jokes which have no authorship and which passed the test of oral retelling. Author's jokes as well as author's anecdotal evidence from life were not included. However, with the growth of the site's popularity, the visitors began sending, along with traditional jokes, many "real stories", accounts of true anecdotal events. Sometimes they were really amazing; it would be a pity to lose them, and Verner began to include them in regular issues of jokes. This, in its turn, provoked a chain reaction, more texts of this genre were being sent, and in September 1997 Verner began to make weekly issues of "real stories". There was a plenty of material; users started demanding to

---

[59] An Old-Russian chronicler of the 11th and the early 12th century, a monk of Kievo-Pechersky Monastery, who wrote the Story of Former Years (*Povest' vremennyx let*), the first all-Russian chronicle code.

have issues of the stories daily, which finally occurred on January 1, 1998. A month later, new sections were introduced – those of *aphorisms* (phrases) and *rhymes* (short funny poems). When artists, both professional and amateur, began to send their drawings, this resulted in the launch of the *caricature* section. The role of the users in the evolution of *Jokes* web site has been extremely high. All of new sections that appeared after jokes, emerged unplanned, under the influence of the materials posted to the site and the expressed wish of the users.

Over time, the relative "weight" of the sections within the site has changed, and a shift from jokes to stories occurred. The story section is not homogeneous; it consists of at least three main groups.

The first group is folklore stories in the proper sense, transmitted from one person to another. The most popular have been posted to the site dozens of times, and in order to increase the effect the storyteller often identifies himself as the story's witness or claims that it occurred with his close acquaintances. Some of these stories were in use in the pre-Internet époque, and some can be traced back to the depth of ages.

The second group is authentic accounts of events that the storyteller really witnessed. The best of them tend naturally to move into the first group and begin their own life, independent of the original storyteller.

The third group includes author's short stories, usually fiction (but not always) disguised as a narrative about real events.

One of the favourite activities of the site's visitors is debates about the authenticity of the story. Often the truth is in between: the tale is based on a real occurrence but is enhanced by the storyteller.

The popularity of stories in comparison with jokes is continuously growing. This can be seen from both the statistics of visits by sections and the grades put down by readers. From July 1999, a system of grades is active on the site from '-2' (terrible) to '+2' (excellent). The averaged grade shows the degree of success of a given text with the audience.

	Jokes	Stories
1999	84.3	93.0
2000	80.8	92.9
2001	74.8	91.8
2002	68.5	91.5
2003	59.4	87.8
2004	57.9	87.3

Table 3. The percentage of jokes and stories positively graded by users.
Data source: Verner (2003) and private communication.

The percentage of jokes with averaged positive response has quickly decreased and dropped by a factor of almost one and a half. Verner (2003) points out that this can be explained by the fact that the share of classic jokes has decreased and more and more "attempts at jokes" or the "raw material" for jokes has appeared. A small decrease in positively graded stories, he believes, has resulted not so much from the deterioration of their quality by rather from the increased exactingness of the audience, accustomed to the high quality of the materials in this section. The contrast between jokes and stories becomes even more striking if you analyze the relative quality of the most successful texts with the average grade higher than +1.0. According to Verner's data, the number of such stories exceeded the number of such jokes by 3 times in 1999, 4 times in 2000, 7 times in 2001, 10 times in 2002, and 14 times in 2003.

Many of the stories' authors are people with authentic literary abilities. However, most of them are known only by their pseudonyms. The stories section seems practically inexhaustible: something interesting has happened with any person at least once. The policy of Anekdot.ru to publish everything guarantees that no message will be lost. Even if the text is boring and unconvincing it will be published nevertheless, if only in the "additional" section. If the editor overlooked a really interesting text and included it in the "additional" section, the readers grading texts in this section would "raise" it into a "readers' top ten".

7.9 Users' participation and collaboration

While the core staff of Anekdot.ru has always consisted of Verner alone, at various stages other people were involved in the project on a voluntary basis. Verner's first assistant, who compiled "second tens" from "repeating jokes" since 1997, was Aleksei Tolkachev, a Russian programmer living in the US, known also as the first Russian LiveJournal user (see chapter 6). Then Arieh Edelstein joined the project in 1998. He began as a compiler of stories issues and then edited the aphorism and poetry sections. In late 1998, a literary Salon was launched on Anekdot.ru, edited by Galya Anni (Parfenov, 2000). Since 2005, when *Jokes* became an independent enterprise, they have a paid staff. However, *Jokes from Russia* would be impossible without users' contribution.

First, users have provided the lion's share of material published on *Jokes* – not only jokes in the proper sense but also stories, poems, caricatures and megabytes of discussion. Second, users have influenced and sometimes determined the ways of the site's development.

In the beginning Verner collected jokes from outside sources; later on the majority of jokes were sent to him by e-mail. When in the late 1996 the web site was redesigned, an interactive form appeared enabling users to post jokes. At the same time the Discussion club was opened to discuss the censorship issue[60]. These innovations were significant since they gave users an opportunity to become co-producers rather than passive readers of the web site. Discussions in the Discussion club and, since September 1998, in the "Book of complaints and suggestions", in

---

[60] http://anekdot.ru/d0.html

which the most active and concerned part of the audience participated, have influenced the further evolution of the web site.

As is the case with folklore, the authors of jokes and stories at Anekdot.ru usually remain anonymous or hide themselves under nicknames and pseudonyms. The most successful authors are known under the name such as Philipp, Cadet Bigler, Vadim, Mikhail, Allure, and Rocketeer. All of them get no material reward for their creative work and invent new jokes "for the art sake'" A reporter from one Moscow newspaper got in touch (through Verner) with three of these authors (Lyamina, 2004). She found out that two of them were lecturers at universities and the third was lieutenant colonel; one lived in Paris, two others in Moscow. Their ages were 37, 48 and 50. All of them had a good consensus that the best reward for their work is when they hear jokes they created from their friends. However, it is considered bad form to admit one's own authorship. The authors of jokes believe that authorship kills the joke. Verner himself confessed elsewhere that he invented a few jokes which received high grades from the readers. He was very proud of it but he also refused to reveal which jokes these were. Such is the nature of true folklore, the people's creativity. What is important is the thing itself, not authorship or copyright.

7.10 Creator's motivation and character traits

Although the users' contribution cannot be overestimated, *Jokes from Russia* would not become what they are without the insight, enthusiasm and daily work of its originator. In this section we shall consider the motivation that has driven Dima Verner all these years in his work on its creation. We shall also touch upon his personal qualities which made possible this ongoing creative process.

Verner liked to read jokes and read them every day in the relcom.humor news group in mid-1990s. However, soon he found out that were many repetitions and irrelevant discussions. Sergei Naumov published from time to time selected jokes from this group on his page *Dazhdbog's Grandsons* (Verner knew about its existence from there) but Verner wanted daily issues. Since there was no such page, he decided to make it himself. In his own words (Verner, 2005), his initial motivation was curiosity, the interest in the subject, the desire to make something which did not exist.

At that time most Russian web pages had an English-language version (this tradition remained in the following years as well: thus, in 1997, the home pages of Rambler and Rambler's Top 100[61], a Russian search engine and a catalogue, were in English). Verner decided to make a web site in which would be no words in English; the Latin script was used only in his e-mail address. Later on, it turned out that *Jokes from Russia* was the first Russian web site updated daily. But then he did not think about it and he had no motivation to be the first.

Moreover, he felt shy for his passion for such an insignificant thing as jokes. He showed his web site to a few friends; their judgements were critical: 'half of the jokes are old stuff; three fourths are not funny, etc.' It was then when he decided that he would collect not "good" jokes but all jokes without exception and selection. A new motivation began to operate: to provide a complete picture of Russian life through jokes. Verner (1996) clearly formulated this principle in his note devoted to the first anniversary of *Jokes* in which he pointed out that it is the lack of subjective selection and the completeness of the collection that makes it a mirror of contemporary Russian society and a valuable source of raw material for researchers. He decidedly resisted when his collection was presented as "Jokes from Verner" emphasizing its transpersonal and national nature (Verner, 1998). The scientific objectivity and impersonality, natural for an astrophysicist, became a foundation of Verner's jokes collection and one of his personal motivations.

---

[61] http://web.archive.org/web/19970327091534/www.rambler.ru/top100/

Figure 10. Dima Verner. Photo by Eugene Gorny (2005).

However, he had to overcome a psychological barrier before presenting his site to the world. It is only after four months of daily issues that he decided to send the link to *Jokes* to Alex Farber who maintained in Germany a popular web site *Russian Literature on the Internet* and only in response to Farber's appeal to the audience to send links. After Farber put the link to *Jokes*, the site's traffic drastically increased. Now, when Verner missed a day, people sent him messages 'what happened; where is the new issue?' Thus a new motivation developed – a responsibility to the audience. This increased even more after *Jokes* moved to *Chertovy Kulichki*,[62] and a means of feedback was introduced. The response from the audience was generally very positive. Verner found out that many people needed his web site. As he wrote in his article published in the last issue of *Zhurnal.ru* (Verner, 1998),

---

[62] http://www.kulichki.com/anekdot

284

How does the working day begin for an employee of a St Petersburg commercial bank and a secretary of the Moscow office of a Western company, a post-graduate at the University of Ohio and a system programmer in London, a visiting professor in Tokyo and a Russian engineer in a small town in Southern Korea? They sit down at their computer, look through their e-mails and open a fresh issue of *Jokes from Russia*. A few thousand people in fifty countries throughout the world do the same.

This provided Verner additional motivation to develop his project.

When Rambler's Top 100 was launched in March 1997 to measure the popularity of web sites on the Russian Internet, Verner decided to participate "for the sport of it". Emulation, competition with others – which Kroeber (1944) considered the main moving force of the development of "cultural configuration" – entered the scene. By the end of March, *Jokes from Russia* took the first place in the rating and held it for more than a year.

In May 1997 Verner experienced a personal crisis. Moreover, he began to feel that the web site distracted him from his main work. At the beginning, he spent about 15 minutes to make an issue: it was enough to scan through fresh news group's articles, copy jokes and paste them in a file (Exler, 2003). Now he spent 3 to 4 hour daily (WashProFile, 2002; Lyamina, 2004) and the work on the *Jokes* tend to devour all its time if he did not control himself enough. He discovered that his head is busy not with science but with *Jokes from Russia*. He decided to discontinue the project and wrote about his decision to Valera Kolpakov, the chief of Kulichki. Kolpakov posted an announcement to the Hussar Club's mailing list that he was looking for a replacement for Verner. To this list was subscribed Anton Nosik, who wrote *The Evening Internet* on Cityline. As the result, in a few days Verner received a call from Cityline and he was asked to continue the project for money. The material stimulus, Verner accepts, was a powerful argument –

especially for his family which was extremely dissatisfied that he spent his time and energy for such rubbish as jokes.

In June 1, 1997 *Jokes from Russia* moved to a new server and obtained the domain name anekdot.ru registered by Cityline. From this day on, there was not a single break in Verner's work; the web site has been updated every day without breaks for holidays and weekends – regardless of his journeys from one country to another, illnesses, etc. Once Verner published an issue in the morning, had an operation under general anaesthetic in the afternoon and posted a new issue next morning. I remember that when I met Verner in Moscow in 2002 in one of the O.G.I. restaurants and we had a nice evening surrounded by exalted girls talking, joking and drinking beer and vodka, I was struck by the fact that he was going home to make a new issue of jokes. And he did so. He is a really strong man; all I managed to do after the evening with Verner is to get back home by taxi. Next morning, I found myself lying on the bed in my coat and shoes with all the lights on! Persistence, stubbornness and passion constitute the basis for one more of Verner's motivations: "To see how long I can stand!"

Next is the motive of recognition and fame. Verner has gained recognition among both the Internet audience and professionals. He was listed as one of the three most famous figures on the Russian Internet in the Celebrities of the Russian Internet online survey in 1999 and 2000. In 2004, he was ranked the sixth in the Magnificent Twenty list of the persons who made the most significant contribution to the development of the Russian Internet. *Jokes from Russia* had won the title "Humorous web site of the year" three years in a row (2001, 2002 and 2003) in POTOP (Russian Top) online contest. Beyond the Internet, Verner's personal fame is less widespread because the Russian media tend to quote jokes from his website without references. However, articles about *Jokes from Russia* and interviews with Verner have appeared in such popular publications as Izvestia, Vechernyaya Moskva, Komsomolskaya Pravda, Moskovsky Komsomolets, Zhurnal.ru, Mir

Internet, etc.; he has been often invited to speak on the radio and television.[63] Ridiculous situations happened as well. Verner (2005) tells about one of them:

> In Lexington, Kentucky, I lived for some time on campus where many Russian members of the University rented apartments and we spent a lot of time together. Once my Kentuckian friends went for a holiday to Moscow and there, while visiting someone, mentioned my name. The host's children, when they heard it, first could not believe and then called their friends to look at the "people who knew Dima Verner". For them I was a mythological, legendary figure. It made a strong impression on my American friends: they knew that I made a humorous web site but they did not suspect that it was so popular in Russia.

But for Verner (2005) it provided one more motivation: the involvement in Russian life and the feeling that Russia needs him.

> It's already the fifteenth year that I have been working abroad. On the Internet, I don't feel that I lost contact with the motherland; my web site is a part of Runet, it lives by the life of Russia and it influences it (both directly and indirectly – because the site's materials are being republished by the biggest Russian newspapers and magazines, broadcast on the television and radio). In other words, *Jokes from Russia* is my participation in Russian life, my work for Russia.

Verner case clearly shows that the motivation for creativity on the Internet (as well as in other domains) is a complex mixture and includes both intrinsic and extrinsic elements. It also has its dynamics – the specific weight of different elements changes over time. Let us summarize particular motivations mentioned by Verner:

- curiosity, interest in the subject, love, pure joy of doing what one likes to do

---

[63] See the list of these publications and broadcasts at http://www.anekdot.ru/interview.html.

- the desire to produce something new, which has not existed before;
- responsibility to the audience, their support, the feeling of usefulness of the site to people;
- scientific motivation: an attempt to gather the most complete collection of contemporary folklore, to trace social processes and psychological moods in society (response to actual events; voting for jokes and stories); working for the idea;
- involvement in Russian life, working for Russia;
- material reward (extrinsic motivation);
- passion and emulation; testing one's own abilities;
- perfectionism, a desire to do something as well as possible;
- popularity and fame; recognition of the audience and peers.

Like most Runet creators, Verner started working from a pure love, interest and the pleasure of doing what he liked; then, when he began to spend more and more time on this work it gradually became his main activity, and the issue of material reward arose. The combination of intrinsic and extrinsic motivations (see section 2.2.2 of chapter 2) is typical in the later stages of a creative activity. However, the actual structure of motivation is much more complex; it consists of a variety of elements ranging from the practical and utilitarian to the most abstract and immaterial. It may be assumed that the actual set of motivational elements varies from one creator to another but it is the complexity of motivation which enables them to keep working and developing their creative projects.

I asked Verner if his personal qualities, in his view, have played a decisive role in the fact that he began and is still working on the *Jokes* project. He replied with a joke – that it has been the mixture of German pedantry and Russian disorganization (*bezalabernost'*). The first means that one carries what one began to its conclusion and the second that one carries to conclusion not what one began, but something completely different. The serious answer is that to work so many years without any breaks one needs to have responsibility, patience and perseverance.

The creative process includes both pleasure and hard work. As Verner points out, at the beginning it was a pure pleasure and fun to develop the *Jokes* web site; now it is mostly hard work but there are moments that bring about a great satisfaction. Another question was what his work on the project gives to him in the sense of self-actualization and self-appraisal. He replied that he has been a successful astrophysicist, the author of several dozen scientific articles, four of which have a citation index higher than 100. However, he felt that he missed something. This something was Russia which he missed in America. Now the web site he created has more than a half million visitors per month, and he feels that he makes a difference.

Let us generalize what has been said. Public recognition of a creative work is essential because, if the creative work is about producing change in the world, then it is mostly made through its reception and influence upon minds and feelings of the audience. Creativity is producing a value which is accepted by a society. The significance of creative contribution is measured by the number of people considering it valuable as well as by the time span in which its value is recognized. *Jokes from Russia*, with its ten-year history and more that a half million visitors monthly is undeniably a successful creative work. The basis of this success has been talent, one-pointed concentration, perseverance and daily work. If on the societal plane it led to producing a socially recognized cultural value, then on the personal plane it led to creative self-realization, a feeling of fulfilled duty and growing material well-being.

7.11 Individual and collective creativity

Jokes from Russia illustrate the principle common for many successful web sites. Their development and public recognition presuppose two main components. First, a creator or charismatic leader who sets the form, its initial content, shows by his example how it can be used and builds up an infrastructure enabling participation of others. Second, the others, that is, the active users who are given the opportunity to realize their own creative potential and who become co-producers of the project by contributing content, suggesting ways of its improvement and influencing its development. Both components are necessary: it is difficult to create a really big thing alone, participants are needed; on the other hand, the mass left on its own usually cannot find the point of force application and needs a leader who sets the vector. The correlation between the two components may vary but their interplay is essential.

There are projects in which the creator, after discovering a successful form of the organization of the masses, switches the process to automatic mode (for instance, giving users a means of self-publishing) or to semi-automatic mode (moderation by assistants or volunteers). Verner (2005) admits that he tried to reduce his direct participation in *Jokes* for several times: for example, to get rid of the "editor's top ten" of jokes and stories and replace them by those selected by readers' voting. But observers and friends told him that it makes the web site more mediocre and faceless. Therefore, Verner argues, one of the reasons for the lasting popularity of *Jokes form Russia* is the feel of its hand-made nature, the daily personal contribution of the editor. One more important element of its success, he continues, is its total openness and the constant feedback. Verner, as the editor-in-chief, responds to endless e-mails and comments of the readers, trying to answer all, even the most difficult questions – an unthinkable situation for 'normal' entertainment web sites, let alone serious publications. Finally, if the majority of commercial projects cannot afford to publish something which can be harmful to its immediate success, Anekdot.ru does it regularly. As Verner (2005) put it, 'For me, the principle is more important than the immediate commercial component. In a long-term perspective it leads to more solid success because it creates a reputation.'

7.12. Conclusion

As I have outlined in this chapter, the web site *Jokes from Russia* contains the most comprehensive collection of urban folklore which had circulation in the Russian language before the époque of the Internet. It has deeply influenced the process of diffusion of folklore and facilitated creation of new folklore. It is a web site created by a private person living abroad "just for fun"', which became one of the most visited web site on the Russian Internet. Not only was the first Russian web site updated daily, it is probably the only web site in the world updated daily by the same person for more than ten years of which eight years were without any breaks (a fact worthy of the Guinness Book of Records). But it could not succeed without the active contribution of users, who became its co-authors and the audience of the Russians worldwide, who are its grateful readers. The lack of censorship and subjective selection supplemented by multilevel sorting of the texts by readers allow adequately representing the picture of the modern daily life of the Russians. Thus, a one-person creation gave voice to the joking and laughing masses and became an "encyclopedia of Russian life" with all its turmoil and painful problems. *Jokes from Russia* is also a mirror of Russian psyche inasmuch as it reflects humorist reactions of the people to all kinds of domestic and international events. The comprehensive and constantly updated online collection of Russian humor promotes a cultural consolidation of the Russians all over the world and serves an active factor of Russian culture.

Chapter 8

CONCLUSIONS

8.1 Introduction

The study makes a distinct contribution to the body of knowledge through an original investigation and testing of ideas found in previous research. The contribution is made on theoretical, factual and methodological levels.

On the theoretical level, the study develops the concept of Internet creativity as production and communication of cultural values in the online environment. As shown in chapter 2, the concept of Internet creativity has not been consistently used in the previous research which focused upon particular forms and aspects of creativity on the Internet. The lack of a common conceptual framework resulted in the incommensurability of findings and a parochial compartmentalization of knowledge. The operational construct of Internet creativity introduced in this study allows developing a unifying approach which can cover a wide range of seemingly unrelated phenomena and reveal regularities which could not be grasped by other approaches. The concept of Internet creativity has emerged as the result of the generalization of findings obtained by empirical research into various forms and practices on the Russian Internet, in which creativity can be identified as a key element. The case studies prove the validity of this approach by applying it to diverse aspects of Russian Internet culture.

This study also contributes to ongoing debates about how historical experience and cultural identity influence the uses and interpretations of communication technologies. It argues that the Internet as a space of cultural production, communication and exchange of values is connected to wider historical and cultural contexts. The study argues that the uniqueness of the Russian civilization and culture accounts for the specificity of the Russian Internet in comparison with the English-language segment of the Internet.

On the factual level, the study introduces material concerning the historical development of the Russian Internet, including both primary and secondary sources, most of which were previously unavailable for English-language scholarship. The analysis of this factual evidence resulted in the development of interpretive theories concerning the dynamics of historical change on the Russian Internet and the interrelationship between a national culture and Internet culture. The sources and factual evidence upon which the study is based can be also used by other researchers of Russian culture and history even if they may disagree with the author's generalizations or approach the material with a different research problem or methodology.

On the methodological level, the study develops an innovative approach by combining methods of history and creativity research in a single methodological framework. Although the historical approach has proved its usefulness and validity in both technological and cultural histories of the Internet, history is a relatively unusual methodology in the field of Internet studies. The application of creativity research methods in Internet studies is even rarer. However, the application of these methods to the study of Internet culture in its historical development may be useful and fruitful. This project justifies these methods as the key methods for the study of dimensions, forms, actors and dynamics of Internet creativity. The attempted methodological synthesis is a response to the challenge which the Internet provides for traditional disciplines. The study thus contributes to ongoing debates of methodological adequacy and to the negotiation of new research strategies in Internet studies. The theoretical and methodological framework developed in the study can provide a model for further research.

8.2 Conclusions about research questions

The following sections summarise the findings for research questions stated in section 1.2 of chapter 1. The research questions have been explained and justified within the context of prior research examined in chapter 2 and explored in chapters 4-7 using the methodology outlined in chapter 3. Specific research questions have been developed and answered in case studies and the emerging interpretive theories have been used to find a solution to the research problem.

8.2.1 Internet as a domain of creativity

The study follows a communicative approach to creativity which defines creativity as production and communication of cultural value (Negus and Pickering, 2004), i.e. of a creative work which is accepted as both novel and useful in a given sociocultural context. Internet creativity is defined as creativity which takes place in the Internet domain and which uses Internet technologies to produce, publish and distribute creative works. The operational construct of Internet creativity allows approaching phenomena which otherwise would be perceived as separate and incomparable using a common theoretical and methodological framework.

The results of the study give grounds to assert the Internet as a specific domain of creativity (Gardner, 1983; Csikszentmihalyi, 1999) comparable with such recognized domains as art, literature, music, philosophy, science and technology. Its specificity is defined, firstly, by material, functional and communicative properties of the medium and, secondly, by skills and understandings required for producing significant innovations in this medium. At the same time, the Internet, as well as other new media, absorbs and transforms domains of creativity that existed separately before. Thus, art, literature, mass media and technology in the Internet domain can be considered as its microdomains (Karmiloff-Smith, 1992), while the Internet, in respect of the latter, serves as a meta-medium or a post-medium (Manovich, 2001).

294

8.2.2 How is Internet creativity distributed among users and who are the actors of creativity on the Russian Internet?

The research shows that creating new forms and content is an important aspect of Internet users' activity. Moreover, users/producers of the Internet (Castells, 2001) governed primarily by intrinsic motivation (Amabile, 1996) contribute to the technocultural systems on many levels thus defining its historical shaping and development. The creative processes on the Russian Internet have been analysed in case studies devoted to the development of online media, an artistic genre, an online community and a humorous web site. The findings of the research corroborate the validity of the co-construction of users and technologies approaches (Oudshoorn, 2003) which consider users as active agents of technocultural change rather than passive consumers of a technology.

It is noteworthy that the Russian Internet from the very beginning developed as a private enterprise. In the Western countries, the Internet was founded (and owned) by the state and the first commercial provider (world.std.com) emerged not earlier than in 1990 (Zakon, 2005). By contrast, in the late Soviet Russia which was synonymous with anti-market, the state played virtually no role in the emergence of the Internet; Internet technology and infrastructure were developed by private commercial companies such as Relcom and Demos. This fact startled foreign observers who could not understand how privately owned and operated networks can exist outside of the Soviet state's social control (Rohozinsky, 1999).

If private companies created the necessary technological prerequisites for the development of the Internet in Russia, the foundation of the Russian Internet as a cultural phenomenon was created by private persons – a relatively small group of young people who studied or worked in the West (in the US, Israel, Germany, Estonia, Finland, etc.) They had a high level of creative drive and passion, access to the new technology and spare time to play with it. They considered the internet as a hobby and a toy rather than work. These individuals felt their unity and energetically collaborated, making up a kind of creative cyber-élite, as opposed to passive users. In a few years, they managed to create successful projects of different types (media, online services, digital libraries, art, and entertainment). Through continuous experimentation, they developed forms and patterns that were socially accepted and became commonly used and reproduced by others. Most of the creators of Russian Internet culture overcame their marginal social status, moved to Moscow as the financial and cultural centre of Russia, reached high social positions and converted their creative experience into money and fame. At present, some of them continue to work in the Internet field as experts or top-level managers. Some left and turned their energy to other realms, such as media, politics, business, education and research.

As in other domains, the distribution of Internet creativity is uneven. The number of users/producers is less that the number of users/consumers; and the number of those who have introduced a significant creative contribution into the Internet is even less. The approximate number of persons who have been credited as the creative élite of the Russian Internet and whose names can be found throughout this study is just two or three dozens. This fact corroborates the findings of sociology and creativity research about a highly skewed distribution of creative contributions in any given domain formulated by Lotka (1926) and Price (1963) and generalized by Simonton (1984) as a law of historiometry. Moreover, most of the members of the "Runet élite" were early Internet adopters. This corresponds to "Matthew's effect" (Merton, 1968) or the principle of cumulative advantage (Simonton, 1984).

The typology of users/producers who create Internet culture proposed by Castells (2001) includes techno-élites, hackers, virtual communitarians and Internet entrepreneurs. This typology was described and discussed in section 2.6 of chapter 2. All these types can be found on the Russian Internet. However, there is a significant deviation of the Russian Internet culture from this model. The eminent users/producers of the Russian Internet have been journalists, writers, philosophers and artists rather than scientists or programmers. Even if they had had a

296

background in the natural or computer sciences, their creative contribution concerned literature, ideology or art. Sometimes it has been supplemented with business and/or organizational activity which increased their leadership. However, it can be argued that on the Russian Internet the cultural aspect has generally prevailed over the technical one.

8.2.3 What is the correlation between individual and collective creativity on the Russian Internet?

There is a dialectical relationship between personal and group creativity. Various forms of creative collaboration pervade the Internet; however, in most cases there are informal leaders who inspire others by example and define the patterns of creative behaviour. The case studies have revealed this process in various sub-domains of the Russian Internet.

8.2.4 Which historical and cultural factors have influenced creative production on the Russian Internet?

The analysis of the case studies reveals recurrent themes, topics and regularities. It can be concluded that the Russian Internet culture follows fractal logic: its structure is characterized by recursiveness and self-similarity, where the same regularities are found in different segments and on different levels. It has been found that the forms or Internet creativity are influenced by the historical background, the sociocultural context and the cultural identity of the users. The main findings concerning the interrelationships between Russian culture and Russian Internet culture are summarized below.

The technological inferiority of Russia in comparison to the West and socio-economic factors such as the population's low income level and undeveloped payment systems have influenced the uses and interpretations of the Internet in Russia. Whereas in developed countries the Internet quickly became available to the majority of the population and developed into an extension of everyday life, in Russia it has long remained a luxury, "an acquisition of the élite" (Delitsyn, 2005) and been used predominantly as a tool for professional activities or self-expression and play.

The authoritative political regime and the underdevelopment of the civic institutes in Russia led to the fact that the function of the public sphere has been traditionally performed by literature. The traditional literature centricity of Russian culture has been reflected on the Russian Internet. The first Russian sites were devoted to literature and culture. The first Russian interactive projects were literary games such as *Bouts-rimés*. The first consolidation of the Russian net community occurred around the online literary contest *Teneta*. The most popular web site on the Russian Internet for a long time was *Jokes from Russia* to which users contributed jokes, real-life stories and other literary genres. Writers are among the most popular users in the Russian-language segment of LiveJournal. The high role of literature and the abundance of literary-related web sites is a striking characteristic of the Russian Internet which seems to have no direct parallel in the West (Schmidt, 2002b).

The lack of respect for private property, including intellectual property, found in Russian culture, is in strong contrast to the West where private property is a cornerstone of the social system (Maly, 2003). The lax attitude to intellectual property and copyright accounts for the high level of computer piracy (BSA, 2003; McDonald, 2003; MPAA, 2003; MosNews, 2004), tacitly encouraged by the government and eloquently advocated by intellectuals. It also accounts for the flourishing of free online libraries unprecedented in the West because of copyright restrictions (Lessig, 2001; Vaidhyanathan, 2001). Virtually any book ever published in the Russian language can be found online and freely downloaded. The authors themselves encourage online publication of their work because it contributes to their popularity and hence to the growing sales of printed books. Some literary reputations in Russian have been made almost exclusively online. Victor Pelevin, one of the most popular authors in modern Russia, can serve an example. Unlike the West, writers' web sites normally include full texts of their work, not only excerpts and links to online bookshops where their books can be bought. However, no matter how deeply the disrespect for intellectual property and the tradition of samizdat may be rooted in Russian mentality, it might have been otherwise if free online libraries had not been established and developed on the Russian Internet since its very beginning, and if the creators of Russian Internet culture had not actively promoted the idea of free content (Gorny, 2000d). The tradition of free online libraries on the Russian Internet did not "naturally emerge" but resulted from practice, ideological struggle and establishing norms which were not evident from the outset. There have also been opposing trends which tried to introduce the Western attitude to copyright and to suppress the free circulation of literary texts on the Internet. The attempts at restricting the free flow of information for the sake of private commercial interests has provoked a strong resistance among the Russian users and generally failed so far.

Political authoritarianism in Russia resulted in the alienation of the population from both the government and the official media. Contrary to the conclusions of Western observers who relied mostly on secondary sources (Alexander, 2003), the Internet in Russia has not been subject to censorship (although the *fear* of censorship among the users has persisted throughout the entire Internet history in Russia). This led to the fact that the Internet in Russia has become a substitute for the public sphere – much the same way as Russian literature substituted for civic institutions during the previous époque. The case studies of Russian online media (chapter 4) and the Russian community on LiveJournal (chapter 6) have provided evidence in favour of this theoretical generalization.

8.3 Conclusions about the research problem

The findings disagree with the conclusions of the "everyday life" approach to the Internet which insists that the Internet is a mere extension of the "world we live in" (Robins 1996/2000) rather than a separate domain of cultural production. It was found that the Russian Internet is often perceived by its users in terms of an alternative space for social and cultural creativity. It is argued that the opposition between the offline and the online worlds, which was a key characteristic for early cyberculture, has been retained on the Russian Internet, although it has been transformed into the opposition between "official" Russia and "non-official" Russia. If the first is perceived as a realm of compulsion, censorship and alienation, then the Internet is perceived as a space of freedom, personal sovereignty and creativity. The Internet serves as a model and representation of "Russia-2" which has little in common with the politicized image of Russia imposed by the official media. The validity of the "everyday life" approach to the Russian Internet has proved to be limited. The emphasis on consumption and conformity to established patterns in rules found in this type of research should thus be supplemented by the study of resistance to the established order and social and cultural creativity.

It has been found that the creative processes on the Russian Internet are governed by two processes described by sociologists and anthropologists. These are imitation or adoption of innovation, and emulation, rivalry, the desire to surpass one's contemporaries. Imitation favours co-production of technology and cultural values and facilitates the continuity of culture (Tarde 1895). Emulation provides a powerful motive for creativity and accounts for the emergence of "cultural configurations" (Kroeber 1944) of creative people.

The dynamics of creative forms on the Russian Internet corroborates the model of literary evolution suggested by Tynyanov (1924/1977) as a sequence of automatisation and de-similarisation by contrast. This model accounts for continuity and discontinuity of experience and provides a link between creativity and history.

The findings are consistent with the historical approach to creativity which contends that novelty – one of the major elements in definitions of creativity – is derived from contrast with the immediate context and is produced by transformation of what was borrowed from the past. The types of transformation include the combination of the common elements into a singular structure, the

300

deformation of a habitual form and the shift of the function of constructive elements. The introduction of new elements and functions derived from the culture pool is yet another source of the development of a cultural form.

8.4 Implications for further research

The findings of this study can provide a reference point for further research into Russian Internet culture. Removing some limitations mentioned in sections 1.7 and 1.8 will provide opportunities for further research by broadening the thematic scope. This will allow introducing the topics which were included into the initial plan of this research but have not been investigated due to the narrowing of the research focus, although the relevant literature has been reviewed in section 2.5 and 2.6 of the literary review in order to develop the concept of Internet creativity. These topics include:

- Personality, motivation and experience of the creative persons who obtained eminence for their contribution to the Russian Internet's development.
- Imitation, emulation and interaction in creative processes on the Russian Internet.
- Technological innovations in Russian computer, telecommunications and Internet industries in broader economic, social and cultural contexts of the late Soviet and post-Soviet reality.
- The role of literature in the formation of the Russian Internet and the issues of Internet literature production, including literary contests, online literary games, digital libraries and archives and, finally, literary web sites publishing both traditional and experimental literature (net-literature, cyberliterature, etc.).
- Net art and other forms of Internet and media art in Russia.
- Russian online activism as a form of social creativity.

301

8.5 Implications for theory

This study has not only made a significant contribution to knowledge in the field of Internet studies as outlined in sections 8.2 and 8.3, but also has theoretical implications for the wider body of knowledge, including creativity research and Russian studies.

As was shown in chapter 2, creativity theories have not been used in Internet research although the latter has incorporated a wide range of theories and methods from both social sciences and humanities. This study attempts to compensate for this omission by applying concepts and methods of creativity research to the study of Internet culture. However imperfect this attempt may be, hopefully it can provide an example and stimulate further research into creative processes on the Internet using the theoretical and methodological tools of creativity research. This is deemed especially important taking into account the growing role of creativity in post-industrial society discussed in the section 2.3 of the chapter 2.

On the other hand, creativity researchers have not paid enough attention to the Internet as a new domain of creativity, restricting themselves to the study of more conventional domains. However, as this study shows, creativity is flourishing on the Internet; it has many aspects and forms and it is manifested on both personal and collective levels. The Internet provides rich opportunities for the study of the traditionally distinguished aspects of creativity such as the creative person, the creative process, the creative work and the creative environment. The case studies touch these topics but their scope is limited by both the material and the research questions. Hopefully, the integration of creativity research and Internet research developed in this study can inspire other researchers who will develop this approach even further and will apply it to a wide range of topics and questions.

The study also contributes to the field of Russian studies by introducing the Russian Internet as a meaningful formation which has a culture and history of its own. It argues that, on the one hand, Russian Internet culture is a part of Russian culture, i.e. that both share certain semiotic characteristics and patterns. Yet on the

302

other hand, it is a specific domain of cultural production and interaction having its own cultural leaders and governed by its own customs and unwritten rules. Russian Internet culture has traditionally opposed itself to "offline" culture including both official and non-official cultures. At the same time, there are many points of convergence between these cultural segments. The study investigates the interrelations, the interplay of similarities and differences between Russian Internet culture and others segments of Russian culture. It shows that Internet culture which has been generally ignored by researchers of Russian culture as something marginal, shallow and insignificant is actually a subject worthy of research.

REFERENCES

Abbate, J. (1999). *Inventing the Internet*. Cambridge, Mass.: The MIT Press.

Adamovich, M. (2000). Etot virtual'nyj mir: Sovremennaya russkaya proza v Internete: ee osobennosti i problemy. *Novy mir*, 4, <http://magazines.russ.ru/novyi_mi/2000/4/adamov.html>

Adler, A. (1956). *The individual psychology of Alfred Adler: A systematic presentation in selections from his writings*. New York: Basic Books.

Adler, A. and Wolfe, W. B. (1927). *Understanding human nature*. Garden City, N. Y: Garden City Pub. Co.

Aksenov, S. (2000). Vecher s Vernerom. *InterNet*, 24, <http://www.gagin.ru/internet/24/22.html>

alex_and_r (2004). *LiveJournal*, 02.06.2004, <http://www.livejournal.com/users/alex_and_r/155286.html>.

Alexander, M. (2003). "The Internet in Putin's Russia: Reinventing a Technology of Authoritarianism". *Department of Politics and International Relations, University of Oxford.* <http://www.psa.ac.uk/cps/003/marcus%0alexander.pdf>.

alliances <Boris Bazyma> (2004a). Empiricheskaya klassifikaciya tipov LJ pol'zovatelej. Chast' 1. *LiveJournal*, 25 March, <http://www.livejournal.com/community/cyberpsy/657.html>.

alliances <Boris Bazyma> (2004b). Empiricheskaya klassifikaciya tipov LJ pol'zovatelej. Chast' 2. *LiveJourna*, 26 March 2004, <http://www.livejournal.com/community/cyberpsy/1191.html>.

alliances <Boris Bazyma> (2004c). Empiricheskie formuly dlya opredeleniya svoego tipa. *LiveJournal*, 27 March 2004, <http://www.livejournal.com/community/cyberpsy/1415.html>.

altimate <Ksjushka> (2004). zhzhizn'. *LiveJournal*, 28.10.2004, <http://www.livejournal.com/users/altimate/49636.html>.

Amabile, T. M. (1983). *The social psychology of creativity*. New York: Springer-Verlag.

Amabile, T. M. (1996). *Creativity in context: update to the social psychology of creativity*. Boulder, Colo.; Oxford: Westview Press.

Amabile, T. M. and Collins, M. A. (1999). Motivation and creativity. In Sternberg, R. J. (Ed.) *Handbook of creativity*, (pp. 297-312). Cambridge: Cambridge University Press.

Andreyev, A. (2002). Webl' protiv hudla. *Fakel*, 3, pp. <http://www.fakel.org/art.php?id=20&art_id=232>

Androunas, E. (1993). *Soviet media in transition: structural and economic alternatives*. Westport, Conn.: Praeger.

Anisimov, V. (2002). "Tajna ZhZh Lexi Andreyeva". *Runet.ru.* <http://www.runet.ru/interview/1304.html>.

Anni, G. (2002, January 14). "Ya vyzhila i smeyus': Chernyj yumor kak lekarstvo ot straha". *Novaya Gazeta.* <http://2002.novayagazeta.ru/nomer/2002/02n/n02n-s25.shtml>.

another_kashin <Kashin> (2005). Bud'te bditel'ny. *LiveJournal*, 06.03.2005, <http://www.livejournal.com/users/another_kashin/1267911.html>.

Anthony, J. B. and Anthony, M. M. (1981). *The gifted and talented: a bibliography and resource guide*. Pittsfield, Mass: Berkshire Community Press.

Arasteh, A. R. and Arasteh, J. D. (1976). *Creativity in human development: an interpretive and annotated bibliography*. Cambridge, Mass.: Wiley.

Arieti, S. (1976). *Creativity: the magic synthesis*. New York: Basic Books.

Aronowitz, S. (Ed.) (1995). *Technoscience and Cyberculture: A Cultural Study*. London: Routledge.

Ashuratova, N. (1999a). "The Self-identification System"" <http://namniyas.velikanov.ru/ident/>.

Ashuratova, N. (1999b). "Enemy Processing System". <http://namniyas.velikhanov.ru/enemy/>.

avva <Anatoly Vorobey> (2004). Russkij ZhZh. *LiveJournal*, 4 February, <http://www.livejournal.com/users/avva/1096134.html>.

Babayev, M. (1995). Pensioner Mukhin v pautine Interneta. *Den za Dnem*, 6 October. <http://www.zhurnal.ru/staff/Mirza/muxin.htm>

Babayev, M. (1996). Mukhin on-line. *Den za Dnem*, 16 February. <http://www.zhurnal.ru/staff/Mirza/muxin2.htm>

Babayev, M. (1999). Apologiya khoumpejdzha. *Internet*, 14. <http://www.zhurnal.ru/staff/Mirza/apology.htm>.

Baer, J. (1993). *Creativity and divergent thinking: A task-specific approach.*, Hillsdale, NJ: Eribaum.

Bagdasarjan, N. <A.Nune> (2003). Slovo I delo, ili Zhizn' i smert'. (Zhivoj zhurnal slovami pisatelej. Vypusk 6), *Russkij zhurnal*. 18 June, <http://old.russ.ru/krug/0030718_nb.html>.

Baranov, V. S. and Nosachev, G. N. (1995). *Semiotika psikhicheskih zabolevanij*. Samara: Samar. gos. med. un-t, Kaf. psikhiatrii i psihoterapii.

Barbrook, R. (1998). "The hi-tech gift economy". *First Monday*. <http://www.firstmonday.dk/issues/issue3_12/barbrook/>.

Barbrook, R. and Cameron, A. (1997). "Kalifornijskaya ideologiya. (Translated into Russian by M. Nemtsov)". *Zhurnal.ru*. 4. <http://zhurnal.ru/4/calif0.htm>.

Barbrook, R. and Cameron, A. (2001). Californian Ideology. In Ludlow, P. (Ed.) *Crypto Anarchy, Cyberstates, and Pirate Utopias*, (pp. 363-387). Cambridge, Massachusets; London: The NIT Press.

Barlow, J. P. (1996). A Declaration of the Independence of Cyberspace. <http://www.eef.org/~barlow/Declaration-Final.html>

Barrett, E. (1992). *Sociomedia: multimedia, hypermedia, and the social construction of knowledge*. Cambridge, Mass.: MIT Press.

Barrett, E. (2001). Series Foreword. In Ludlow, P. (Ed.) *Crypto Anarchy, Cyberstates, and Pirate Utopias*, (p. XIII). Cambridge, Massachusets; London: The NIT Press.

Bavilsky, D. (2002a). Bes metafory (Katahreza #2: Ten', znaj svoe mesto!). *Russkij zhurnal.* <http://www.russ.ru/krug/20020304.html>.

Bavilsky, D. (2002b). Zhivoj kak zhizn': Katachreza #17: «Mitin zhurnal» #60 na fone «Zhivogo zhurnala» . *Russkij zhurnal.* 8 June, <http://old.russ.ru/krug/000708_bav.html>.

Beard, G. (1874). *Legal responsibility in old age.* New York: Russel.

Bell, D. (1973). *The Coming of Post-Industrial Society: A Venture in Social Forecasting.* New York.

Bell, D. (2001). *An Introduction to Cybercultures.* London - New York: Routledge.

Bell, D. and Kennedy, B. M. (2000). *The cybercultures reader.* London: Routledge.

Bell, D., Loader, B. D., Pleace, N. and Shuler, D. (2004). *Cyberculture: The key concepts.* London: Routledge.

Belsie, L. (1991). Technology thwarted coup leader success. *Christian Science Monitor,* 9.

Benedikt, M. (2000). Welcome to Cyberia: Notes on the anthropology of cyberculture. In Bell, D. and Kennedy, B. M. (Eds.) *The cybercultures reader,* (pp. 57-76). London: Routledge.

Bennis, W. G. and Biederman, P. W. (1997). *Organizing genius: the secrets of creative collaboration.* Reading, Mass.: Addison-Wesley.

Berdyaev, N. A. (1947). *The Russian Idea.* (Translated by R. M. French.), Geoffrey Bles, London.

Berdyaev, N. A. (1990). Russkaya ideya. Osnovnye problemy russkoj mysli XIX i nachala XX veka. *O Rossii i russkoj kul'ture: Filosofy russkogo posleoktyabr'skogo zarubezh'ya.* (pp. 43- 271) Moscow: Nauka.

Berger, P. L. and Luckmann, T. (1966). *The Social Construction of Reality: A Treatise in the Sociology of Knowledge.* Garden City, New York: Anchor Books.

Berk, E. and Devlin, J. (1991). *Hypertext/hypermedia handbook.* New York: Intertext Publications: McGraw-Hill.

Berners-Lee, T. (1997). "Realising the Full Potential of the Web". *World-Wide Web Consortium.* <http://www.w3.org/1998/02/Potential.html>.

bes (2005). *LiveJournal,* 01.03.2005, <http://www.livejournal.com/users/bes/240698.html>. Unavailable.

Bey, H. (1998). Information War. In Broadhurst, J. and Cassidy, E. J. (Eds.) *Virtual futures: Cyberotic, technology and post-human pragmatism,* (pp. 3-8). London - New York: Routledge.

Bijker, W. E. (1995). *Of bicycles, bakélites, and bulbs: toward a theory of sociotechnical change.* Cambridge, Mass.: MIT Press.

Bijker, W. E. and Law, J. (1992). *Shaping technology/building society: studies in sociotechnical change.* Cambridge, Mass.: MIT Press.

Bijker, W. E., Hughes, T. P. and Pinch, T. J. (1987). *The Social construction of technological systems: new directions in the sociology and history of technology.* Cambridge, Mass.: MIT Press.

Bloomberg, M. (1973). *Creativity: theory and research.* New Haven, Conn.: College & University Press 1973.

Boden, M. A. (1991). *The creative mind: Myth and mechanisms.* New York: Basic.

Boden, M. A. (1999). Computer Models of Creativity. In Sternberg, R. J. (Ed.) *Handbook of creativity*, (pp. 351-372). Cambridge: Cambridge University Press.

Bolter, J. D. (1991). *Writing Space: The Computer, Hypertext, and the History of Writing.* Hillsdale, NJ: Lawrence Erlbaum.

Bonnell, V. E. (1997). *Iconography of power: Soviet political posters under Lenin and Stalin.* Berkeley: University of California Press.

bopm <Prezident vselennoj v izgnanii> (2000). I am a legal alien. Nezatejlivye dni, *LiveJournal*, 7 October, <http://www.livejournal.com/users/bopm/00/10/7/> (18.09.005).

Bowles, A. (2006). The Teapots are Coming: the Changing Face of RuNet. In Schmidt, H., *et al.* (Eds.) *Control + Shift: Public and Private Usages of the Russian Internet,.* Norderstedt: Books on demand, 2006. (pp.21-33)

boyd, d. (2002). Faceted Id/entity: Managing Representation in a Digital World. *Media Arts and Sciences School of Architecture and Planning.* Cambridge, MA: Massachusetts Institute of Technology. <http://www.danah.org/papers/Thesis.FacetedIdentity.pdf>

Brackett, V. (2003). *Steve Jobs: computer genius of Apple.* Berkeley Heights, NJ: Enslow Publishers.

bradfitz <Brad Fitzpatrick> (2000). UTF-8. *LiveJournal News*, 14 April, <http://www.livejournal.com/users/news/54041.html>.

bradfitz <Brad Fitzpatrick> (2001). Good news! *LiveJournal News*, 4 November, <http://www.livejournal.com/users/news/48745.html>.

Brashares, A. (2001). *Linus Torvalds: software rebel.* Brookfield, Conn.: Twenty-First Century Books.

Bray, J. and Institution of Electrical, E. (2002). *Innovation and the Communications Revolution: From the Victorian Pioneers to Broadband Internet.* London: Institution of Electrical Engineers.

Brief, M. (1997). "The Internet Élite". <http://www.advancedtalent.com/About_Us/News/internetélite.pdf>.

Briggs, A. and Burke, P. (2002). *A social history of the media: from Gutenberg to the Internet.* Cambridge: Polity.

Brockman, J. (1996). *Digerati: encounters with the cyber élite.* San Francisco: HardWired : Distributed to the trade by Publishers Group West.

Brown, R. T. (1989). Creativity: what we are to measure? In Torrance, E. P., et al. (Eds.) *Handbook of creativity*, (pp. 3-32). New York; London: Plenum.

Brown, R. T. (1989). Creativity: what we are to measure? In Torrance, E. P., et al. (Eds.) *Handbook of creativity*, (pp. 3-32). New York; London: Plenum.

BSA (2003). *Global Software Piracy Study.* <www.bsa.org/globalstudy/2003_GSPS.pdf>

Bucher, H.-J. (2004). Is there a Chinese Internet? Intercultural investigation on the Internet in the People's Republic of China: Theoretical considerations and empirical results. In F. Sudweeks and C. Ess (Eds.), *Proceedings of the Fourth International Conference on Cultural Attitudes towards Technology and Communication.* Karlstad, Sweden, 7 June-1 July 004. Murdoch: Murdoch university, pp. 416-428.

Bukatman, S. (1995). "Virtual textuality".
<http://virtual.park.uga.edu/~hypertxt/bukatman.html>.

Burzhuaznyj zhurnal (2004). Vasha sekretarsha Lilu. *Burzhuaznyj zhurnal*, 13 March, <http://www.bj.ru/trends/004/3/13/658.html>.

Bush, V. (1945). As We May Think. *The Atlantic Monthly*, July.

Busse and Mansfield (1980). Theories of the creative process: A review and a perspective. *Journal of Creative Behavior*, **13**, 91-103.

buzhbumrlyastik <Apsyr Jekzjuskin> (2005). *LiveJournal*, <http://www.livejournal.com/users/buzhbumrlyastik/59908.html>.

Campbell, D. T. (1960). Blind variation and selective retention in creative thought as in other knowledge processes. *Psychological Review*, 67, pp. 380-400.

Castells, M. (1996). *The rise of the network society.* Malden, Mass.; Oxford: Blackwell.

Castells, M. (1997). *The power of identity.* Massachusetts ; Oxford: Blackwell.

Castells, M. (1998). *End of millennium.* Malden, Mass.: Blackwell.

Castells, M. (2001). *The Internet galaxy: reflections on the Internet, business, and society.* Oxford: Oxford University Press.

Castells, M. and Himanen, P. (2002). *The information society and the welfare state: the Finnish model.* Oxford: Oxford University Press.

Castells, M. and Kiselyova, E. (1995). *The Collapse of the Soviet Communism: The View from the Information Society.* Berkeley: University of California International and Area Studies Book Series.

Castells, M. and Kiselyova, E. (1998). *Rossiya i setevoe obshschestvo: Analiticheskoe issledovanie.* <http://www.socio.ru/wr/00-1/Castells.htm>

Certeau, M. de. (1988). *The Writing of History.* New York: Columbia University Press.

Chenitz, W. C. and Swanson, J. M. (1986). *From Practice to Grounded Theory.* Menlo Park CA: Addison-Wesley Publishing.

Chernov, A and Prostospichkin, E. (1997). Robot Sergej Datsyuk™, <http://rosd.org.ru>.

Clarke, R. (2001). "A brief History of the Internet in Australia".
<http://www.anu.edu.au/people/Roger.Clarke/II/OzIHist.html>.

Clarke, R. (2004). "Origins and Nature of the Internet in Australia".
<http://www.anu.edu.au/people/Roger.Clarke/II/OzI04.html>.

Clifford, J. and Marcus, G. E. (1986). *Writing Culture: The Poetics and Politics of Ethnography.* New York: University of California Press.

Cohen, L. M. (1989). A continuum of adaptive creative behavior. *Creativity Research Journal*, 2, 169-183.

Cohen, L. M. and Ambrose, D. (1999). Adaptation and Creativity. In Runco, M. A. and Pritzker, S. R. (Eds.) *Encyclopedia of Creativity,* vol. 1, (pp. 9-22). San Diego, Calif. ; London: Academic Press.

Colebrook, C. (1997). *New Literary Histories: New historicism and contemporary criticism.* Manchester: Manchester University Press.

Cook, A. (1988). *History writing.* New York: Cambridge University Press.

Cooley, C. H. (1969). *Sociology Theory and Social Research.* New York: A.M. Kelly.

Creswell, J. W. (1998). *Qualitative inquiry and research design: choosing among five traditions.* Thousand Oaks, Ca.: Sage.

Cropley, A. J. (1999). Definitions of Creativity, in: M. A. Runco and Pritzker, S. R. (Eds), *Encyclopedia of Creativity*, Vol. 1, pp. 511-524, San Diego, Calif. ; London: Academic Press.

Crutchfield, R. (1962). Conformity and creative thinking. In Gruber, G., *et al.* (Eds.) *Contemporary approaches to creative thinking*, (pp. 120-140). New York: Athrton.

Csikszentmihalyi, M. (1988). Society, culture, and person: a system view of creativity. In Sternberg, R. J. (Ed.) *The Nature of creativity : contemporary psychological perspectives*, (pp. 325-339). Cambridge: Cambridge University Press.

Csikszentmihalyi, M. (1996). *Creativity: Flow and the psychology of discovery and invention.* New York: HarperCollins.

Csikszentmihalyi, M. (1999). Implications of a System Perspective for the Study of Creativity. In Sternberg, R. J. (Ed.) *Handbook of creativity*, (pp. 313-325). Cambridge: Cambridge University Press.

Cummings, D., Watts, P., Evans, C., Dixon, R., Gulberg, H. and Starr, S. (2002). *The Internet: Brave New World?* London: Hodder and Stoughton / Institute of Ideas.

Curran, J. and Park, M.-J. (2000). *De-Westernizing media studies.* London: Routledge.

Currie, R. (1974). *Genius: An ideology in literature.* London: Chatto & Windus.

Cuypers, Stefan E. (2001). *Self-identity and personal autonomy: an analytical anthropology.* Ashgate New Critical Thinking in Philosophy. Aldershot; Burlington, USA: Ashgate.

Dahlstrom, W.G. Welsh, G.S. (1960). *An MMPI Handbook. A guide to use in clinical practice and research.* Minneapolis, University of Minnesota Press.

Datsyuk, S. (1997a). Skomorosh'i vol'nosti Kati Detkinoj: Predshestvenniki i prototipy. *Kul'turnye provokatsii.* <http://www.uis.kiev.ua/russian/win/~_xyz/kat_det.html>.

Datsyuk, S. (1997b). Shipy i rozy Mery Shelley. *Kulturnye provokatsii.* <http://www.uis.kiev.ua/russian/win/~_xyz/mary.html>.

Datsyuk, S. (1998a). Virtualografija robota "Sergejj Dacjuk". *Kul'turnye provokacii,* <http://www.uis.kiev.ua/russian/win/~_xyz/drobot.html>

Datsyuk, S. (1998b). Interaktivnaya depersonalizatsiya avtora: K probleme giperavtorstva - kazus "Robot Sergej Dacyuk". *Kul'turnye provokatsii.* <http://www.uis.kiev.ua/russian/win/~_xyz/depersonalisation.html>.

Davis, E. (1988). *Techgnosis: Myth, magic + mysticism in the age of information.* New York: Harmony Books.

Davis, G. (1999). Barriers to Creativity and Creative Attitudes. In Runco, M. A. and Pritzker, S. R. (Eds.) *Encyclopedia of Creativity,* vol. 1, (pp. 165-174). San Diego, Calif.; London: Academic Press.

Davis, S., Elin, L. and Reeher, G. (2002). *Click on democracy: the Internet's power to change political apathy into civic action.* Boulder, Colo.: Westview Press.

ddb <dmitry> (2003). Itogi. EXIT POLL pol'zovatelej ZhZh. *LiveJournal*, 8 December, <http://www.livejournal.com/users/ddb/375573.html>.

ddb <dmitry> (2004). exit poll zhzh-juzerov. *LiveJournal*, 15 March, <http://ddb.livejournal.com/004/03/15/>.

Debord, G. (1967). *La Société du Spectacle.* Paris: Editions Buchet-Chastel.

Delany, P. and Landow, G. P. (1991). *Hypermedia and literary studies.* Cambridge, Mass.: MIT Press.

Delitsyn, L. (1996). "Sex sells sex... i ne tol'ko". *Zhurnal.ru.* 3. <http://zhurnal.ru/3/delisex.htm>.

Delitsyn, L. (2005). *Diffuziya innovatsij i razvitie informacionno-kommunikatsionnykh tehnologij v Rossijskoj federatsii* (unpublished PhD thesis).

Denning, D. (2000). *Activism, Hacktivism, and Cyberterrorism: The Internet as a Tool for Influencing Foreign Policy.* Washington, D.C.: Georgtown University.

Dery, M. (1996). *Escape Velocity: Cyberculture at the End of the Century.* London: Hodder and Stoughton.

Detkina, K. (1997). Nablyudeniya KaDetkinoy. *Chertovy Kulichki.* <http://www.kulichki.com/kadet/index1.htm>.

Dibbel, J. (1993). A rape in cyberspace; or how an evil clown, a Haitian trickster spirit, two wizards, and a cast of dozen turned a database into a society. *Village Voice*, 21, pp. 36-42.

Dilthey, W. (1976). *Selected Writings.* Cambridge: Cambridge University Press.

dm_lihachev <Dima Likhachev> (2000). tipa ustal ja ignorirovat' zhanr przdravljalok ;). *LiveJournal*, 1 January, <http://www.livejournal.com/users/dm_lihachev/00/01/01/>.

Dray, W. H. (1964). *Philosophy of history.* Engelwood Cliffs, NJ: Prentice Hall, Inc.

e_neo <Vladimir Jakovlev> (2003). No 215. *LiveJournal*, 10.10.2003, <http://www.livejournal.com/users/e_neo/88315.html>.

Ellis, F. (1999). *From glasnost to the Internet: Russia's new infosphere.* New York: St. Martin's Press.

Ellule, J. (1967). *The Technological Society.* New York: Vintage Books.

Escobar, A. (2000). Welcome to Cyberia: Notes on the anthropology of cyberculture. In Bell, D. and Kennedy, B. M. (Eds.) *The cybercultures reader*, (pp. 57-76). London: Routledge.

Ess, C. and Sudweeks, F. (Eds.) (2001). *Culture, Technology, Communication: Towards an Intercultural Global Village.* Albany, NY: SUNY Press.

evan <Evan Martin> (2004a). preliminary language detection results. *LiveJournal*, January, <http://www.livejournal.com/community/lj_research/606.html>.

evan <Evan Martin> (2004b). language identification, another run. Comment. *LiveJournal*, 9 March, <http://www.livejournal.com/community/lj_research/5607.html?thread=34279#t3427>.

Exler, A. (2000). Zapiski zheny programmista: vystavka (okonchanie). *Exler.ru.* <http://www.exler.ru/ezhe/21-04-00.htm>.

Exler, A. (2003, November 18). "Dima Verner - prostye sekrety Anekdot.ru". *Hostinfo.* <http://hostinfo.ru/tree/internet/vip/content/verner/>.

Feist, Gregory J. (1999). Autonomy and Independence. *Encyclopedia of Creativity.* Editors Mark A. Runco, and Steven R. Pritzker, 157-63. Vol. 1. San Diego, Calif.; London: Academic Press.

Fekete, L. (2001). Rights, Rules, and Regulations in Cyberspace. *International Journal of Communications,* 1-2, pp. 73-103.

Fischer, G. (2002). Beyond 'Couch Potatoes': From Consumers to Designers and Active Contributors. *First Monday.* 7 (12). <http://firstmonday.org/issues/issue7_12/fischer/index.html>. (December 2002)

Fisher, D. H. (1971). *Historical Fallacies: Towards a Logic of Historical Thought.* London: Routledge & Kegan Paul.

Florida, R. L. (2002). *The rise of the creative class: and how it's transforming work, leisure, community and everyday life.* New York, NY: Basic Books.

Fox, K. (2005). *Watching the English: The hidden rules of English Behaviour.* London: Hodder & Stoughton.

Frankel, D. (1987). *The Post-Industrial Utopians.* Madison, WI.

Freeland, C. (2000). *Sale of the century: Russia's wild ride from communism to capitalism.* New York, N.Y: Crown Business.

Freeman, J., Butcher, H. J. and Christie, T. (1968). *Creativity: a selective review of research.* London: Society for Research into Higher Education Ltd.

Frei, M. (1999). O romane Mery Shelly i Persy Shelley "Pautina". *Znanie - sila,* 9-10, <http://www.znanie-sila.ru/online/issue_584.html>

French, L. (2001). *Internet pioneers: the cyber-élite.* Berkeley Heights, NJ: Enslow Publishers.

Freud, S. (1900). The Interpretation of Dreams. *SE* 4-5.

Freud, S. (1908). Creative Writers and Day-Dreaming. *SE* 9, 143-153.

Freud, S. (1910). Leonardo da Vinci and a Memory of his Childhood. *SE* 11, 59-137.

Freud, S. (1928) Dostoevsky and Parricide. *SE* 21, 175-196.

Frey, L. R. (Ed.) (2002). *New directions in group communication.* Thousand Oaks, Calif.: Sage Pub.

Fridman, Y. (1998). Dmitrij Vulis, Ph.D., i pol'zovatel' Krasnaya Shapochka. *Russkij Zhurnal.* <http://www.russ.ru/journal/netcult/98-08-18/fridmn.htm>

Fried, E. (1980). *The courage to change: from insight to self-innovation.* New York: Brunner/Mazel.

Gagin, A. (1998). Glasnost' + Network = Lyubov'. *Internet,* 8 (11), <http://inter.net.ru/11/32.html>.

Gan, S., Gomez, J. and Johannen, U. (2004). *Asian cyberactivism: freedom of expression and media censorship.* Bangkok: Friedrich Naumann Foundation, East and Southeast Asia Regional Office in association with Journalism and Media Studies Centre, Eliot Hall, University of Hong Kong.

311

Gardner, H. (1993). Seven creators of the modern era. In Brokman, J. (Ed.) *Creativity*, (pp. 28-47). New York: Sinom & Shuster.

Gardner, H. and Wolf, C. (1988). The fruits of asynchrony: Creativity from a psychological point of view. *Adolescent Psychiatry*, 15, pp. 105-123.

Garty, J. (2003). *Jeff Bezos: business genius of Amazon.com.* Berkeley Heights, NJ: Enslow Publishers.

Gashkova, E. M. (1997). Ot ser'eza simvolov k simvolicheskoj ser'eznosti (teatr i teatral'nost' v XX veke). *Metafizicheskie issledovaniya. Vypusk 5. Kul'tura. Al'manah Laboratorii Metafizicheskih Issledovanij pri Filosofskom fakul'tete SPbGU*, (pp. 85-95). SPb: SPbGU.

Gauntlett, D. (2000). *web.Studies: Rewiring Media Studies for the Digital Age.* London: Edward Arnold.

Gere, C. (2002). *Digital Culture.* Reaktion Books.

Gerovitch, S. (2002). *From newspeak to cyberspeak: a history of Soviet cybernetics.* Cambridge, Mass.: MIT Press.

Gibbs, J. (1999). *Gorbachev's glasnost: the Soviet media in the first phase of perestroika.* College Station: Texas A & M University Press.

Gillis, D. (1966). *Instant music: an experience in group creativity, for band, orchestra, or ensemble.* New York,: Frank Music Corp.

Glaser, B. G. and Strauss, A. (1967). *Discovery of Grounded Theory. Strategies for Qualitative Research.* New York: Sociology Press.

GlobalReach (2004). Global Internet Statistics (by Language). *GlobalReach.* <http://global-reach.biz/globstats/index.php3>.

Goffman, E. (1956). *The presentation of self in everyday life.* Edinburgh: University of Edinburgh, Social Sciences Research Centre.

Goggin, G. and McLelland, M. (2006). "Internationalizing Internet Studies: A Workshop and Edited Volume Convened by Gerard Goggin, University of Sydney and Mark McLelland, University of Wollongong". *Capstrans Conferences and Workshops 2006.* <http://www.capstrans.edu.au/resources/conferences/2006/conferences-2006-inet-studies.html>.

Goldman, M. I. (2003). *The piratization of Russia: Russian reform goes awry.* New York: Routledge.

Goralik, L. (2001). Comment on this. *Russkij zhurnal*, 30 March, <http://old.russ.ru/netcult/0010330_goralik.html>.

Gorny, E. (1996a). "Obraschenie k deyatelyam Russkogo Veba (an e-mail message of 7 July 1996)". *Moshkov Library.* <http://lib.ru/WEBMASTER/gorny.txt>.

Gorny, E. (1996b). "ZR - FAQ: Voprosy, kotorye chasto zadayut o Zhurnal.Ru, i otvety na nikh (November 18)". *Zhurnal.ru.* <http://web.archive.org/web/19970525082201/www.zhurnal.ru/zr-faq.htm>.

Gorny, E. (1999a). Amphiblestronic Fragments. *Zhurnal.ru*, <http://www.zhurnal.ru/staff/gorny/english/amphiblestron.html>

Gorny, E. (1999b). O gestbukakh. *Internet*, 15.
<http://www.zhurnal.ru/staff/gorny/texts/gb.html>

Gorny, E. (1999c). Elita.Ru: kto rulit? *Internet Magazine*. 13.
<http://gagin.ru/internet/13/1.html>.

Gorny, E. (2000a). Evgenij Gornyj: (re)konstruktsiya virtual'noj lichnosti.
<http://www.zhurnal.ru/staff/gorny/ego_net.html>

Gorny, E. (2000b). Internet i kiberkul'tura v Rossii: Sbornik statej.
<http://www.zhurnal.ru/staff/gorny/texts/icr_contents.html>

Gorny, E. (2000c). Letopis' russkogo Interneta: 1990-1999.
<http://www.zhurnal.ru/staff/gorny/texts/ru_let/>

Gorny, E. (2000d). Problema kopirajta v russkoj Seti: bitva za "Goluboe salo". *Internet*, 17.
<http://zhurnal.ru/staff/gorny/texts/salo.html>

Gorny, E. (2001a). *Chuzhie slova [The words of others].*
<http://www.litera.ru/slova/gorny/chslova/show.cgi>

Gorny, E. (2001b), *Simvolicheskie situatsii [Symbolic situations].*
<http://www.russ.ru/netcult/20010731_gorny.html>

Gorny, E. (2003a). "Dynamics of Creativity in Russian Cyberculture." Presentation at the Oxford Internet Institute. <http://www.zhurnal.ru/staff/gorny/english/dynamics_of_creativity-oii2003.html>.

Gorny, E. (2003b). "The virtual self: Self-presentation and self-knowledge on the Internet (A working draft)." <http://zhurnal.ru/staff/gorny/english/self/>.

Gorny, E. (2003c). Poslednij lytdybr: Predislovie k "Elektricheskim snam" Romana Leibova. *Setevaja slovesnost'*, 1 June, <http://www.litera.ru/slova/gorny/e-sny.html>.

Gorny, E. (2004a). Ontologiya virtual'noj lichnosti. *Bytie i yazyk: Sb. statej po materialam mezhdunarodnoj konferencii*, (pp. 78-88). Novosibirsk.

Gorny, E. (2004b). "Russian LiveJournal: National specifics in the development of a virtual community". *Russian-Cyberspace.org*. <http://www.ruhr-uni-bochum.de/russ-cyb/library/texts/en/gorny_rlj.pdf>.

Gorny, E. (2004c). Zhivoj zhurnal v zerkale russkoj pressy. Vebografija i citatnik. Version 4.0, 3 April, <http://www.zhurnal.ru/staff/gorny/texts/lj/rlj_biblio.html>.

Gorny, E. and Itzkovich, D. (1997). "Internet kak nravstvennaya problema" in InterNovosti, issue 9-1 of 21.02.1997. *Zhurnal.ru*. <http://www.zhurnal.ru/news/drevnosti/news9-1.htm>.

Gorny, E. and Pil'schikov, I. (2000). Lotman v vospominaniyakh sovremennika. *Novaya russkaya kniga*, 1, pp. 75-76.

Gorny, E. and Sherman, A. (1999). Infokratiya, ili Konets otchuzhdennogo truda. *Guelman.ru*.
<http://www.guelman.ru/vse_obozrev/gorniy.html>

Gorny, E., Litvinov, V. and Pil'schikov, I. (2004). Russkaya virtual'naya biblioteka. *Mir PK. Disk. Lyudi i komp'yutery. Istoriya v litsakh*, **12**.
<http://www.rvb.ru/about/meta/2004_12_mir_pk.htm>

Goryunova, O. (2005). Ob odnoj nenormativnoj subkul'ture russkoyazychnoj seti: Udaff.com kak "kontrkul'turnoe", mejnstrimnoe, fol'klornoe hudozhestvennoe techenie. *Russian-Cyberspace.org*. <http://www.ruhr-uni-bochum.de/russ-cyb/library/seminars/Russian_Cyberspace/info/info_og.htm>.

Gorz, A. (1982). *Farewell to the Working Class: An Essay on Post-Industrial Socialism.* London.

Gottlieb, N. and McLelland, M. J. (Eds.) (2002). *Japanese cybercultures.* New York; London: RoutledgeCurzon.

Govorun, M. (2002). Anekdot bez borody. *Mir Internet,* 5 (68), pp. <http://www.iworld.ru/magazine/index.phtml?do=show_article&p=9978168>

Gowan, J. C. (1961). *An annotated bibliography on the academically talented.* Washington: National Education Association Project on the Academically Talented Student.

Gowan, J. C. (1965). *Annotated bibliography on creativity & giftedness.* Northridge, Calif.: San Fernando Valley State College Foundation.

Greenblatt, S. (1988). *Marvelous Possessions: The Wonder of the New World, Oxford, Clarendon Press.* Oxford: Clarendon Press.

Greene, R. (2004). *Internet art.* New York, N.Y.: Thames & Hudson.

Gromov, G. (2002). *Roads and Crossroads of Internet History.* <http://www.netvalley.com/cgi-bin/intval/net_history.pl?chapter=1>

Gruber, H. (1999). Evolving Systems Approach. In Runco, M. A. and Pritzker, S. R. (Eds.) *Encyclopedia of creativity,* vol. 1, (pp. 689-693). San Diego, Calif. ; London: Academic Press.

Gruber, H. E. and Wallace, D. B. (1999). The Case Study method and Evolving Systems Approach for Understanding Unique Creative People at Work. In Sternberg, R. J. (Ed.) *Handbook of creativity,* (pp. 93-115). Cambridge: Cambridge University Press 1999.

Guilford, J. P. (1954). *Psychometric methods.* New York: McGraw-Hill.

Gumilev, L. N. (1990). *Ethnogenesis and the Biosphere.* Moscow: Progress.

Gundry, L. K. and LaMantia, L. (2001). *Breakthrough teams for breakneck times: unlocking the genius of creative collaboration.* Chicago: Dearborn Trade.

Gusejnov, G. (2000). Zametki k antropologii russkogo Interneta: osobennosti yazyka i literatury setevyh lyudej. *Novoe literaturnoe obozrenie,* **43**. <http://magazines.russ.ru/nlo/2000/43/main8.html>

Gusejnov, G. (2005). Berloga vebloga. Vvedenie v erraticheskuyu semantiku. <http://www.speakrus.ru/gg/microprosa_erratica-1.htm>.

Hafner, K. and Markoff, J. (1991). *Cyberpunk: Outlaws and Hackers on the Computer Frontier.* New York: Simon and Schuster.

Hage, J., and Ch. H. Powers. (1992). *Post-Industrial Lives: Roles and Relationships in the 21st Century.* Newbury Park, CA.

Hamilton, P. (1996). *Historicism.* London: Routledge.

Haraway, D. (1991). A Cyborg Manifesto: Science, Technology, and Socialist-Feminism in the Late Twentieth Century. *Simians, Cyborgs, and Women: The Reinvention of Nature*, (pp. 149-181). New York: Routledge.

Hargrove, R. A. (1998). *Mastering the art of creative collaboration.* New York: McGraw-Hill.

Harrington, D. M. (1990). The ecology of human creativity: A psychological perspective. In Runko, M. A. and Albert, R. S. (Eds.) *Theories of creativity*, (pp. 134-169). Newburry Park, CA: Sage Publications.

Harrington, D. M. (1999). Conditions and Settings/Environment. In Runco, M. A. and Pritzker, S. R. (Eds.) *Encyclopedia of Creativity,* vol. 1, (pp. 232-340). San Diego, Calif.; London: Academic Press.

Hayward, P. (1990). Technology and (trans)formation of culture. In Hayward, P. (Ed.) *Culture, technology & creativity in the late twentieth century*, (pp. 1-12). London: Libbey.

Heim, M. (1987). *Electric language: a philosophical study of word processing.* New Haven: Yale University Press.

Henderson, H. (2002). *Pioneers of the Internet.* San Diego, CA: Lucent Books.

Henle, M. (1962). The birth and death of ideas. In Gruber, G., *et al.* (Eds.) *Contemporary approaches to creative thinking*, (pp. 31-62). New York: Athrton.

Hennessey, B. and Amabile, T. (1999). Consensual Assessment. In Runco, M. A. and Pritzker, S. R. (Eds.) *Encyclopedia of Creativity,* vol. 1, (pp. 347-359). San Diego, Calif.; London: Academic Press.

Herman, A. and Swiss, T. (2000). *The World Wide Web and Contemporary Cultural Theory: Magic, Metaphor, Power.* New York: Routledge.

Herring, S. C., Scheidt, L. A., Wright, E., Bonus S. (2003). Beyond the Unusual: Weblogs as Genre. Paper presented at the Association of Internet Researchers "Broadening the Band" Conference. Toronto, Canada, Oct. 16-19, 003, <http://www.blogninja.com/air.abs.doc>.

Hill, S. (1988). *Tragedy of technology: Human liberation versus domination.* New York: Vintage.

Himanen, P. (2001). *The Hacker Ethic and the Spirit of the Information Age.* London: Vintage.

Hine, C. (2000). *Virtual ethnography.* London; Thousand Oaks, Calif.: SAGE.

Hiraoka, L. S. (2004). *Underwriting the internet: how technical advances, financial engineering, and entrepreneurial genius are building the information highway.* Armonk, N.Y.: M.E. Sharpe, Inc.

Hixson, W. L. (1997). *Parting the curtain: propaganda, culture and the Cold War, 1945-1961.* Houndmills: Macmillan.

Ho, K. C., Kluver, R. and Yang, C. C. (Eds.) (2003). *Asia.com: Asia Encounters the Internet.* New York: Routledge.

Hoffman, D. E. (2001). *The oligarchs: wealth and power in the new Russia.* New York: Public Affairs.

Hogan, B. T. and Hogan, M. (1991). *Computer Networking in the USSR: Technology, Uses and Social Effects.* Syracuse: School of Information Studies, Syracuse University.

holmogorova_v (2005). Untitled. *LiveJournal*, 14.06.2005,
<http://www.livejournal.com/users/holmogorova_v/400347.html>.

Honig, B. and Rostain, A. (2003). *Creative collaboration: Simple tools for inspired teamwork.*
Menlo Park, CA: Crisp Publicatons.

Huberman, A. M. and Miles, M. B. (1994). Data management and analysis methods. In Denzin,
N. K. and Lincoln, Y. S. (Eds.) *Handbook of qualitative research*, (pp. 428-444). Thousand Oaks,
CA: Sage.

Hunsinger, J. (2005). Towards a Transdisciplinary Internet Research. *The Information Society*,
21, 4, pp. 277-279.

Ignacio, E. N. (2005). *Building Diaspora: Filipino Cultural Community Formation on the
Internet.* New Brunswick, NJ: Rutgers University Press.

Ihde, D. and Selinger, E. (Eds.) (2003). *Chasing Technoscience: Matrix for Materiality.*
Bloomington: Indiana University Press.

Inglehart, R. (1977). *The silent revolution: changing values and political styles among Western
publics.* Princeton, N.J.: Princeton University Press.

Inozemtsev, V. L. (2000). *Sovremennoe postindustrial'noe obshchestvo: priroda,
protivorechiya, perspektivy.* Moscow: Logos.

Intelros (2004). Rejting rossijskih sociogumanitarnyh myslitelej: 100 veduschih pozicij. God
2003/2004. *Intelros.ru.* <http://www.intelros.ru/rating/rating_1.htm>.

Ioffe, D. (2005). Konstantin K. Kuz'minskij kak monumental'naya Konstanta Russkogo
poeticheskogo Avangarda. *Setevaya Slovesnost.* <http://www.litera.ru/slova/ioffe/kuzm.html>.

Ivanov, D. (2004). Maksim Kononenko: "Vse dolzhno povtoryat'sya - v etom zalog uspeha".
Istoriya Interneta v Rossii. <http://www.nethistory.ru/memories/1076437726.html>.

Ivanov, I. (2004). Intellektual'nye "seti" virtual'nykh prostranstv. *Rossijskie vesti.* 41 (1749).
<http://www.rosvesty.ru/numbers/1749/socium/a_02.phtml>.

Jacobson, L. (1992). *CyberArts: exploring art & technology.* San Francisco: Miller Freeman.

James, W. (1908). *Talks to teaches on psychology.* New York: Henry Holt.

Jausovec, N. (1994). Metacognition in creative problem solving. In Runco, M. (Ed.) *Problem
finding, problem solving, and creativity*, (pp. 77-95). Norwood, NJ: Ablex.

John-Steiner, V. (2000). *Creative collaboration.* Oxford ; New York: Oxford University Press.

Jones, S. (Ed.) (1997). *Virtual culture: identity and communication in cybersociety.* London;
Thousand Oaks: Sage Publications.

Jones, S. (Ed.) (1999). *Doing Internet Research: Critical Issues and Methods for Examining the
Net.* London: SAGE.

Jordan, T. and Taylor, P. A. (2004). *Hacktivism and cyberwars: rebels with a cause?* New
York, N.Y.: Routledge.

Jorgensen, D. L. (1989). *Participant Observation: A Methodology for Human Studies.* London:
SAGE publications.

Kalathil, S. and Boas, T. C. (2003). *Open Networks, Closed Regimes: The Impact of the
Internet on Authoritarian Rule.* Washington, D.C: Carnegie Endowment for International Peace.

Kalkinen, G. (2002). Vesti dnevnik snova stalo modno: „Zhivoj zhurnal" kak sreda obitanija kollektivnogo razuma. *Nezavisimaja gazeta*, 73 (627), 12 April, <http://www.ng.ru/internet/002-04-12/11_notebook.html>.

Kapustin, I. (1998). Razoblachenie Il'i Kapustina. *Sumasshedshij dom Mistera Parkera.* <http://parker.paragraph.ru/archive/apr98.htm>.

Karttaavi, T. (2004). "History of Internet in Finland". <http://www.isoc.fi/internet/internethistory_finland.html>.

Karush, S. (1998, September 25). wwwhat's online in russia. *The St. Petersburg Times, #402.* < http://www.sptimesrussia.com/secur/402/features/online.htm>

Kas'yanova, K. (2003). *O russkom nacional'nom haraktere.* Moskva: Akademicheskij proekt.

Kataevy, brothers. (1999-2000). Bodalsya telenok so stulom. *Ezhe.ru.* <http://www.ezhe.ru/15/index.shtml>.

Katz, R. L. (1988). *The Information Society: An International Perspective.* New York.

Kelly, K. (2002). The Web Runs on Love, Not Greed. *Wall Street Journal*, 04.01.2002, <http://www.scripting.com/stories/2002/01/09/kevinKellyTheWebRunsOnLoveNotGreed.html>

Kelly, O. (1996). *Digital creativity.* London: Caloust Gulbenkian Foundation.

Kenez, P. (1985). *The birth of the propaganda state: Soviet methods of mass mobilization, 1917-1929.* Cambridge [Cambridgeshire]; New York: Cambridge University Press.

khodorkovsky <Mihail Hodorkovskij> (2005). Zapiski molokom. *LiveJournal*, <http://www.livejournal.com/users/khodorkovsky/>.

Kiesler, S., B. (1997). *Culture of the internet.* Mahwah, N.J.: Lawrence Erlbaum Associates.

Kireev, O. (2006). *Povarennaya kniga media-aktivista.* Moscow: Ultra.Kultura. <http://macb.media-activist.ru/>.

Kirton, M. J. (1994). *Adaptors and innovators: styles of creativity and problem solving.* London: Routledge 1994.

Kitchner, K. S. (1983). Cognition, metacognition, and epistemic cognition: A three-level model of cognitive processing. *Human Development*, 26, pp. 222-232.

Klebnikov, P. (2000). *Godfather of the Kremlin: Boris Berezovsky and the looting of Russia.* New York: Harcourt.

Koestler, A. (1964). *The act of creation.* New York: Macmillan.

Kolko, B. E., Nakamura, L. and Rodman, G. (1999). *Race in cyberspace.* London: Routledge.

Kozhemyakin, V. (2003, October 22). "Aleksandr Nevzorov: 'U nas takie ushi – lapsha soskal'zyvaet!'". *Argumenty i fakty.* 43 (1200). http://www.aif.ru/online/aif/1200/18_01. (2004, 2 December)

Kozinets, R. V. (1998). On Netnography: Initial Reflections on Consumer Research Investigations of Cyberculture, *Advances in Consumer Research*, **25**, 366-371.

Kroeber, A. L. (1944). *Configurations of cultural growth.* Berkeley: University of California Press.

Krotov, N. (1993). Aleksandr Nevzorov. *Obozrevatel*, 21 (25), <http://www.nasledie.ru/oboz/N21_93/21_06.htm>

Kuipers, G. "The Social Construction of Digital Danger: Debating, Diffusing and Inflating the Moral Dangers of Online Humor and Pornography in the Netherlands and the United States," *New Media & Society* 8, no. 3 (2006): 379-400.

Kuritsyn, V. (1999). Kuritsyn Weekly, 13, 25 March. *Guelman.ru.* <http://www.guelman.ru/slava/archive/25-03-99.htm>

Kuznetsov, S. (1998). Pust' poka vsego chetyre kopii (Samizdat bez politiki). *Russkij zhurnal.* <http://www.russ.ru/journal/netcult/98-04-14/kuznets.htm>.

Kuznetsov, S. (2000). Poganka sovremennogo iskusstva. *Internet.ru.* <http://www.internet.ru/index.php?itemid=52>.

Kuznetsov, S. (2001). NasNet: vypusk 44. *Russkij zhurnal*, 4 May, <http://old.russ.ru/netcult/nasnet/0010504.html>.

Kuznetsov, S. (2004). *Oschupyvaya slona. Zametki po istorii russkogo Interneta.* Moscow: Novoe literaturnoe obozrenie.

Landow, G. (1997). *Hypertext 2.0: The Convergence of Contemporary Critical Theory and Technology.* Johns Hopkins University Press.

Langdon, C. and Manners, D. (2001). *Digerati Glitterati: high-tech heroes.* Chichester ; New York, N.Y.: Wiley.

Lanham, R. (1993). *The Electronic Word: Democracy, Technology and the Arts.* Chicago, IL: University of Chicago Press.

Lebedev, A. (2005). Personal communication with the author, 26.04.2005. Moscow.

Ledeneva, A. (1998). *Russia's economy of favours: blat, networking, and informal exchanges.* New York: Cambridge University Press.

Ledeneva, A. (2001). *Unwritten rules: how Russia really works.* Centre for European Reform.

Ledeneva, A., Kurkchiyan, M. (Eds.) (2000). *Economic crime in Russia.* Hague, London: Kluwer Law International.

Legewie, H. and Schervier-Legewie, B. (2004). "Anselm Strauss interviewed by Heiner Legewie and Barbara Schervier-Legewie". *Forum: Qualitative Social Research On-line Journal.* 5(3). <http://www.qualitative-research.net/fqs-texte/3-04/04-3-22-e.htm>.

Leibov, R. (1997). Yazyk risuet Internet. *Internet.* 4. <http://www.gagin.ru/internet/4/9.html>.

Leibov, R. (1998). Bessrochnaya ssylka. Vypusk ot 9 marta 1998 goda. *Russkij zhurnal.* <http://www.russ.ru/ssylka/98-03-09.htm>.

Leibov, R. (2003). Nezhivoj nezhurnal: Samyj modnyj adres v Seti. *GlobalRus.ru,* 3 January. <http://www.globalrus.ru/opinions/131813/>.

Lenhart, A., Fallows, D. and Horrigan, J. (2004). "Content Creation Online". *Pew Internet and American Life Report.* <http://www.pewinternet.org/pdfs/PIP_Content_Creation_Report.pdf>.

Lennon, J. A. (1997). *Hypermedia systems and applications: World Wide Web and beyond.* Berlin; New York: Springer.

Lessig, L. (2001). *The future of ideas : the fate of the commons in a connected world.* New York: Random House.

Lessig, L. (2004). *Free culture: how big media uses technology and the law to lock down culture and control creativity.* New York: Penguin Press.

Levkin, A. (1998). "Polit. ru" ot chastnogo lica. *Russkij zhurnal.*
<http://www.russ.ru/journal/politics/98-12-17/levkin.htm>.

Levy, S. (2001). *Hackers: Heroes of the computer revolution.* London: Penguin Books.

Lewin, R. A. (1997). *Creative collaboration in psychotherapy: making room for life.* Northvale, N.J.: J. Aronson.

Lialina, O. (2000). RUNET: NetCulture in Russia. Interview by Florian Schneider and James Allan. *Telepolis. magazin der netzkultur*, 1 February,
<http://www.heise.de/tp/english/inhalt/on/5819/1.html>.

ligreego <Verochka> (2004): vsya pravda pro virtualov. *LiveJournal*, 02.09.2004,
<http://www.livejournal.com/users/ligreego/146181.html>.

Littman, J. (1996). *The fugitive game: online with Kevin Mitnick.* Boston: Little, Brown.

Littman, J. (1997). *The watchman: the twisted life and crimes of serial hacker Kevin Poulsen.* Boston, Mass.: Little, Brown and Co.

LiveJournal (2006a). About LiveJournal. LiveJournal Press area. Statistics,
<http://www.livejournal.com/stats.bml>.

LiveJournal (2006b). About LiveJournal. Paid accounts,
<http://www.livejournal.com/paidaccounts/>.

Long, C. R. and Averill, J. R. (2003). Solitude: An Exploration of Benefits of Being Alone. *Journal for the Theory of Social Behaviour*, **33**, 1, pp. 21-44.

Lotka, A. J. (1926). The frequeny distribution of scientific productivity. *Journal of the Washington Academy of Science*, 16, pp. 317-374.

Loughran, D. (2003). *Internet history.* Austin: Raintree Steck-Vaughn.

Lubart, T. I. (1999). Creativity Across the Cultures. In Sternberg, R. J. (Ed.) *Handbook of creativity*, (pp. 339-350). Cambridge: Cambridge University Press.

Lyamina, M. (2004, March 14). Tajnye anekdoty otcov. *MK-Voskresenie.*
<http://syy.narod.ru/wordmk.htm>

M. Nemtsov)". *Zhurnal.ru.* 4. <http://zhurnal.ru/4/calif0.htm>.

maccolit <Aleksandr Zhitinskij> (2003). Filosoficheskoe. *LiveJournal*, 6 December,
<http://www.livejournal.com/users/maccolit/90148.html>.

maccolit <Aleksandr Zhitinskij> (2004). Spasibo, druz'ja. *LiveJournal*, 19 January,
<http://www.livejournal.com/users/maccolit/98826.html>.

maccolit <Aleksanr Zhitinskij> (2003). LYTDYBR. *LiveJournal*, 19.04.2003,
<http://www.livejournal.com/users/maccolit/220392.html>.

Macek, J. (2005). "Defining Cyberculture (v. 2)".
<http://macek.czechian.net/defining_cyberculture.htm>.

Machlup, F. (1962). *The Production and Distribution of Knowledge in the United States.* Princeton.

Machlup, F. (1984). *Knowledge: Its Creation, Distribution and Economic Significance*. Vol. I - III. Princeton, NJ.

Machlup, F. and Mansfield, U. (1983). *The Study of Information*. New York.

MacIver, R. M. (1942). *Social Causation*. Boston: Ginn.

Magyari-Beck, I. (1990). An introduction to the framework of creatology. *The Journal of Creative Behavior*, 3, 151-160.

Magyari-Beck, I. (1999). Creatology. In Runco, M. A. and Pritzker, S. R. (Eds.) *Encyclopedia of Creativity*, vol. 1, (pp. 443-448). San Diego, Calif. ; London: Academic Press.

Majzel, E. (2003). Anton Nosik. Intelligent (Zhivoj Zhurnal slovami pisatelej Vypusk 7.). *Russkij Zhurnal*, July 25. <http://www.russ.ru/krug/20030725_an.html>.

Makhlis, L. (2006). Na "Svobode" – s chistoj sovest'yu. *Sovershenno sekretno*, #4 (203), pp. 28-29.

Maly, M. (2003). *Russia As It Is: Transformation of a Lose/Lose Society*. Booklocker.com.

Malyukov, A. and Romadanov, A. (1997). "Margarita i Master". *Ezhe.ru*. <http://www.ezhe.ru/MiM/>.

Manin, D. (1997). Zadushit li kommerciya utopiyu? *Zhurnal.ru*. 4. <http://www.zhurnal.ru/4/utopia.htm>.

Manovich, L. (1999). *Avant-garde as Software*. <http://www.manovich.net/DOCS/avantgarde_as_software.doc>

Manovich, L. (2001). *The Language of New Media*. Cambrigde, Mass. - London: The MIT Press.

Marcuse, Herbert. (1955). *Eros and civilization: a philosophical inquiry into Freud*. Boston, Mass.: Beacon Press.

Markham, A. N. (2003). "Metaphors Reflecting and Shaping the Reality of the Internet: Tool, Place, Way of Being". http://faculty.uvi.edu/users/amarkha/writing/MarkhamTPWwebversion.htm.

Marshall, C. and Rossman, G. B. (1989). *Designing Qualitative Research*. Newbury Park, CA: Sage.

Maslow, A. (1968). *Toward a psychology of being*. New York: Van Nostrand, Reinhold.

Maslow, A. (1973). *The Farther Reaches of Human Nature*. Harmondsworth.

Maslow, A. (1987). *Motivation and Personality*. New York: Longman.

Masuda, Y. (1981). *The Information Society as Post-Industrial Society*. Washington, DC.

Mayer, R. E. (1999). 'Fifty Years of Creativity Research', in: R. J. Sternberg (ed.), *Handbook of creativity*, pp. 449-460, Cambridge: Cambridge University Press.

McCaughey, M. and Ayers, M. D. (Eds.) (2003). *Cyberactivism: online activism in theory and practice*. New York: Routledge.

McDonald, M. (2003). "Piracy and counterfeiting on the rise in Russia". *charleston.net*. October 26. <http://www.charleston.net/stories/102603/bus_26russia.shtml>.

McLeish, J. A. B. and Varey, J. R. (1992). *Creativity in the later years: An annotated bibliography*. New York; London: Garland.

McNair, B. (1991). *Glasnost, perestroika, and the Soviet media*. London; New York: Routledge.

Mednick, S. A. (1962). The associative basis of the creative process. *Psychological Review*, no. 69: 220-232.

Medvedev, Z. A. (1969). *The rise and fall of T. D. Lysenko*. New York; Columbia University Press.

Meier, A. (2003). *Black earth: a journey through Russia after the fall*. New York: Norton.

Meikle, G. (2002). *Future active: media activism and the Internet*. Annandale, N.S.W.; New York, N.Y.: Pluto Press; Routledge.

Melihova, E. M. and Abalkina, I. L. (2003). *Dialog po voprosam riska: Prakticheskie sovety*. Moscow.

Merton, R. K. (1968). The Matthew effect in science. *Science*, 159, pp. 56-63.

Mickiewicz, E. P. (1997). *Changing channels: television and the struggle for power in Russia*. New York: Oxford University Press.

Miller, D. and Slater, D. (2001). *The Internet: An Ethnographic Approach*. Oxford: Berg Publishers.

Miller, W.W. (1960). *Russians as people*. Phoenix House, London.

Misa, T. J. (2004). *Leonardo to the internet: technology & culture from the Renaissance to the present*. Baltimore: The Johns Hopkins University Press.

Mitnick, K. D. and Simon, W. L. (2002). *The art of deception: controlling the human element of security*. Indianapolis, Ind.: Wiley.

Mitnick, K. D. and Simon, W. L. (2005). *The art of intrusion: the real stories behind the exploits of hackers, intruders, and deceivers*. Indianapolis, IN: Wiley Pub.

moon_lady (2004). Vzglyad na mir poverkh ochkov. *LiveJournal*, 28.09.2004, <http:/www.livejournal.com/users/moon_lady/565434.html>.

Moore, D. W. (1995). *The Emperor's Virtual Clothes: the Naked Truth About Internet Culture*. Chapel Hill: Algonquin Books.

Moschovitis, C. J. P. (1999). *History of the Internet: a chronology, 1843 to the present*. Santa Barbara, Calif.: ABC-CLIO.

MosNews (2004). "MPAA Accuses Russia of Rampant Piracy". *MosNews*. June 10. <http://www.mosnews.com/money/2004/06/10/mpaarussia.shtml>.

MPAA (2003). "2003 Russia Piracy Fact Sheet: MPA Worldwide Market Research". <http:// www.mpaa.org/PiracyFactSheets/PiracyFactSheetRussia.pdf>.

Muller-Prove, M. (2002). "Vision and Reality of Hypertext and Graphical User Interfaces". <http://www.mprove.de/diplom/index.html>.

Mungo, P. and Clough, B. (1992). *Approaching zero: the extraordinary underworld of hackers, phreakers, virus writers, and keyboard criminals*. New York: Random House.

Muxin, M.I. (1997) [M.I.Muxin's Home Page], <http://www.cs.ut.ee/~roman_l/muxin_old.html>

N., A.B. (1998). Gumanitarnoe Izmerenie (beseda s Romanom Leibovym i Kubom). *Internet*, 7. <http://www.gagin.ru/internet/7/6.html>

nabokov (2005): Mr. Vladimir Nabokov's journal. *LiveJournal*, <http://www.livejournal.com/users/nabokov/>.

Nakamura, L. (2002). *Cybertypes: race, ethnicity, and identity on the Internet*. New York: Routledge.

Nechaev, S. (1999). "Robot Verbitsky". *Inache*. <http://www.inache.net/virtual/rob_ver.html>.

Negus, K. and Pickering, M. (2004). *Creativity, communication, and cultural value*. London; Thousand Oaks; New Delhi: SAGE Publications.

Neroznak, V. P. (Ed.) (2001). *Sumerki lingvistiki. Iz istorii otechestvennogo yazykoznaniya. Antologiya*. Moscow: Academia.

Newsru.com (2004). Rasstreljan moskovskij student, kotoryj borolsja protiv milicejskogo proizvola. *Newsru.com*, 12 April, <http://newsru.com/crime/12apr2004/german.html>.

nnikif (2003). Untitled. *LiveJournal*, 22 March, <http://www.livejournal.com/users/nnikif/>.

Nosik, A. (1996-). Vecherny Internet. <http://vi.cityline.ru/vi/>.

Nosik, A. (1997a). "Ne zhu-zhu, no mumu". *Vechernj Internet*. 76, 09.03.1997. <http://vi.cityline.ru/vi/09mar1997.htm>.

Nosik, A. (1997a). "Ruka ruku moet", *Vechernij Internet*. 20, 12.01.1997<http://www.cityline.ru/vi/12jan1997.htm>.

Nosik, A. (1997b). "Elektronnyj Datsyuk". *Vecherni Internet*. 333, 06.12.1997. <http://vi.cityline.ru/vi/06dec1997.htm>.

Nosik, A. (1997c). "Robot Mafusailovich Prostospichkin". *Vecherni Internet*. 336, 10.12.1997. <http://vi.cityline.ru/vi/10dec1997.htm>.

Nosik, A. (2001). "SMI russkogo Interneta: teoriya i praktika". *Mediasoyuz*. <http://www.mediasoyuz.ru/guild.asp?id=2&lvl=79>.

Nosik, A. (2004). "Russkie reshili zarabotat na amerikantsakh'" *Gazeta.ru*. <http://www.gazeta.ru/2004/03/11/oa_114510.shtml>.

Nosik, A. (2005). Blogging: tochki peresecheniya s internet-SMI i vozmozhnoe razvitie v rossijskoj real'nosti (doklad na festivale "Internit'", Novosibirsk, 2005). <http://www.cn.ru/internit/news/reports/260/>.

Now, E. (2000). What it is doing to us (sociocultural implications of the Internet in Russia). *Russian Studies in Literature*, **36**, 2, pp. 34-42.

Ochse, R. (1990). *Before the gates of excellence the determinants of creative genius*. Cambridge, New York: Cambridge University Press.

Okanagan Bookworks (n.d.). About Weblogs and Blogging, <http://www.booksokanagan.com/weblogs.html>.

Orlowski, A. (2003). Most bloggers 'are teenage girls' – survey. In The Register. Internet, 30 May, <http://www.theregister.co.uk/content/6/30954.html>.

Osborn, A. F. (1953). *Applied Imagination*. New York: Scribner's.

Oudshoorn, N. and Pinch, T. J. (Eds.) (2003). *How users matter: the co-construction of users and technologies.* Cambridge, Mass.: MIT Press.

Ovchinnikov, I. (1997). "Internet ub'et kino, vino i domino (interv'yu s Maksimom Moshkovym)". *Russkij Zhurnal.* <http://www.russ.ru/journal/media/97-10-03/moshkw.htm>.

Ovchinnikov, I. and Ivanov, D. (1997). "Iz "abort, retry, ignore" Zhurnal.ru vybiraet "ignore"". *Russkij Zhurnal.* <http://old.russ.ru/journal/media/97-11-05/ovchin.htm>.

Paasilinna, R. (1995). *Glasnost and Soviet television: a study of the Soviet mass media and its role in society from 1985-1991.* Helsinki: Finnish Broadcasting Company.

Paravozov (1997). IRC-konferencija s duchom Ivanom Paravozovym. *Zhurnal.ru*, 25 September.. <http://www.zhurnal.ru/transcripts/paravozov.htm>

Parfenov, S. (2000). "Anekdot.ru: 1257 dnej bez edinogo vyhodnogo". *Netoscope*, 11 November. <http://www.netoscope.ru/news/2000/11/08/764.html>.

parker <M. Kononenko> (2005). *Vladimir Vladimirovich™*, <http://vladimir.vladimirovich.ru>

Paulus, P. B. and Nijstad, B. A. (2003). *Group creativity: innovation through collaboration.* New York: Oxford University Press.

Pavlovsky, G. (1997a). "K predvaritel'noj koncepcii zhurnala". *Russkij Zhurnal.* <http://russ.ru/journal/dsp/97-07-14/pavlov1.htm>.

Pavlovsky, G. (1997b). "Pochemu - Russkij Zhurnal?" *Russkij Zhurnal.* <http://www.russ.ru/journal/zloba_dn/97-07-14/index.html>.

Pavlovsky, G. (2003). Agitprop ili samizdat: Beseda G. Pavlovskogo, V. Kurennogo, I. Zasurskogo. *Otechestvennye zapiski*, **4**. <http://magazines.russ.ru/oz/2003/4/2003_4_18.html>.

Peabody, D. (1985). *National characteristics.* Cambridge: Cambridge University Press.

Perfiliev, Y. (2002). Development of the Internet in Russia: Preliminary observations on its spatial and institutional characteristics. *Eurasian Geography and Economics*, **43**, 5, pp. 411-421.

Perseus Blog Survey (2003). The Blogging Iceberg - Of 4.12Million Hosted Weblogs, Most Little Seen, Quickly Abandoned, <http://www.perseus.com/blogsurvey/iceberg.html>.

Perseus Blog Survey (2005). Blog studies, <http://www.perseus.com/blogsurvey/index.html>.

Peters, C. (2003a). *Bill Gates: software genius of Microsoft.* Berkeley Heights, NJ: Enslow Publishers.

Peters, C. (2003b). *Larry Ellison: database genius of Oracle.* Berkeley Heights, NJ, USA: Enslow Publishers.

Peters, C. (2003c). *Steve Case: Internet genius of America Online.* Berkeley Heights, NJ, USA: Enslow Publishers.

Petrova, A. (1998). Moskovskaya auditoriya fil'ma Aleksandra Nevzorova "Chistilische". *FOM.* <http://bd.fom.ru/report/map/projects/finfo/finfo1998/619_12135/of19981406>.

Pfitzmann, A., Kohntopp, M., Shostack, A., Jaquet-Chiffelle, D.-O., Hansen, M., Diaz, C., Hogben, G., Kriegelstein, T. and Schreurs, W. (2004). "Anonymity, Unobservability, Pseudonymity, and Identity Management – A Proposal for Terminology. Draft v0.21 Sep. 03, 2004". <http://dud.inf.tu-dresden.de/Literatur_V1.shtml>.

Plucker, J. A. and Renzulli, J. S. (1999). Psychometric Approaches to the Study of Human Creativity. In Sternberg, R. J. (Ed.) *Handbook of creativity*, (pp. 35-61). Cambridge: Cambridge University Press.

Poincaré, H. (1921). *The foundations of science*. New York: Science Press.

Polanyi, M. (1958). *The study of man*. London: Routledge & K. Paul.

Policastro, E. and Gardner, H. (1999). From Case Studies to Robust Generalizations: An Approach to the Study of Creativity. In Sternberg, R. J. (Ed.) *Handbook of creativity*, (pp. 213-225). Cambridge: Cambridge University Press.

Porat, M. and Rubin, M. (1978). *The Information Economy: Development and Measurement*. Washington, DC.

Porter, D. (Ed.) (1997). *Internet culture*. New York: Routledge.

Postman, N. (1992). *Technopoly: The Surrender of Culture to Technology*. New York: Alfred A. Knopf.

POTOP <Russian Online Top> (2002). <http://ezhe.ru/POTOP/>

Press, L. (1991). *Relcom, an Appropriate Technology Network*. Los Angeles: California State University.

Price, D. (1963). *Little science, big science*. New York: Columbia University Press.

Protasov, P. (2005). P@utina, vypusk 5. *Russkij Zhurnal*, 3 May, <http://old.russ.ru/culture/network/0050523.html>.

pushkin (2002). Alexander Pushkin's journal. *Live journal*, <http://www.livejournal.com/users/pushkin/>.

r_l <Roman Leibov> (2001). Proba pera. *LiveJournal*, 1 February, <http://www.livejournal.com/users/r_l/13503.html>.

r_l <Roman Leibov> (2004). Razgovor studentov s A. Gaginym, paravozom i chelovekom. *LiveJournal.com*, 3.12.2004. <http://www.livejournal.com/users/r_l/1462391.html>.

Rancour-Laferriere, D. (1995). *The slave soul of Russia: moral masochism and the cult of suffering*. New York University Press, New York; London.

Rank, O. (1968). *Art and artist: Creative urge and personality development*. New York: Agathon Press.

Raymond, E. (Ed.) (1996). *The New Hacker's Dictionary*. Canbridge, MA: The MIT Press.

Razik, T. A. (1965). *Bibliography of creativity studies and related areas*. Buffalo, N.Y.: State University of New York c1965.

Reed, I. (2004). "Interpretive Theory and Socio-Historical Research". <http://research.yale.edu/ccs/workshop/reed_interpretivet&r.pdf.>.

Reestr russkojazychnych soobsshestv "Zhivogo zhurnala" (2005). <http://lj.com.ru/>.

Remington, T. F. (1988). *The truth of authority: ideology and communication in the Soviet Union*. Pittsburgh, Pa.: University of Pittsburgh Press.

Rheingold, H. (1993/2000). *The virtual community: homesteading on the electronic frontier*. Reading, MA: Addison Wesley.

Riasanovsky, N.V. (1952) *A study of Russia and the West in the Teaching of the Slavophiles.* Cambridge, Mass.: Harvard University Press.

Rice, R. E. (2005). New Media/Internet Research Topics of the Association of Internet Researchers. *The Information Society,* **21,** 4.

Richmond, Y. (2003). *From Nyet to Da: Understanding the Russians* (Third edition). Yarmouth, ME: Intercultural Press.

Robertson, R. (1985). Modernization, Globalization and the Problem of Culture in World-Systems Theory (with Frank Lechner). *Theory, Culture & Society,* **II** (3) 1985, pp. 103-118.

Robins, K. (2000). Cyberspace and the world we live in. In Bell, D. and Kennedy, B. M. (Eds.) *The cybercultures reader,* (pp. 77-95). London: Routledge.

Robins, K. and Webster, F. (1999). *Times of the Technoculture: Information, Communication and the Technological Order.* London: Routledge.

Rogers, C. R. (1976). Towards a theory of creativity. In Rothenberg, A. and Hausman, C. R. (Eds.) *The creativity question.* Durham, NC: Duke University Press.

Rogers, C. R. (1980). *A way of being.* Boston: Houghton Mifflin.

Rogers, E. M. (1962). *Diffusion of innovations.* New York: Free Press of Glencoe.

Rohozinski, R. (1999). *Mapping Russian Cyberspace: Perspectives on Democracy and the Net.* <http://unpan1.un.org/intradoc/groups/public/documents/UNTC/UNPAN015092.pdf>.

Rohozinski, R. (2000). How the Internet did not transform Russia. *Current History,* **99,** 639, pp. 334-338.

Roll-Hansen, N. (2004). *The Lysenko effect: the politics of science.* Amherst, N.Y.: Humanity Books.

Romadanov, A. (1998). "Vse obozrevately". *Guelman.ru.* <http://www.guelman.ru/obzory/>.

Romanova, G. (2004). Aleksandr Nevzorov: Loshadi uchat lyudej terpeniyu. *Rossijskaya gazeta.* <http://www.rg.ru/2004/05/28/nevzorov.html>

Rose, M. A. (1991). *The Post-Modern and the Post-Industrial: A Critical Analysis.* Cambridge.

Rosenberg, S. (1999). Fear of links. *Salon.com.* 8 May, <http://www.salon.com/tech/col/rose/1999/05/8/weblogs>.

Roszak, T. (1969). *The making of a counter culture: reflections on the technocratic society and its youthful opposition.* Garden City, N.Y.,: Doubleday.

rualev (2004). Proisshestvie v ZhZh. *LiveJournal,* 29.07.2004, <http://www.livejournal.com/users/rualev/70927.html>.

Runco, M. A. (1991). *Divergent Thinking.* Norwood, N.J.: Ablex Pub. Corp.

Runco, M. A. (1997). *The creativity research handbook.* Vol.1, Cresskill, N.J.: Hampton Press.

Runco, M. A. and Pritzker, S. R. (1999). *Encyclopedia of Creativity.* Vol 1-2, San Diego, Calif.; London: Academic.

Runco, M. A. and Sakamoto, S. O. (1999). Experimental Studies of Creativity. In Sternberg, R. J. (Ed.) *Handbook of creativity,* (pp. 62-92). Cambridge: Cambridge University Press.

Runko, M. A. and Albert, R. S. (Eds.) (1990) *Theories of creativity.* Newburry Park, CA: Sage Publications.

Ryback, T. W. (1990). *Rock around the bloc: a history of rock music in Eastern Europe and the Soviet Union.* New York: Oxford University Press.

Sakaiya, T. (1991). *The Knowledge-Value Revolution or A History of the Future.* Tokyo - New York.

sandra_and_me (2002a). Elita runeta. *LiveJournal*, 14 January, <http://www.livejournal.com/users/sandra_and_me/002/01/14/>.

sandra_and_me (2002b). Uninvolved. *LiveJournal*, 8 January, <http://www.livejournal.com/users/sandra_and_me/002/01/8/>.

Saunders, R. A. (2004). A New Web of Identity: The Internet, Globalization, and Identity Politics In Post-Soviet Space. *Russia in Global Affairs*, 4. <http://www.globalaffairs.ru/docs/saunders.doc>

Sawyer, R. K. (2003). *Group creativity: music, theater, collaboration.* Mahwah, N.J.: L. Erlbaum Associates.

Schmidt, H. (2001). Literaturnyj russkoyazychnyj internet: mezhdu grafomaniej i professionalizmom. *Setevaya slovesnost.* <http://litera.ru/slova/schmidt/liternet.html>.

Schmidt, H. (2002). Evgenij Gornyj: "Ya soglasen na vypadenie iz sovremennosti..." Beseda s Henrikoj Schmidt o Setevoj Slovesnosti, skorosti vremeni, passionarnosti i bespochvennosti. *Russkij Zhurnal.* <http://www.russ.ru/netcult/20020425_gorny.html>.

Schmidt, H. (2002a). CyberRus. Blicke in die russische Internetkultur und-literatur. <http://www.ruhr-uni-bochum.de/lirsk/sphaeren/pages/seite.htm>.

Schmidt, H. (2004). "Virtual (re)unification? An investigation into cultural identity performances on the Russian Internet". *Russian-Cyberspace.org.* <http://www.ruhr-uni-bochum.de/russ-cyb/project/en/project.htm>.

Schmidt, H. and Teubener, K. (2005a). "Our RuNet"? Cultural identity and media usage. *Russian-Cyberspace.org.* <http://www.ruhr-uni-bochum.de/russ-cyb/library/seminars/Russian_Cyberspace/info/info_intro.htm>.

Schmidt, H. and Teubener, K. (2005b). "(Counter)Public Sphere(s) on the Russian Internet". *Russian-Cyberspace.org.* <http://www.ruhr-uni-bochum.de/russ-cyb/library/seminars/Russian_Cyberspace/info/info_hs_kt_1.htm>.

Schmidt, H. and Teubener, K. (2005c). "Russian-cyberspace.org. Kulturelle Identitatsbildung im russischsprachigen Internet". *Russian-Cyberspace.org.* <http://www.ruhr-uni-bochum.de/russ-cyb/library/texts/de/sammelband.htm>.

Schmidt, H., Teubener, K. and Konradova, N. (Eds.) (2006). *Control + Shift: Public and Private Usages of the Russian Internet,.* Norderstedt: Books on demand, 2006.

Schmidt, H., Teubener, K. and Zurawski, N. "Virtual (Re)Unification? Diasporic Cultures on the Russian Internet," in Henrike Schmidt, Kati Teubener and Natalia Konradova (Eds.) *Control + Shift: Public and Private Usages of the Russian Internet.* Norderstedt: Books on demand, 2006, pp. 120-146.

Scholder, A. and Crandall, J. (2001). *Interaction: artistic practice in the network.* New York, NY: Eyebeam Atelier: D.A.P./Distributed Art Publishers.

326

Schrage, M. (1995). *No more teams!: mastering the dynamics of creative collaboration.* New York: Currency Doubleday.

Sekretarev, N. (2004). "Tri goda naedine so vsemi: Russkoyazychnoe soobschestvo pol'zovatelej «Zhivogo Zhurnala» otmechaet den' svoego rozhdeniya". *Nezavisimaya gazeta.* <http://ng.ru/internet/2004-02-20/10_livejournal.html>.

serg_a <Sergej Akhmetov> (2001). Elita runeta. *LiveJournal,* 1 December, <http://www.livejournal.com/users/serg_a/96697.html>.

shakaka <Denis> (2002). Lytdybr. *LiveJournal,* 6 June, <http://www.livejournal.com/users/shakaka/002/06/6/>.

Shane, S. (1995). *Dismantling utopia: how information ended the Soviet Union.* Chicago: I.R. Dee.

Sheldon, K. M. (1999). Conformity. In Runco, M. A. and Pritzker, S. R. (Eds.) *Encyclopedia of Creativity,* vol. 1, (pp. 341-347). San Diego, Calif. ; London: Academic Press.

Shelley, M. (1997). Domovaya stranica Mery Shelley. *Fuga.ru.* <http://fuga.ru/shelley/>.

Shelley, M. (1998a). Legko li byt' virtual'noj. *Internet,* 5, <http://www.gagin.ru/internet/5/2.html>

Shelley, M. (1998b). Manifezd Antigramatnasti. *Fuga.ru.* <http://www.fuga.ru/shelley/manifest.htm>.

Shelley, M. (2002). *Pautina.* SPb: Amfora.

Shelley, M. (2004). 2048. *Fuga.ru.* <http://fuga.ru/shelley/2048/>.

Shepovalov, D. (2002). Interv'yu s Mery Shelly. *Xaker.* <http://www.fuga.ru/articles/2002/02/mary-haker.htm>

Sherman, A. (1997a). Svoya igra: Otkrytoe pis'mo glavnomu redaktoru Zhurnal.Ru. *Zhurnal.ru.* <http://zhurnal.ru/nepogoda/svoya_igra.html>.

Sherman, A. (1997b). Dve zametki: o russkoj Seti i o "Russkom zhurnale. *Setevaya slovesnost.* <http://www.litera.ru/slova/sherman/rzh1.htm>.

Sherman, J. (2003). *The history of the Internet.* New York: F. Watts.

Limor Shifman, "Cyber-Humor: The End of Humor as We Know It?" Oxford Internet Institute seminar, 23 March, 2006, http://www.oii.ox.ac.uk/collaboration/?rq=seminars/20060323.

Shifman, L. and Varsano, H.M., "The Clean, the Dirty and the Ugly: A critical Analysis of 'clean joke' Web sites," *First Monday* 12, no. 2 (2007), <http://firstmonday.org/htbin/cgiwrap/bin/ojs/index.php/fm/article/view/1621/1536>.

Shimomura, T. and Markoff, J. (1996). *Take-down: the pursuit and capture of Kevin Mitnick, America's most wanted computer outlaw – by the man who did it.* New York: Hyperion.

Shirky, C. (2003). Power Laws, Weblogs, and Inequality. *Clay Shirky's Writings About the Internet,* 8 February, <http://www.shirky.com/writings/powerlaw_weblog.html>.

Shpileva, M. (2004). My – svobodny. Skol'ko nas? Reportazh s malen'kogo mitinga. *Novaya gazeta,* 19 April, <http://004.novayagazeta.ru/nomer/004/7n/n27n-s02.shtml>

Shulgin, A. (1998). "Net Art / klassifikatsiya". *Zhurnal.ru.* <http://www.zhurnal.ru/netart/classification/>.

Silver, D. (2000). Looking Backwards, Looking Forward: Cyberculture Studies 1990-2000. In Gauntlett, D. (Ed.) *web.Studies: Rewiring Media Studies for the Digital Age*, (pp. 19-30). Oxford University Press.

Silver, D. (2004). Internet/cyberculture/digital culture/new media/fill-in-the-blank studies. *New Media and Society*, **6**, 55-64. <http://nms.sagepub.com/cgi/reprint/6/1/55.pdf>

Simonton, D. K. (1984). *Genius, creativity, and leadership: Historiometric inquiries.* Cambridge, Mass: Harvard University Press.

Simonton, D. K. (1988). *Scientific genius.* Cambridge: Cambridge University Press.

Simonton, D. K. (1994). *Greatness: Who makes history and why.* New York: Guilford.

Simonton, D. K. (1997). *Genius and creativity: selected papers.* Greenwich, Conn.: Ablex.

Simonton, D. K. (1999). *Origins of genius: Darwinian perspectives on creativity.* New York: Oxford University Press.

skotina <Skotina nenuzhnaja> (2005). Dlja tekh komu ne bezrazlichno. LiveJournal, 24 May, <http://www.livejournal.com/users/skotina/>

Slatalla, M. and Quittner, J. (1995). *Masters of deception: the gang that ruled cyberspace.* New York: HarperCollins Publishers.

Smith, H. (1976). *The Russians.* New York: Quadrangle/New York Times Book Co.

Smith, H. (1990). *The New Russians.* London: Hutchinson.

Smith, J. (1999). *Internet culture in easy steps.* Southam: Computer Step.

Snow, C. P. (1959). *The two cultures and the scientific revolution.* New York,: Cambridge University Press.

Sorokin, P. A. (1957). *Social and cultural dynamics: A study of change in major systems of art, truth, ethics, law and social relationships. Revised and abridged in one volume by the author.* Boston: Extending horizons books; Porter Sargent Publishers.

soros (2003). George's Journal. *LiveJournal*, <http://www.livejournal.com/users/soros/>.

Sottocorona, C. and Romagnolo, S. (2003). *I protagonisti della rivoluzione digitale.* Roma: F. Muzzio.

Soyfer, V. N., Gruliow, L. and Gruliow, R. (1994). *Lysenko and the tragedy of Soviet science.* New Brunswick, N.J.: Rutgers University Press.

Spengemann, W. C. (1980). *The forms of autobiography: Episodes in the history of a literary genre.* New Haven and London: Yale University Press.

Spengler, O. (1928). *The decline of the West.* Vol.1-2, Perspectives of world history, London: Allen & Unwin.

Sputnik ZhZhista (2005). Putevoditel' po russkojazychnomu LiveJournal, <http://lj.eonline.ru/>.

Stahlman, M. (1996). "The English Ideology and WIRED Magazine". *REWIRED.* <http://www.rewired.com/96/Fall/1118.html>.

Stallabrass, J. (2003). *Internet art: the online clash of culture and commerce.* London: Tate Pub.

Stefik, M. J. and Cerf, V. G. (1997). *Internet Dreams: Archetypes, Myths, and Metaphors.* MIT Press.

Stein, M. I. and Heinze, S., J. (1960). *Creativity and the Individual. Summaries of selected literature in psychology and psychiatry ... A McKinsey Foundation annotated bibliography.* Glencoe, Ill.: Free Press 1960.

Sternberg, R. J. (1999). *Handbook of creativity.* Cambridge: Cambridge University Press.

Sternberg, R. J. and Grigorenko, E. (1997). *Intelligence, heredity, and environment.* New York: Cambridge University Press.

Sternberg, R. J. and Lubart, T. I. (1995). *Defying the crowd: cultivating creativity in a culture of conformity.* New York; London: Free Press.

Sternberg, R. J. and Lubart, T. I. (1999). The Concepts of Creativity: Prospects and Paradigms. In Sternberg, R. J. (Ed.) *Handbook of creativity*, (pp. 3-15). Cambridge: Cambridge University Press.

Stonier, T. (1983). *The Wealth of Information. A Profile of the Post-Industrial Economy.* London.

Storr, A. (1989). *Solitude.* New York: Free Press.

Strauss, A. and Corbin, J. (1990). *Basics of qualitative research: Grounded theory procedures and techniques.* Thousand Oaks: Sage Publications.

Strauss, A. L. (1987). *Qualitative Analysis for Social Scientists.* Cambridge: Cambridge University Press.

Suler, J. R. (1996-2005). "Psychology of Cyberspace". <http://www.rider.edu/~suler/psycyber/>.

Sullivan, A. (2002). A Blogger Manifesto: Why online weblogs are one future for journalism. *The Sunday Times of London*, 4 February, <http://www.andrewsullivan.com/main_article.php?artnum=0020224> .

Sztompka, P. (1993). *The Sociology of social change.* Oxford: Blackwell.

Tarde, G. (1895). *Les lois de l'imitation : Étude sociologique.* Paris: [s.n.].

Taylor, I. A. and Getzels, J. W. (1975). *Perspectives in creativity.* Chicago: Aldine Pub. Co.

Taylor, J. (1959). The nature of the creative process. In Smith, P. (Ed.) *Creativity*, (pp. 51-82). New York: Hastings House.

Taylor, P. A. (1999). *Hackers: crime in the digital sublime.* London; New York: Routledge.

Teneta (1998). Orgkomitet literaturnogo konkursa Teneta-98. *Teneta.* <http://www.teneta.rinet.ru/1998/orgkomitet.html>.

Teneta (2003). Teneta: Konkurs russkoj setevoj literatury. <http://www.teneta.ru>.

Terent'eva, I. (2002). Osobennosti russkojazychnych diaspor v raznych stranach. Chast' 6. Runet. *Russkij zhurnal*, 6 October, <http://www.russ.ru/ist_sovr/0021003_ter.html>.

Teubener, K., Schmidt, H. and Zurawski, N. (2005). Virtual reunification? Diasporic Culture(s) on the Russian Internet. *Media Studies*, 23, pp. 118-148.

Thorn, D. (1996). *Digital delinquents: computer hackers, cyberpunks and electronic criminals.* San Diego: Index Publishing Group.

329

tiphareth <Misha Verbickij> (b.d.). <http:/www.livejournal.com/users/tiphareth>. Suspended.

Toffler, A. (1980). *The Third Wave*. New York: Bantam Books.

Tofts, D., Jonson, A. and Cavallaro, A. (Eds.) (2002). *Prefiguring cyberculture: an intellectual history*. Cambridge, Mass.; Sydney: MIT Press; Power Publications.

Torrance, E. P., Glover, J. A., Ronning, R. R. and Reynolds, C. R. (1989). *Handbook of creativity*. New York ; London: Plenum.

Torvalds, L. and Diamond, D. (2001). *Just for fun: the story of an accidental revolutionary*. New York, NY: HarperBusiness.

Tosh, J. (1984). *The pursuit of history: Aims, Methods and New Directions in the Study of Moder History*. London: Longman.

Touraine, A. (1974). T*he Post-Industrial Society. Tomorrow's Social History: Classes, Conflicts and Culture in the Programmed Society*. New York.

Toynbee, A. J. and Somervell, D.C. (1948). *A study of history. Abridgement of volumes I-[X] by D. C. Somervell*, London: Oxford University Press.

Travis, M. W. (2002). *Directing feature films: the creative collaboration between directors, writers, and actors*. Studio City, CA: Michael Wiese Productions.

Treanor, P. (1996). Internet as hyper-liberalism. <http://web.inter.nl.net/users/Paul.Treanor/net.hyperliberal.html>.

Tresschanskaja, M. (2001). Udalennaja zhizn': Vesti virtual'nyj dnevnik – eto modno. *Izvestiya.ru*, 4 July, <http://main.izvestia.ru/rubr.cgi?idr=530&idbl=&id=054>.

Trofimenko, A. V. (2004). The Legal Regulation of Information Relations: A Note on the Use of the Internet in the Russian Federation. *Review of Central and East European Law,* **29**, 3, pp. 407-420.

Trofimov, A. (2003). Kak bylo to, chto budet. 1. *Russkij Zhurnal*, 12 November, <http://old.russ.ru/netcult/20031112_trofimov.html>.

Turkle, S. (1995). *Life on the Screen: Identity in the Age of the Internet*. New York: Simon & Schuster.

Turner, B. A. (1981). Some practical aspects of qualitative data analysis: one way of organising the cognitive processes associated with the generation of grounded theory. *Quality and Quantity*, 15, pp. 225-247.

Tynyanov, Y. N. (1977). Literaturnyj fakt. *Poetika. Istoriya literatury. Kino.*, (pp. 255-270). Moscow: Nauka.

Utin (2005). *Resident Utin*, <http://utin.ru/>

Vaidhyanathan, S. (2004). *The anarchist in the library: how the clash between freedom and control is hacking the real world and crashing the system*. New York: Basic Books.

Velichko, A. (2004) An email message to the author, 1 May.

Velikanov, A. and Ashuratova, N. (2000). Odin chelovek - dva hudozhnika: Andrei Velikanov - Namniyaz Ashuratova. *Guelman.ru*. <http://www.guelman.ru/dva/para4.html>.

Verner, D. (1996, November 8). "Zametki po povodu pervoj godovshshiny". Anekdot.ru. <http://anekdot.ru/god.html>.

Verner, D. (1997). "Anekdoty NE ot Vernera". Zhurnal.ru. 7.
<http://www.zhurnal.ru/7/anekdot.html>.

Verner, D. (2001, April 22). "Ya vybirayu pedantichnost'. Bessmennyj sostavitel' Anekdot. Ru o SMI, yumore, nepristojnykh stishkakh i anekdotakh, konechno." Echonet.
<http://www.echonet.ru/archive/22Apr01.html>.

Verner, D. (2003). "Anekdoty iz Rossii" i fol'klor internetovskoj epokhi. Russky Zhurnal.
<http://russ.ru/netcult/20030617_verner.html>.

Verner, D. (2005). Re: voprosy po anekdotam. E-mail message to the author, 7 February.

Verner, D. and Leibov, R. (2001, September 17). Anekdoty i/kak terror: beseda s Dmitriem Vernerom. Russky Zhurnal. <http://www.russ.ru/netcult/20010917_verner.html>.

Vernidub, A. (2005). U jazyka est' aftar. *Russian Newsweek*, 17 (47), 16–22 May,
<http://www.runewsweek.ru/theme/?tid=16&rid=15> (13.02.2006).

Vernon, P. E. (1970). *Creativity*. Harmondsworth: Penguin Books.

Vieta, M. (2003). "What's Really Going On With the Blogosphere and Why Should We Care?"
<http://arago.cprost.sfu.ca/marcelo/archives/BlogArticle-BlogosphereIII.pdf>.

Vishnya, L. (2004). Problemy Sazonova ("Proza. ru" i "Stihi. ru"): Literatura v "Nacional'noj literaturnoj seti". *Setevaya slovesnost*. <http://litera.ru/slova/vishnja/nls.html>.

Volchek, D. (2003). Activated or deleted status ili Monolog zhivogo i mertvogo. (Zhivoj zhurnal slovami pisatelej. Vypusk 4). *Russkij zhurnal*, 4 June,
<http://www.russ.ru/krug/0030704_em.html>.

Voronezhsky, R. (1997). „V Zhurnale, kotoryj Ru". *Zhurnal.ru*.
<http://www.zhurnal.ru/rv/explore_zr.htm>.

Walicki, A. (1975). *The Slavophile controversy: history of a conservative utopia in nineteenth-century Russian thought*. Oxford: Clarendon Press.

Wallace, D. B. (1971). *The Logic of Science in Sociology*. Chicago: Aldine.

Wallas, G. (1926). *The Art of Though*. New York: Harcourt, Brace.

Wark, M. (2004). *A hacker manifesto*. Cambridge: Harvard University Press.

Washington ProFile (2002, October 21). "Anekdoty iz Rossii" delayutsya v SShA. Washington ProFile. <http://www.washprofile.org/Interviews/Verner.html>.

Weber, M. (1949). *The Methodology of the Social Science*. Glencoe, Il.: Free Press.

Weber, M. (1992). *Protestant ethic and the spirit of capitalism*. London: Routledge.

Webster, F. (2002). *Theories of the Information Society*. London: Routledge.

Webster, F. (Ed.) (2003). *The Information Society Reader*. London: Routledge.

Wehner, L., Csikszentmihalyi, M. and Magyari-Beck, I. (1991). Current approaches used in studying creativity: An explanatory investigation. *Creativity Research Journal*, **4,** 3, pp. 261-271.

Wellman, B. and Haythornthwaite, C. (Eds.) (2002). *The Internet in Everyday Life*. Oxford: Blackwell Publishers.

Wertheim, M. (1999). *The Pearly Gates of Cyberspace: A History of Space from Dante to the Internet*. W.W. Norton & Company.

331

Wertheim, M. (2002) Internet dreaming: A utopia for all seasons. In Tofts, D. (Ed.) *Prefiguring Cyberspace: An intellectual history.* Cambridge, Mass.; London, England: The MIT Press. P. 216-226.

Wilber K. (2003). "Foreword" in Visser, F. *Ken Wilber: Thought As Passion.* New York: SUNY Press.

Williams, S. (2002). *Free as in freedom: Richard Stallman's crusade for free software.* Sebastopol, Calif. Farnham: O'Reilly.

Wilson, S. (2002). *Information Arts: Intersection of Art, Science, and Technology.* Cambridge, Mass.; London, England: The MIT Press.

Winnicott, D. W. (1969). The capacity to be alone. *The Maturational Process and the Facilitating Environment,* (pp. 29-36). London: The Hogarth Press.

Winston, B. (1998). *Media technology & society: a history from the telegraph to the internet.* London: Routledge.

Wolinsky, A. (1999). *The history of the Internet and the World Wide Web.* Berkeley Heights, N.J.: Enslow Publishers.

Woodhead, N. (1991). *Hypertext and hypermedia: theory and applications.* Wilmslow, England; Wokingham, England; Reading, Mass.: Sigma Press; Addison-Wesley Pub. Co.

Woodman, R. W. and Schoenfield, L. F. (1989). Individual differences in creativity: An interactionist perspective. In Torrance, E. P., *et al.* (Eds.) *Handbook of creativity,* (pp. 77-92). New York; London: Plenum.

Woolgar, S. (1991). Configuring the User: The Case of Usability Trials. In Law, J. (Ed.) *A Sociology of Monsters: Essays on Power, Technology and Domination,* (pp. 58-100). London: Routledge.

xxx (2001). Untitled. LiveJournal, November 2, <http://www.livejournal.com/users/xxx/>.

za_lib_ru (2005). Soobsshestvo v zasshitu ehlektronnoj biblioteki Moshkova. *LiveJournal,* <http://www.livejournal.com/community/za_lib_ru/>.

Zasursky, I. (2001). *Rekonstruktsiya Rossii: Mass-media i politika v 90-e.* Moscow: Izdatel'stvo MGU.

Zasursky, I. (2002). "Karty media-rynka rossii. Samye vliyatel'nye media-gruppirovki. Vesna 2002". <http://www.ricn.ru/media/material/3659>.

Zhitinsky, A. (1997). Virtual'naya zhizn' i smert' Kati Detkinoj. *Setevaya slovesnost':.* <http://www.litera.ru/slova/zhitinski/kadet1.htm>.

Zhitinsky, A. (1999). "Samizdat XXI veka". *Russian Journal.* <http://www.russ.ru/netcult/99-07-08/zhitinsk.htm>.

Znaniecki, F. (1935). *The Method of Sociology.* New York: Holt, Rienhart & Winston.

Zurawski, N. (2001). "[Review of Virtual Ethnography by Christine Hine]". *RCCS.* <http://www.com.washington.edu/rccs/bookinfo.asp?BookID=109&ReviewID=126>

Zusne, L. (1976). Age and achievement in psychology: The harmonic means as a model. *American Psychologist,* 31, pp. 805-807.